DALLAS & THE SOUTHWEST

JOB SEEKERS

SOURCEBOOK

The most complete and accurate source for fast access to the key contacts within the placement industry to help find a job, change careers, or promote yourself.

Donald D. Walker and Valerie A. Shipe

Net-Research
160 S. Bolingbrook Road
Suite 114
Bolingbrook, Illinois 60440

JOB SEEKER'S SOURCE BOOK

Published by: **NET-RESEARCH**
16731 East Iliff
Suite B 183
Aurora, Colorado 80013

Cover Design by: Salvatore Concialdi

Disclaimer of All Warranties and Liabilities

Although the authors have exhaustively researched all sources to ensure the accuracy and completeness of the information contained in this book, we assume no responsibility for errors, omissions, inaccuracies, or any other inconsistencies herein. Any mistakes or slights against people or organizations are unintentional.

For information on distribution or quantity discount rates, contact: Net-Research at (303) 690-7349 or (303) 690-9430.

Distribution to the trade is by Independent Publishers Group.

To order copies of this or other SourceBooks, contact the Independent Publishers Group at: 1 (800) 888-4741

ISBN: 1-882499-08-5

Library of Congress Catalog Card Number: 93-24726

TABLE OF CONTENTS

ACKNOWLED V

DEDICATION VII

1. INTRO: JOB SEEKERS SOURCEBOOK 1

the most out of this book -- A special note to employers -- Using this book effectively

2. SPECIALTY CODES - FOR YOU 7

What are they -- How to use them efficiently -- Specialty Code Table -- Specialty Code Definitions

3. GUIDELINES TO A SUCCESSFUL JOB SEARCH 17

Organizing your job search -- Additional help getting started -- General preparation -- Creating the perfect resume -- Secrets to writing a cover letter -- Preparations before the interview -- Handling the interview -- Important questions to ask -- After the interview follow-up -- Stress management made easy -- How people find jobs

4. EMPLOYMENT AGENCIES/RECRUITERS 47

What is an employment agency? -- How to select an employment agency -- Questions to ask to qualify a employment agency -- Working with an employment agency -- Questions to ask about job openings -- Topics you should not discuss with recruiters -- Recap

Arizona Employment Agencies/Recruiters 57

Index Cross Reference by Specialty -- Alphabetical list of Arizona employment agencies/recruiters

New Mexico Employment Agencies/Recruiters 79

Index Cross Reference by Specialty -- Alphabetical list of New Mexico employment agencies/recruiters

Oklahoma Employment Agencies/Recruiters 87

Index Cross Reference by Specialty -- Alphabetical list of Oklahoma employment agencies/recruiters

Texas Employment Agencies/Recruiters 103

Index Cross Reference by Specialty -- Alphabetical list of Texas employment agencies/recruiters

5. **EXECUTIVE SEARCH FIRMS** 185

How executive recruiters differ from employment agencies -- How to select an executive recruiter -- Key questions to ask to qualify an executive recruiter -- Working with an executive recruiter -- Questions to ask about job openings -- Topics you should not discuss with executive recruiters -- Recap -- Index Cross Reference by Specialty -- Alphabetical list of Executive Recruiters

6. **DATABASE, NETWORK, REFERRAL SERVICES** 261

Overview -- How to select a database, network, referral service -- Questions to ask to qualify a service -- Using a database, network, or referral Service -- Recap -- Alphabetical list of Database, Network, Referral Services

7. **CAREER CONSULTANTS** 281

Consultant services, What are they? -- How to select the right career consultant -- Questions to ask to qualify a career consultant -- Working with a career consultant -- Recap -- Alphabetical list of Career Consultants

8. **OUTPLACEMENT SERVICES** 307

A definition of Outplacement Services -- How to select the right outplacement service -- Questions to ask to qualify an outplacement service -- Working with a outplacement service -- Recap -- Alphabetical list of Outplacement Services

9. RESUME PREPARATION SERVICES 329

Resume preparation services, How they differ -- How to select a resume preparation service -- Questions to ask to qualify a resume preparation service -- Working with a resume preparation service -- Recap -- Alphabetical list of Resume Preparation Services

CONTACT LOG FORMS 349

Placement Firm Contact Form -- Hiring Company Contact Form

READER FEEDBACK FORM 351

CATALOG OF NET-RESEARCH BOOKS 353

ACKNOWLEDGEMENTS

This book could not have been produced without the dedication and cooperation of several people. In the months that it took to research and write this book, Val Shipe and I along with our research team contacted thousands of businesses to create the database of information included.

Most firms listed inside this book were first contacted by telephone to obtain critical source information such as: contact names, current addresses, phone numbers, and specialty disciplines.

Then to double check the information gathered, a letter containing the proposed business listing was sent back to each business for confirmation. Using the results of these confirmation returns, we finally put our book in its final form.

Our special thanks to the many firms listed in this book for their contribution and cooperation in helping us make this book the most current source of information available to job seekers, hiring companies, and firms in the placement industry.

Without their cooperation, we would not have been able to provide you with this valuable book.

Additionally, we wish to acknowledge the countless organizations, companies, and individuals who offered ideas, information, and review comments. The Job Seekers SourceBook grew out of personal experiences - our own and that of others, which enabled us to recognize the need to provide this consolidated source of timely information that would be beneficial to job seekers, hiring companies, and members of the placement industry.

And finally, thanks to you, our readers who continue to share our books with others. We are glad that people have been found "The Job Seekers SourceBooks" helpful in making the job search process more productive.

We value the comments and advice given to us by our readers. To enable you to help us improve this book and help others, we have provided a Reader's Comment form at the back of the book. Please share your comments with us by using this form.

Donald D. Walker
August, 1993

DEDICATIONS

This book is dedicated to my friends, Anna cp Stoelting, her husband Tom, and their two wonderful daughters, Samantha and Jessica, for their understanding, support, and unfailing belief in my dreams to continue to help others.

Donald D. Walker
Author

This book is also dedicated to my daughter Bonnie and her husband Mark whose faith and support of our family has helped us grow as individuals and as a family.

Valerie A. Shipe
Author

*"Let another man praise thee,
and not thine own mouth"*

Proverbs: 27:2

IMPORTANT NEWS FOR THOSE JOB SEEKERS LOOKING FOR A JOB OUT-OF-STATE !!!

Net-Research produces regional Job Seekers SourceBooks for areas across the entire United States.

Other Job Seekers SourceBooks currently in print include:

- Boston & New England
- Chicago & Illinois
- L.A. & Southern California
- Northern Great Lakes
- Ohio Valley
- Pacific Northwest
- Southern Atlantic Coast

Future Job Seekers SourceBooks due out soon include:

- New York & New Jersey
- Plaines States
- Denver & Mountain States
- Washington D.C. & Mid-Atlantic
- Southern States

Job Seekers SourceBooks are available at special quantity discounts for bulk purchases for sales promotions, premiums, or fund raising.

For details, contact the Vice President of Special Sales, Net-Research, 160 S. Bolingbrook Rd, Suite 114, Bolingbrook, Illinois 60440

DALLAS & THE SOUTHWEST JOB SEEKERS SOURCEBOOK

Section 1

Getting The Most Out Of This Book

Introducing:

The "Dallas & The SouthWest" Job Seekers SourceBook"!

IMPORTANT !!!

For the most effective use of your time, read this section first prior to attempting to use the materials contained within this book.

This book has been especially prepared for the individual who has decided to look for a new job. Unlike other books which provide lists of placement firms and related services, this source book provides detailed information to give you **fast** and **direct** access to organizations that can do you the most good.

Recognizing the frustration of trying to find the right resources for your job search, we have created the most comprehensive regional source listing of employment agencies, recruiters, executive search firms, database services, career consultants, outplacement services, and resume preparation services in the United States.

Proper use of this book will enable you to pinpoint the right organization for your particular needs. It contains services and helpful hints to aid everyone from entry-level to CEO, and covers virtually every field and profession.

Turn the pages and you'll find useful information about developing the most effective resume or cover letter, perfecting interview techniques and getting your foot in the door of a new career. This book will help you find the right contacts to aid in your personal marketing strategy.

Whether you are just beginning your job search or if you've been pounding the pavement for a long time, you will find this book to be absolutely the best source of helpful information.

<u>Whether expanding your business or in the middle of a reorganization, this book is indispensable to you!</u>

When in need of people with certain skills and qualifications, it is important to quickly find the placement professionals who specialize in particular fields.

The Job Seekers SourceBook helps you do just that.

With the information contained within this book, you can quickly and accurately reference resources by specialty and location to improve the effectiveness of your match.

The Job Seekers SourceBook provides the most up-to-date and complete regional list of placement firms for use by hiring companies.

Every entry has been verified by phone and/or mail to ensure that you have the right tool at your finger tips to save you time.

During the difficult times of a reorganization, the Job Seekers SourceBooks provide your Human Resource departments with the best tool to help your former employees find a new job elsewhere.

Companies that provide their former employees with free copies of this book as part of an outplacement package have found that they have been able to help these people find jobs sooner.

This book contains the most comprehensive listing of employment agencies, executive search firms, specialty recruiters, outplacement firms, career counselors, resume preparation firms, and database/referral services. Altogether there are over **1000** listings in this book, all of them verified as to type of business and as to being active in business.

This book is designed to be user-friendly. Throughout the book, we have listed firms in alphabetical order and categorized them as to type of firm. In addition, employment agencies and recruiters have been separated into distinct geographic areas: Florida, Georgia, North Carolina, and South Carolina. We have also provided vital identifying information with each listing to help make your job search easier.

The first section of the book is devoted to guidelines for a successful job search. Included are tips for interviewing, resume preparation, better writing, stress management, networking and overall preparation for your job search. Each topic is designed in an easy to read outline format that makes quick reference easier when the need arises.

The remaining sections cover the different types of firms functioning in the placement industry. Each section contains several pages of introduction which is filled with information designed to educate the reader on the type of firms listed and how to find and use these firms for maximum benefit.

Following each introduction (where appropriate) is a cross reference by specialty to that section's list of resources that may be beneficial to your search. All businesses contained in the cross reference are then listed in alphabetical order for ease of access. Under each listing you will find the organization's specialty, the type of positions and clients they serve, and other pertinent information.

To maximize the benefit of using this book, first read the section titled "Guidelines to a Successful Job Search".

Next read the introduction to each of the other sections to determine which types of firms you will need to use in your job search.

Finally, review the Section of this book on Specialty Codes to familiarize yourself with the different industry fields and disciplines prior to selecting any firm for use.

Practical examples are presented in the Specialty Codes Section to quickly guide you to only those firms that you need to contact.

The goal of this book is to provide you with the right information to focus your job search efforts for timely success.

<u>This can be best achieved by following the suggestions identified above on this page.</u>

Good luck, and we hope you find this book a most valuable tool to assist you in finding a new career opportunity.

Important Job Hunting Fact

Two thirds of all job hunters spend five hours or less a week on their job search.

To be successful in your job search, work full-time on your search, spend at least 30 hours per week on this task.

DALLAS & THE SOUTH WEST JOB SEEKERS SOURCEBOOK

Section 2

Specialty Codes

What are they?

Specialty codes within this book are the identifying codes which enable the reader to quickly find those employment agencies, recruiters or executive recruiters that can be most helpful during a job search.

The full definition of specialty codes by industry disciplines and types of positions is contained within this section on the pages that follow.

Within this book every business listed in the sections for employment agencies/recruiters or executive recruiters has been tagged with one or more specialty codes based upon the information we have gathered.

The Index Cross References by Specialty Codes provide the reader with quick access to those firms that should be contacted first when conducting a job search.

<u>**How to use them!**</u>

If for example, you were in computer programming, then you would scan our list of specialty code definitions, until you found "C" for computers.

Reading the definition associated with this code you would see that one of the positions handled by firms that deal in area is that of computer programmer.

Knowing that your salary level is less than $70,000, you would next look to find those firms in the sections for "Employment Agencies Recruiters" that were tagged with this code.

The easiest way to do this is use the Index Cross Reference for one of these sections and scan down until you found firms listed under the heading: "Specialty C: Computers & Data Processing", which would appear like this:

Specialty: C
(Computers & Data Processing)

Business Management Personnel
Computer Futures Exchange Inc <----If you selected this entry
Data Career Center then you would scan the
Data Resource Consultants alphabetical list until
you found that entry.

(You would have found this entry)

Rick Ceater, Pres
Computer Futures Exchange Inc
727 N Hudson Ave, Ste 3
Chicago, IL 60610
(312) 951-0102
Specialty: C
Employment Agency

Reviewing this entry, you now have the contact name of who to call or write, the correct phone number and address, and the knowledge that this firm **only** specializes in placements within the computer industry since that is the only Specialty Code listed for this entry.

To maximize your efforts, always contact those firms first that deal exclusively in placements within your industry or discipline. Read the Introduction to each section to learn how to evaluate and locate the best firms to use in your job search.

SPECIALTY CODE TABLE

A	-	ADVERTISING
B	-	BANKING
C	-	COMPUTERS & DATA PROCESSING
E	-	ENGINEERING
F	-	FINANCE & ACCOUNTING
G	-	GENERAL APPLICATIONS
H	-	HEALTH CARE
I	-	INSURANCE
L	-	LEGAL
M	-	MANUFACTURING
O	-	OFFICE ADMINISTRATION
P	-	PERSONNEL & HUMAN RESOURCES
R	-	RESEARCH & DEVELOPMENT
S	-	SALES & MARKETING
T	-	TRAVEL, FOOD & HOSPITALITY

Specialty codes identify the specific industry areas that are served by Employment Agencies, Recruiters, or Executive Search firms.

SPECIALTY CODE DEFINITIONS

A - ADVERTISING

Disciplines: Advertising

Positions: Administrative Assistant, Advertising Worker, Media Specialist, Receptionist, Secretary, Typist, Word Processor

B - BANKING

Disciplines: Auditing, bookkeeping, branch management, consulting, financial analysis, loan processing/origination, operations management

Positions: Bank Officer, Branch Manager, Clerk, Credit Manager, Customer Service Representative, Data Entry Clerk, Loan Processor, Receptionist, Secretary, Teller, Trust Officer, Word Processing Specialist

C - COMPUTERS & DATA PROCESSING

Disciplines: EDP audit, programming, systems development

Positions: Computer Operator, Data Entry Clerk, LAN Specialist, MIS Specialist, Programmer, Software Engineer, Systems Analyst, Systems Programmer, Technical Writer, Telecommunication Specialist

SPECIALTY CODE DEFINITIONS

E - ENGINEERING

Disciplines: Aeronautical, chemical, civil, electrical, environmental/hazardouswaste,HVAC, industrial, manufacturing, mechanical, nuclear, & packaging

Positions: Architectural Engineer, Biochemical Engineer, Ceramics Engineer, Chemical Engineer, Civil Engineer, Construction Engineer, Electrical Engineer, Environmental Engineer, HVAC Engineer, Industrial Engineer, Mechanical Engineer, Metallurgical Engineer, Mining Engineer, Nuclear Engineer, Plastic Engineer, Petroleum Engineer

F - FINANCE & ACCOUNTING

Disciplines: Auditing, bookkeeping, commodities broker, budgeting, consulting, financial analysis, public accounting, tax accounting

Positions: Accountant, A/P Clerk, A/R Clerk, Auditor, CFO, Controller, Cost Accountant, Payroll Clerk, Tax Accountant

G - GENERAL APPLICATIONS

Disciplines: No specialty implied, usually used for entry level support, staff office worker/clerical, mid-level management, mid-level professional/technical

Positions: All general support positions

SPECIALTY CODE DEFINITIONS

H - **HEALTH CARE**

Disciplines: Dental, Nursing, Pharmaceuticals

Positions: Dental Assistant, Medical Secretary, Nurse, Receptionist

I - **INSURANCE**

Disciplines: Actuarial, Claims, Life/Health, Property/Casualty, Rating, Reinsurance, Underwriting

Positions: Actuary, Claims Adjuster, Clerk, Insurance Agent, Receptionist, Secretary, Underwriter

L - **LEGAL**

Disciplines: Legal

Positions: Attorney, Court Recorder, Legal Administrator, Legal Secretary, Paralegals, Receptionist

SPECIALTY CODE DEFINITIONS

M - MANUFACTURING

Disciplines: Factory automation, logistics, manufacturing/production, plant management, quality control, robotics, safety, supervisory, textiles, traffic management

Positions: Factory Worker, General Manager, Inventory Controller, Personnel & Labor Relations Specialist, Production Manager, Purchasing Agent, Quality Control Supervisor, Shift Supervisor, Traffic Manager, Warehouse Manager

O - OFFICE ADMINISTRATION

Disciplines: Administrators, clerks, management, receptionists, secretaries, supervisors

Positions: Clerk, Data Entry Clerk, Customer Service Representative, Legal Secretary, Medical Secretary, Office Manager, Office Worker, Secretary, Stenographer, Technical Writer/Editor, Typist, Word Processing Specialist

P - PERSONNEL/HUMAN RESOURCES

Disciplines: Personnel, Human Resources

Positions: Benefits Coordinator, Human Resources Manager, Payroll Administrator, Personnel Director, Personnel & Labor Relations Specialist

SPECIALTY CODE DEFINITIONS

R - RESEARCH & DEVELOPMENT

<u>Disciplines:</u> Product development, R&D, sales, technicians

<u>Positions:</u> Product Developer, Project Manager, Quality Control Specialist, Technical Writer/Editor

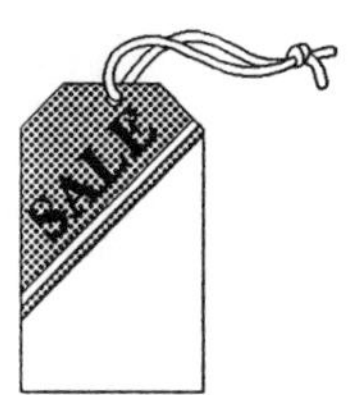

S - SALES & MARKETING

<u>Disciplines:</u> Business products, computers, consumer products, industrial products, real estate, retail, services/intangibles, trainees

<u>Positions:</u> Customer Service Representative, Marketing Specialist, Public Relations Specialist, Regional Manager, Sales Manager, Sales Representative, Sales Trainee

T - TRAVEL

<u>Disciplines:</u> Airlines, Hospitality, Hotel, Restaurant, Travel Agencies

<u>Positions:</u> Assistant Manager, Chef, Cook, Front Desk Clerk, Hotel Manager, Reservation Agent, Ticket Agent

SPECIALTY CODE DEFINITIONS

OTHER SPECIFIC SPECIALTIES

Where a particular specialty does not fit into any of the above classifications, it is listed as a specific specialty and placed in alphabetical order under a general category titled "Other Specific Specialties".

DALLAS & THE SOUTH WEST JOB SEEKERS SOURCEBOOK

Section 3

Guidelines to a Successful Job Search

Organizing Your Job Search

Getting organized for your job search is the most critical step you can take in finding the right position in the least amount of time.

Finding a job is kind of like solving a detective novel mystery. There are certain predefined activities that must be performed before the mystery can be solved. In the case of a job search these activities involve the following:

1. *Identifying sources for leads*

   Be creative in your thinking about possible source of job leads. Some good possibilities often overlooked by job seekers include: equipment manufacturers, special interest publications, trade publications, service directories, manufacturer's directories, books, and business newspapers.

   Take note of announcements about a company moving into the area, acquiring another company, or expanding its product line. All are potential sources for new job openings. Write down everything and keep track of it.

2. *Fill in the blanks*

Once you have identified a lead, then spend the time to gather supporting information such as: contact names (include department heads), type of company, addresses, phone numbers, company size, growth potential and stability.

3. *Probe for information on openings*

Find out who is in charge, then call and get an answer as to whether they have any openings now or in the future. Using an indirect approach such as: "Where can I put my knowledge of telemarketing to work?" often will help you obtain the best information about possible openings and who else to contact.

4. *Follow up on any openings*

Once you've found where an opening is available, contact the individual in charge to request permission to send them a copy of your resume. Now is the time to do some advance selling of yourself over the telephone. If you found out about an opening through your own search efforts, then don't forget to sell them on your creative ingenuity as one of your skills.

Include a carefully tailored and targeted cover letter that highlights how some of your key skills could be beneficial to this company.

Tell them why they should hire you and not someone else...in one paragraph. Be creative and positive in your approach.

5. *Follow up your mailing*

Allow a reasonable amount of time for your letter and resume to arrive, then call the company contact. Make this call to find out if there is further interest on their part and to schedule a convenient time for a personal interview.

If there is no interest on their part, then probe to find out why. This is very important. You may find out that their objection has to do with experience or skills not listed on your resume. If so, then cover this on the phone to overcome their objections.

Remember, the purpose of this follow up call is to validate their interest, overcome any objections, and to set a time for a personal interview.

6. *Attending the interview*

Smile, and go into the interview with a positive attitude. Make that first impression of you a pleasant experience, because people like to be around pleasant people.

No matter how badly you may need a job, never, never appear desperate.

Appear confident without appearing arrogant. Remember, you know more about yourself and your previous job history than they do.

Be prepared, review our guidelines titled: "The Interview".

Take notes during the interview on key points, especially on any information that you promise to get back to them.

Audition for the part, sell yourself without being overbearing. Demonstrate why they should hire you. Relate your skills and experience to their needs.

After you have identified all of the reasons why they should hire you, then ask for the job. Too often, job seekers give a perfect sales pitch, then forget to close the sale by asking for the job.

If they're not ready to make a decision, then find out when the decision will be made and where you fit in the running. Mark this date down and follow up later with a letter and a phone call.

7. *Critique your interview*

Immediately after the interview, identify what was good and what needs changing, then improve those areas that need to be better.

8. *One more time*

Now is the opportunity to put your name in front of the interviewer again. Send out a thank you letter, recap how your background can be beneficial to their company, and ask for the job...one more time.

9. *Move forward and re-loop*

Repeat your efforts as a good detective, and continue through this process again with other job leads.

Persistence and perseverance will prevail.

Maintain a positive mental attitude and learn from any rejection.

Only by using the experience gained from each interview can you polish your performance.

Remember, by being better prepared than the other people applying for the same position, your opportunity of being selected as the right match is greater, which would result in you soon having the job you want.

Additional Help Getting Started

To assist you in being better prepared to conduct your successful job search, we have provided a set of useful guidelines on the next few pages of this book.

These guidelines are designed to help you handle the important aspects of your job search. They contain information on:

- General preparation needed prior to starting a job search.
- Instructions for creating the perfect resume.
- Cover letter creation for responding to job openings.
- The Interview Process (Before/During/After).
- Stress management during your job search.
- An overview of how people find jobs.

It is recommended that you read and follow them carefully.

Keep the faith, stay positive, and happy sleuthing.

General Preparation

1) If you are unemployed now, obtain some business cards that have your name, address and specialty listed. Hand these out to everyone you meet in your efforts to obtain employment.

   One of the best cards I've seen used by a job seeker had in large bold type, right in the middle of the card, the words: "**Between Successes**". I contacted that person and interviewed him just because of the ingenuity displayed with this phrase.

2) If you want to relocate, check the job market in the area by reading local newspapers or information from the Bureau of Labor Statistics. Try to arrange and coordinate multiple interviews during trips to this new area to cut expenses.

3) Maintain a contact file with names, companies, titles, addresses, phone numbers, etc.

4) Attend job fairs, seminars, meetings, lectures, etc. and introduce yourself to as many people as possible.

5) Contact everyone you can to tell them you are looking. Explain the kind of job you are looking for and the two or three things that you do very well.

6) Try sending out broadcast letters to companies where you'd like to work (expect responses from about 20%, interview opportunities from less than 5%).

7) Find a mentor in your field and cultivate a relationship.

8) Be truthful in your interviews and on your resume/application.

9) Work on small talk.

10) Periodically evaluate your progress to maximize your results.

Creating The Perfect Resume

Think before you write

1) Make a list of your skills, honors, professional/civic organizations, languages, etc.

2) Assemble a list of past jobs with employers' names, addresses, phone numbers, dates that you started, supervisors' names and starting and ending salaries. Different jobs for the same company count.

3) Arrange the information on your resume so that your strongest points are near the top.

4) Jot down brief examples of what you accomplished at each job. Include actions you took and the results produced, showing increases in dollars, percentages and units wherever possible.

5) Identify people you want to use as references. Contact each potential reference to insure that they are aware of your job search and your intentions.

6) Determine what you do best and the kind of job you want.

Structure your resume

1) Think about your reader -- who will receive it and what is it going to tell them?

2) Head the resume with your name, address and phone number(s).

3) Make a single statement that identifies your capabilities and/or your job objective.

4) Use your past accomplishments to demonstrate your ability and experience for handling the new job.

   - Show jobs held, what was done and results achieved.
   - Strengthen the listing with chronological dates.
   - Be accurate.

5) Identify educational background -- especially as it supports your job objective.

6) Support with a list of skills, languages, honors or activities as they apply.

7) Edit for length -- one page if possible, two pages maximum.

Review your work

1) Check spelling, grammar, etc.

2) Avoid clutter -- the resume should give the reader a taste of your capabilities while leaving him or her wanting to know more.

3) Never use abbreviations.

4) Start sentences with verbs -- never use "I...".

5) When providing references, print them on a separate sheet.

6) Choose tasteful, business-like colors for paper and ink (white, ivory, light blue or gray are best for paper).

7) Limit your creativity unless the position you want warrants it.

8). Always keep your resume up-to-date. You never know when you'll need it.

Writing The Cover Letter

1) Prepare each cover letter as a unique personal response to a specific job opportunity.

2) DO NOT use form letters to respond to a job opening.

3) Match your background to the specific needs of the job opportunity.

4) Keep the cover letter brief and to the point, with no more than 3-4 short paragraphs.

5) Avoid long rambling sentences and abbreviations.

6) Ensure that the company and the person's name to whom the letter is being sent are spelled correctly.

7) Check each letter for spelling, grammar, and typo's.

8) Put your name address and phone number(s) on the letter.

9) Be courteous and truthful.

10) Ask for the opportunity of a personal interview to discuss your background and their needs in greater detail.

11) Choose tasteful business-like colors for the paper.

12) Use a heavy quality bond paper for your letters.

Preparations Before The Interview

1) Know who you are, not what you are.

2) Research the company, position and industry by:
   - going to the library
   - reading newspapers, magazines, etc.
   - calling or writing the company and asking them to send you information (annual report)
   - visit the company and ask for information (you might even get an informal interview)

3) Ensure that you have specific directions as to how to get to the interview location. Plan out your travel route, be aware of road construction and traffic patterns in the area.

4) Allow plenty of travel time to reach the interview location. Remember it is better to be there early than to be late. Use spare time to review your notes and check your appearance.

5) Write out a personal inventory of your strongest skills, areas of knowledge and personality traits, including goals and areas of improvement.

6) Prepare examples of past accomplishments with solid evidence of results achieved.

7) Practice a mock interview with a friend or spouse beforehand.

8) Prepare answers to tough questions you anticipate being asked -- especially ones that require comment on your negative traits. Make the response positive.

8) Make a list of past employers, addresses, phone numbers and job responsibilities -- to be able to fill out an application.

9) Check the weather forecast, and dress appropriately.

Handling The Interview

1) Dress appropriately and be well-groomed.

2) Don't eat, chew gum, smoke or drink during the interview.

3) Be polite, on-time and interested.

4) Prepare yourself ahead of time for possible questions.

5) Answer questions succinctly but completely.

6) Be honest about while you are looking for another job, but don't bad mouth you current or previous employer.

7) Ask pertinent questions about the job. You want to know as much about them as they do about you.

8) Remain calm. Many interviewers are more nervous than you.

9) Make good eye contact with the interviewer but don't stare.

10) If a tough question comes up, compose yourself before answering. The interviewer will respect your thoughtfulness.

11) Turn negatives into positives.

12) Keep smiling and sound pleasant.

13) Illustrate points with examples but don't ramble.

14) Bring extra copies of resume, references or samples of work.

15) DO NOT ask about salary, vacation time, etc.

16) Ask to take home a copy of the annual report or other company literature.

17) Be aware of your rights -- employers are not allowed to ask about creed, nationality, race, marital status, family plans or age, nor are they allowed to request a photo of you.

18) When asked about previous salary, be specific as to what you were making and what your benefit package was.

19) If asked what salary you are looking for, inquire as to what is the salary range of the position offered. If less then what you were making, you may want to adjust your requirements to fit their range.

    This can best be done by telling them that an offer in this range taking into consideration your experience and positive attitude would be acceptable.

    Your willingness to accommodate their needs and accept an offer of less than what you were making should be explained by the fact that you believe your future performance with the company will quickly be recognized and rewarded.

20) Don't forget to thank the interviewer for his or her time.

21) Ask for a business card from the interviewer, this will be useful for your follow-up later.

22) Leave one of your own business cards with the interviewer. This is just another way to reinforce the memory of your visit with them.

23) Close by asking the interviewer for a candid evaluation of his/her thoughts about your opportunity of being considered for the position.

24) Set a specific date and time for follow up for further information or for when you can expect a decision.

Important Questions To Ask

Questions to ask about Hiring Companies:

1. What is the overall objective and goal of the company?

   It is important to know whether a company is concerned about growth and expansion or if the company is positioning itself for the possibility of a future takeover. If the latter is true, then job security make be shaky.

2. What is the industry ranking of the company? How has that changed from the previous year?

   If a company is improving in the industry ranking from one year to the next, then this is the right one to hitch your star to.

3. How profitable is the company? How has that changed from the previous year?

   A company that is growing in profitability or has some very good reasons for any downturns is a better place than one which is losing money. You want one that isn't worried about where the next nickel is coming from.

4. What has been the turnover rate of the current staff and management?

   Beware of any company that has a high turnover rate, you could be walking through a revolving door.

Questions to ask concerning a specific job:

1. What are the specific experience requirements?

   The more that you understand in advance the needs of a specific position, the better you will be able to draft a cover letter that is targeted to respond directly to those needs.

2. What are the educational requirements?

   Understanding the educational requirements will allow you to propose experience and training courses as an alternative to overcome any potential objections if you lack the appropriate credentials.

3. What is the reporting structure?

   Knowing the chain of command will give you a better understanding of internal opportunities for advancement.

4. What are the responsibilities associated with the position?

   Identifying the specific responsibilities of a position will give you a measure to gauge your own experience against the needs of the company. It will also give you some insight into how exciting you will find the job if it is offered to you.

5. Where is the job located?

   A simple question, but often the interview for a position is held in a location different from where the position is located. Knowing where the job is will permit you to determine how much travel is required and to weight that factor when evaluating a job opening.

6. What are the normal working hours?

   Another simple but important question that helps prevent misunderstanding if asked up front.

7. Is this a salaried or non-salaried position?

   If this is a non-salaried position, then you need to know what the potential is for overtime and what is the pay scale associated with overtime.

8. What is the long term grow opportunity for this position?

   Everyone likes to have a goal to work towards, and one of the best goals available for employees is the reward and recognition associated with advancement. Know up front what opportunities are available for top performers to avoid any let down later.

Questions to ask concerning a job offer:

1. What is the makeup of the benefit package?

   You need to understand not only what is in the benefit package but also who pays for what portion of these benefits.

2. What is the salary range tied to the position?

   If the salary offered is at the high end of the salary range for a position, then you will know to expect minimal salary increases unless you are promoted into another position.

3. How often will there be performance reviews?

   It nice to know how often a performance review is performed so that you can have frequent feedback concerning your performance.

4. What is the normal schedule for salary reviews?

   Performance reviews and salary reviews are not always performed on the same cycle. Therefore by obtaining this information, it will prevent you from making false assumptions that lead to disappointment at a later date.

5. When do they need expect you to come on board?

   This is important in case you have any special plans that would conflict with their needs, or for you to give your current employer sufficient notice.

6. When do they need your answer to their offer?

   If you are unsure about making a commitment, then at least obtain a breathing period of a day or two to consider your decision. Once you've made your decision, then stick with it.

After the Interview Follow-up

1) On the same day, send brief thank-you notes to everyone encountered that day (receptionists, secretaries, etc.)

2) Send a thank-you note to everyone who interviewed you.

3) End your note to the interviewer(s) by reiterating your interest in the company and the position.

4) Begin follow-up calls one week later, and inquire as to how the selection process is going.

5) Continue to interview at other companies -- don't wait by the phone after each one.

6) Work to get multiple job offers, you will put you in the driver's seat for negotiating salary and benefits.

Stress Management Made Easy!

1) For immediate relief, practice stress-controlling exercises:

   - Alternately contract and relax muscles, counting to 10 in between.

   - Take a long, warm shower or bath.

   - Visit a masseur or masseuse -- a one hour session costs little more than a good haircut.

   - Exercise! It's amazing what sweat and sore muscles can do for improving your outlook.

   - Listen to soothing music in a quiet comfortable area.

2) Create a time-management plan and follow it.

3) Prioritize short- and long-term goals and write them down.

4) Create a financial planning strategy to project current expenses and anticipated expenses for the unemployed period.

5) Assess personal goals in relationship to the job market.

6) Talk with people -- you are not the only one looking for a job.

7) Keep things in perspective, remember that the man with no shoes is not nearly as bad off as the man with no feet.

8) Be easy on yourself and set realistic objectives.

9) Remember all problems have a definite life cycle, persistence will help you to shorten the time required to find a job.

10) Look in the mirror and smile, already you feel good.

How People Find Jobs

There is no sure-fire way to find your next job. It often seems as if luck, and being in the right place at the right time, have a lot to do with it. However, one thing is certain -- the more people you tell about your search for a new opportunity, the better your chance of finding it.

Here are some guidelines and facts for conducting your search:

Networking

- Call all friends and acquaintances, regardless of whether they are in your field or not
- Seek advice from them on finding a suitable job
- Identify 2-3 areas of expertise for them
- Query them for contacts to talk to for advice
- Ask if they will call ahead and introduce you
- Send these contacts a copy of your resume along with a cover letter that refers back to the contact source
- Follow up with a telephone call to determine interest and to establish a time for a personal interview
- Work new contacts for further leads to other potential jobs

Employment Agencies and Recruiters

- Are used more and more frequently to fill positions
- Cover specialized areas and fields
- Typically find people for jobs, not jobs for people
- Retain your information on file for only 6 months to a year
- Often control the best paying positions
- Require you to update information periodically
- Are most effective if they specialize in your field
- Often require the use of more than one firm for maximum exposure to the hiring market
- Require continue followup on your part to ensure that you remain an active presence

Newspaper Ads

- Respond to ads quickly, within 2-3 days
- Provide a brief cover letter -- no more than 3-4 short paragraphs
- Tailor your resume or cover letter to fit the job description covered by the ad
- Beware of ads with only a phone number, P.O. Box number or ones that advertise false positions for job banks
- For maximum response, provide a self addressed, stamped postcard that provides check off boxes for ease of response.

  Examples of check off boxes:

  ___ Interested, will contact for an interview
  ___ Not a match at this time, will hold on file
  ___ Not Interested, however your resume will be routed for consideration to: ________________
  ___ Not interested, however, send your resume to:

  ____
  ____
  ____

- For those jobs of particular interest, send a follow up letter after two weeks to keep your name fresh in their files

Database Services

- Growing in popularity -- used by many employment agencies
- Puts your job history in the hands of more people
- Provide a wider geographic exposure to the job market
- Can help employers find you sooner
- Retain your information on file for only 6 months to a year
- Require periodic information updating
- Access available from many sources such as resume preparation firms, employment agencies, private advertising, non-profit organizations, and college placement offices
- Available free or usually for a small fee

Videotaping Services

- Popular with companies for reducing travel/recruitment costs
- Save money and time, especially if you're planning to relocate
- Speed-up the selection process for hiring companies
- Can ease first-interview tensions
- Make in-person interviews more productive
- Provide wider geographic exposure to the job market
- Require a certain amount of front end preparation
- May require the payment of a small fee
- Provide the greatest flexibility of scheduling time for a screening interview
- On the down side, video interviews are often one shot deals performed at the request of the hiring company after they have received your resume.

Outplacement Firms/Employment Counselors

- Help to accurately evaluate your current skills
- Assist in matching your skills to a field or position
- Help you psychologically with the search process
- Aid in targeting the right hiring companies
- Require dedicated involvement on your part
- Effective in evaluating current job skills
- Assist you in organizing an effective job search process
- Provide an excellent support base
- Are most beneficial for those with special problems or skills
- Require the payment of a fee for services provided
- Are available on an hourly basis or a flat fee depending upon the type of services offered

Resume Preparation Firms

- Help structure your resume to best suit a position sought
- Can be especially helpful when considering a career change
- Assist in creating and supporting an effective mail campaign
- Furnish the means of putting your job credentials in the best written presentation format
- Often provide access to resume database services
- Allow the easy creation of several specifically tailored resumes for emphasizing different job skills depending upon the position sought
- Provide a finished document which creates the best professional image for presenting your job history to potential employers

Job-Finding Facts

- 31.5% of jobs are found by applying directly to the employer
- 25% of jobs are found from networking with friends/relatives
- 12.5% of jobs are found through employment agencies
- 12.5% of jobs are found through newspaper advertisements
- 1.3% of jobs are found from union hiring halls
- 1.3% of jobs are found from civil service testing
- 16% of jobs are found through other methods

The key to finding a job can be found in this summary:

- Obtain and maintain a positive mental attitude.
- Get and stay organized.
- Always be over prepared for an interview.
- Use as many sources as possible to network.
- Follow up all leads and network for more.
- Pursue different avenues to obtain interviews and concentrate your efforts where responses are greatest.
- Remember, finding a job is work, to be successful, you must continually work at the process.
- Keep your sense of humor, even the worst problem looks better through a smile.
- Share with your spouse and family your concerns, it makes the burden smaller and easier to carry.
- Take time out to enjoy a nice day, smell the flowers, take a long walk, to recharges your energy level.
- When there appears to be nowhere else to turn, stop a minute, and pray, all things are possible with His help. Sometimes, we just forget to ask!

To quote the famous radio talk show host
Bruce Williams, who I admire very much...

"I wish you well my friend".

DALLAS & THE SOUTH WEST JOB SEEKERS SOURCEBOOK

Section 4

Employment Agencies/Recruiters

What is an employment agency?

Generally firms that place candidates in support and staff positions that pay $20,000 to $70,000 per year are called employment agencies, personnel consultants or recruiters. For purposes of grouping these firms in our source book, we use the label "Employment agency / Recruiter". For ease of reading this introduction, the terms "agency" and "recruiter" are used to refer to employment agencies/recruiters.

The value of an agency to a job seeker depends upon several things: the quality of the agency, the kind of work or position being sought, and your own level of experience. A good agency may help its candidates develop a strategy and prepare for personal interviews.

The benefit of an agency to a hiring company depends upon: the quality of the agency, the level of expertise contained by an agency's staff, the type of screening support performed by an agency to assist a company to quickly find the right person to meet its needs, and the span of individuals that are accessible to an agency from either the agency's own files or through its affiliations or network services.

Today many agencies are taking advantage of computer automation to share information with other agencies, making such agencies much more beneficial to both job seekers and hiring companies.

The next few pages contain important information on how to:

- Select an employment agency/recruiter to help you
- Work with an agency/recruiter

How To Select An Employment Agency/Recruiter

Finding the right employment agency or recruiter to help you find a job or change jobs requires some careful research on your part.

This is a process that cannot and should not be ignored. To maximize your chances of obtaining a job through this approach means that you must work hard to qualify and then select recruiters that you want to represent you in your job search. To assist you in this process we've outlined some important selection criteria that should be useful.

Selection Criteria:

The selection of the right firm to support your job search efforts should be based upon a combination of the following criteria:

Specialty Does the firm specialize in making placements in your career field and industry?

If so, the firm is more likely to find you a new job. If it deals exclusively in your discipline, so much the better.

Experience How long has the firm and the recruiter been in the placement business? And how long have they been making placements for members of your profession?

It is best to select a recruiter who has at least three years experience specializing in your industry. These recruiters will already have established a network of contacts with a number of hiring companies and will be better sources for job openings.

Proximity Is the firm convenient for you to visit on a regular basis?

Periodic office visits help you maintain high visibility with an individual recruiter.

Personality Does the recruiter like you and do you the recruiter? Are you comfortable with the recruiter's business style and ability to represent you to hiring companies?

If, yes, then you have a better shot at establishing and maintaining a good rapport with your recruiter on an ongoing basis.

Referrals Was this agency referred to you by someone else in your field?

Added to positive responses for the preceding qualifiers, a referral will give you an edge over other job seekers.

Quality Does this agency have a good reputation and do they present themselves in a professional manner?

The best way to determine this is to talk to other job seekers and to visit the recruiter's office to size them up. If you're unhappy with what you see or find, keep looking.

Networks Is this recruiter or employment agency a member of a placement affiliation or shared database network?

If yes, then the chances are better that having them represent you will give you broader exposure to a larger share of the employment market.

Questions to ask to qualify an employment agency/recruiter:

1. How long have they been in the placement business?

   The longer a firm has been in the business, the more contacts it is likely to have, therefore the odds of the firm being able to help you are better.

2. Do they specialize in making placements only in your career field?

   Usually, it is best to concentrate your efforts with just those recruiters that specialize in placing individuals with your background.

3. How many job openings are they working on at any one time?

   Typically ten to fifteen openings per month are good numbers for an individual recruiter.

4. How many placements do they average per month?

   Typically one to two placements per month are good numbers for an individual recruiter.

5. How many candidates are they working with?

   An average agency is likely to have three to four thousand resumes on file with maybe half of these representing people actively seeking new employment. Avoid those agencies that have more than 300 active candidates per agent, because you'll be easily forgotten.

6. How many client companies are they working with?

   Firms which average twenty companies per recruiter are about the right size to support you in your job search. Those below that level unless in a very narrow vertical market (ie. chemical engineers) or without a large number of annual job searches may not be active enough.

   Firms attempting to handle a larger number of hiring companies per agent may be spreading its resources too thin, especially if the number of placements per agent is low.

Working with an Employment Agency/Recruiter

Maximize your success of having an employment agency or recruiter find you a job, by remembering a few important axioms.

Employment agencies or recruiters normally do not get paid until they place an individual into a fee paid position.

Therefore, do everything possible to help make their job easier. This includes having a very good resume available for their use and being prepared and on time for any job interviews that you agree upon.

Employment agencies and recruiters will quickly lose interest in a job applicant that continually turns down job offers.

To prevent problems, be specific with the employment agency or recruiter as to what you are looking for in a company and a position. Do this during your first meeting with the recruiter.

If the job offer, the position, or the company environment isn't right, then by all means turn it down, but discuss it first with your recruiter so he/she understands your reasons. Just remember that you run the risk of losing support if you turn down too many offers.

Employment agencies and recruiters prefer to have an exclusive commitment from a job seeker.

This means that if you are going to use multiple agencies or recruiters to speed up your job search, keep this information to yourself.

The level of interest an agency has in helping you find a job drops to almost zero once they know that you are shopping recruiters. There are more than enough job seekers out looking for a job that a recruiter hesitates to spend time on someone who any day may be placed through another agency. It could be a waste of both time and money to try to place that individual.

Employment agencies and recruiters see as many as a hundred people each day. Also, an equal or greater amount of resumes are received in the daily mail from job seekers.

This means that you must get noticed and stay noticed, but this must be accomplished without becoming a pest. There are a variety of ways of doing this such as:

1. Hand deliver your resume to the firm and spend some time to ask questions, answer questions, and get a contact name.

2. Call on a weekly basis to update them on your status and to obtain an update from your recruiter.

3. Send a thank you note, right up front when a recruiter takes an interest in helping you.

4. Drop in the office once every two weeks to spend a few quick moments with your contact. Avoid Mondays or Fridays, as these days are always busy.

5. From time to time share a small gift (ie. donuts, candy, etc.) when you drop in for a visit.

6. When you come across current articles in newspapers or magazines about company expansions or relocations that could be beneficial to the recruiter, cut out the article and send it to recruiter along with a note.

The service recruiters provide to job seekers is free, but don't abuse this service, recruiters need to make a living too.

Treat them with respect, and be thoughtful enough to at least notify them when you have taken a job offer from another source. If you really appreciated their efforts, send them a thank you card or a little gift to show your appreciation for their efforts.

If you were extremely satisfied with their efforts, refer job openings to them as well as other good job seekers. This will allow you to maintain contact with them and to keep your options open in case you need someone to again help you find a job in a timely manner.

Recruiters know their job, but they don't know you or how well you can perform your job.

This means that they need your help in getting to know you. Remember, you know your job qualifications better than anyone, so tell them what you are good at. Describe and identify the important features of previous accomplishments. Furnish them with a means of measuring performance, such as a list of awards or reference letters.

Questions to ask recruiters about job openings:

1. How long has the job opening been available?

   If just a short time and you've received an offer, then this is a company that can make decisions quickly. If the job has been open a long time, then you need to know why, prior to making any acceptance decision.

2. Why is the job open?

   If someone retired or it's a new position, these are all positive signs. However, if someone has left the company or was terminated, then it would be nice to understand the circumstances before making a long term commitment.

3. When does a decision have to be made?

   Allow yourself some time to sleep on it before getting back to them. Be comfortable with your decision or don't do it.

4. How many people have already been presented?

   If a large number, than the odds are the hiring company has a backup candidate for the same job offer.

5. Why wasn't the position filled from within the company?

   If you don't like the answer, then the odds for future promotions within the company may be slim.

6. What is the long term opportunity for this position?

   Again, if you're looking for future growth, you need to be comfortable with the answer to this question.

Topics you should not discuss with recruiters:

1. Your knowledge about job openings in your field, until you have found and accepted a job yourself.

   Don't create unwanted competition for yourself.

2. Whether you are using other recruiters.

   To do so would reduce the interest in working with you.

- If a placement firm doesn't have the experience in your field or the placement industry, it may not be the firm for you to use.

- If they don't handle a large number or the right type of hiring companies or if they have too many job seekers on file then they may be not be the best avenue for obtaining a job.

- Finally, if they do not handle a large number of job openings, especially in your field, then chances are slim they can be of any meaningful help to you.

Employment Agencies/Recruiters - Arizona

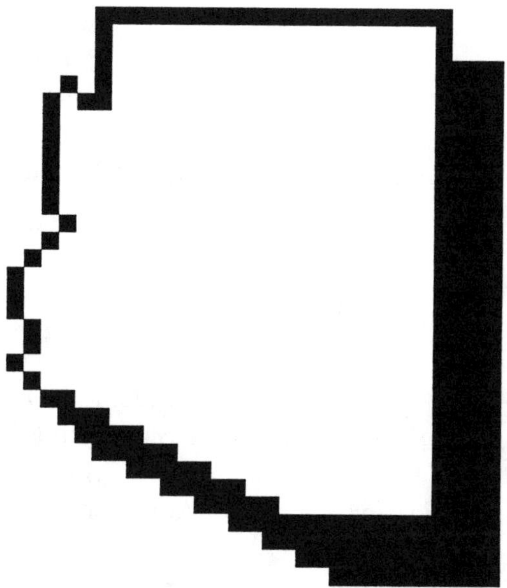

The following pages contain the specialty cross-reference listings to an alphabetical list of active employment agencies/recruiters located in Arizona.

The alphabetical listing is immediately after the cross-reference list.

INDEX CROSS REFERENCE BY SPECIALTY

Specialty: A
(Advertising)

Asosa Personnel

Specialty: B
(Banking)

Asosa Personnel
Robert Half International

Specialty: C
(Computers & Data Processing)

Asosa Personnel
Computer People Inc
Computer Strategies Inc
Exec-2000
Robert Half International
Russell Group The
Source EDP
Southwest Search Inc
Southwest Semiconductor Specialists

Specialty: E
(Engineering)

Asosa Personnel
Connelly Search
Russell Group The

Specialty: F
(Finance & Accounting)

Accountants Registry
Accountemps
Accountemps
Accounting & Bookkeeping Personnel
Asosa Personnel
Robert Half International
Source Finance

Specialty: G
(General Applications)

Academy of Business College
Accent Human Resource Specialists
Adia Personnel Services
Alpha Personnel
American Career Group
Ann Allen Agency
Apple One Employment Services
Arizona Labor Force
Asosa Personnel
B & A-Bishop & Associates
B & B Employment
Best Rates USA
C M of Phoenix Inc
Career Connections Inc
Contract Personnel Systems
Corporate Job Bank
Corporate Personnel Services
Cosmopolitan Personnel Servs
Del Personnel

Delcor Technical Placements
DES-Job Service
Dorado Employment
Dynamic Science Inc
Eleventh Hour Personnel
Executemps In Of Phoenix
Far Western Placement Service
First Choice Personnel Services
Foxie Temps & Advertising
General Employment
Industrial Personnel Inc
International Execusearch Ltd
Job Service
JTPA Career Centers
Kerry's Referrals
Key Personnel
Kingston & Associates Inc
Labor Force
Labor Profesionals Inc
Magic Group The
Mature Resources
Network Personnel II Inc
Norrell Services Inc
North Phoenix Employment Training Center
Orion Personnel Ltd
P D I Corp
Perry Placement Service
Plus-50 Placement Center Inc
Prestige Support 2000/PPS Inc
Professional Career Consultants
Professional Perspectives
Professional Placement Inc
Quantum Associates Inc
R S I Search Division
Ray Rashkin Assocs Inc
Rees Enterprises Inc
Roberson And Company
Scottsdale Employment Agency
SER-Jobs for Progress
Snelling Personnel Services
Source Finance
Staff One Inc
Staffing Solutions of Arizona Inc
Sterling Enterprises Inc
Thomas Laura
Top Personnel
Twin Star Productions Inc
Valley Employment Agency
VSP Personnel Service Inc
Western Personnel Associates
Western Personnel Employment

Specialty: H (Healthcare)

Arizona Medical Exchange
Asosa Personnel
EAI Medical Personnel Services
Exec-2000
Healthcare Recruiters of Arizona
Human Resource Network Medical
Maricopa County Medical Society
Medical Society The
Norrell Health Care
Nursefinders of Phoenix Inc
Professional Nursing Services
Sun Health Corp

Specialty: I (Insurance)

Asosa Personnel

Insurance Personnel Consultants

Specialty: L
(Legal)

Asosa Personnel
Exec-2000
Legal Placement Services Inc

Specialty: M
(Manufacturing)

Asosa Personnel

Specialty: O
(Office Administration)

Asosa Personnel
Office World Personnel Inc
Officeteam
OM5/Office Mates 5

Specialty: P
(Personnel/Human Resources)

Asosa Personnel

Specialty: R
(Research & Development)

Asosa Personnel

Specialty: S
(Sales & Marketing)

Asosa Personnel
Exec-2000
Personnel Resource Corp
Russell Group The

Specialty: T
(Travel,Food & Hospitality)

Asosa Personnel
Ogden Aviation Services

Other Specific Specialties:

Specialty: Automotive

Automotive Opportunities
O'Connor & Associates

Specialty: Domestics

Camelview Domestic Placement

Specialty: Electronic

Exec-2000

Specialty: High Tech

Exec-2000

Specialty: Management/Senior Management

Exec-2000
Source Finance

Specialty: Technical

Technical Search Service

Melissa A Gross
Academy of Business College
3320 W Cheryl Dr Ste 115
Phoenix, AZ 85051
(602) 942-4141
Specialty: G
Employment Agency/Recruiter

Office Manager
Accent Human Resource Specialists
2222 E Camelback Rd
Phoenix, AZ 85016
(602) 955-2222
Specialty: G
Employment Agency/Recruiter

Office Manager
Accountants Registry
1300 E Missouri Av S-D 200
Phoenix, AZ 85014
(602) 264-1108
Specialty: F
Employment Agency/Recruiter

Office Manager
Accountemps
1811 S Alma School Rd
Mesa, AZ 85210
(602) 820-4616
Specialty: F
Employment Agency/Recruiter

Office Manager
Accountemps
100 W Clarendon Av
Phoenix, AZ 85013
(602) 264-6488
Specialty: F
Employment Agency/Recruiter

Office Manager
Accounting & Bookkeeping Personnel
1702 E Highland Ave Ste 213
Phoenix, AZ 85016
(602) 277-3700
Specialty: F
Employment Agency/Recruiter

Office Manager
Adia Personnel Services
333 E Osborn Rd
Phoenix, AZ 85012
(602) 246-1143
Specialty: G
Employment Agency/Recruiter

Office Manager
Adia Personnel Services
123 E Baseline Rd
Tempe, AZ 85283
(602) 831-1131
Specialty: G
Employment Agency/Recruiter

Office Manager
Alpha Personnel
605 E Broadway Rd
Tempe, AZ 85282
(602) 968-9489
Specialty: G
Employment Agency/Recruiter

Office Manager
American Career Group
3333 E Camelback Rd Ste 250
Phoenix, AZ 85018
(602) 381-1667
Specialty: G
Employment Agency/Recruiter

Office Manager
Ann Allen Agency
2425 E Thomas Rd
Phoenix, AZ 85016
(602) 956-2886
Specialty: G
Employment Agency/Recruiter

Office Manager
Apple One Employment Services
9201 N 29th Ave
Phoenix, AZ 85051
(602) 280-1720
Specialty: G
Employment Agency/Recruiter

Office Manager
Apple One Employment Services
3405 N 7th Ave
Phoenix, AZ 85013
(602) 263-5122
Specialty: G
Employment Agency/Recruiter

Office Manager
Apple One Employment Services
7272 E Indian School Rd
Scottsdale, AZ 85251
(602) 280-1700
Specialty: G
Employment Agency/Recruiter

Office Manager
Apple One Employment Services
20 E University
Tempe, AZ 85281
(602) 829-3777
Specialty: G
Employment Agency/Recruiter

Office Manager
Arizona Medical Exchange
2440 W Mission Ln
Phoenix, AZ 85021
(602) 246-4906
Specialty: H
Employment Agency/Recruiter

Office Manager
Arizona Labor Force
2288 S Idaho Rd
Apache Junction, AZ 85219
(602) 644-9009
Specialty: G
Employment Agency/Recruiter

Paul P Payne CPC, Pres
Asosa Personnel
1016 E Broadway
Tucson, AZ 85719
(602) 792-0622
(602) 792-0655 FAX
Specialty: A,B,C,E,F,G,H,I,L,M,O,P,R,S,T
Employment Agency/Recruiter

Office Manager
Arizona Labor Force Inc
88 W Boston St
Chandler, AZ 85224
(602) 821-0974
Specialty: G
Employment Agency/Recruiter

Office Manager
Automotive Opportunities
6845 N Black Canyon Hwy
Phoenix, AZ 85017
(602) 433-9447
Specialty: Automotive
Employment Agency/Recruiter

Paul P Payne CPC, Pres
Asosa Personnel
8601 N Black Canyon Ste 105
Phoenix, AZ 85021-4155
(602) 246-7024
Specialty: G
Personnel Consultant/Recruiter

Office Manager
B & A-Bishop & Associates
2504 E Indian School Rd
Phoenix, AZ 85016
(602) 957-4620
Specialty: G
Employment Agency/Recruiter

Office Manager
Asosa Personnel
1232 E Broadway Rd Ste 108
Tempe, AZ 85282
(602) 968-4481
Specialty: G
Employment Agency/Recruiter

Office Manager
B & B Employment
1702 E Highland Ave Ste 206
Phoenix, AZ 85016
(602) 277-3381
Specialty: G
Employment Agency/Recruiter

Office Manager
Best Rates USA
3625 N 16th St Ste 1006
Phoenix, AZ 85016
(602) 241-1131
Specialty: G
Employment Agency/Recruiter

Office Manager
C M of Phoenix Inc
5308 N 12th St 401
Phoenix, AZ 85014
(602) 248-7979
Specialty: G
Employment Agency/Recruiter

Office Manager
Camelview Domestic Placement
2990 E Northern Ave Ste 8101
Phoenix, AZ 85028
(602) 996-0882
Specialty: Domestics
Employment Agency/Recruiter

Office Manager
Career Connections Inc
301 E Bethany Home Rd
Phoenix, AZ 85012
(602) 277-7222
Specialty: G
Employment Agency/Recruiter

Office Manager
Computer People Inc
3829 N 3rd St
Phoenix, AZ 85012
(602) 248-0010
Specialty: C
Employment Agency/Recruiter

Moira Silver CPC
Computer Strategies Inc
7454 E Broadway Ste 105
Tucson, AZ 85710
(602) 721-9544
Specialty: Systems Analysis
Personnel Consultant/Recruiter

Joseph Connelly CPC
Connelly Search
P O Box 30926
Tucson, AZ 85751-0926
(602) 327-7999
Specialty: E
Personnel Consultant/Recruiter
For Consulting Engineering
Firms ONLY

Office Manager
Contract Personnel Systems
1430 E Missouri Ste 165
Phoenix, AZ 85014
(602) 230-2000
Specialty: G
Employment Agency/Recruiter

Office Manager
Corporate Job Bank
1725 W University Dr 114
Tempe, AZ 85281
(602) 966-0709
Specialty: G
Employment Agency/Recruiter

Office Manager
Corporate Personnel Services
1440 E Missouri Ste 185
Phoenix, AZ 85014
(602) 230-2500
Specialty: G
Employment Agency/Recruiter

Office Manager
Cosmopolitan Personnel Servs
4525 N 12th St
Phoenix, AZ 85019
(602) 248-7766
(602) 263-8214
Specialty: G
Employment Agency/Recruiter

Del Dempewolf
Del Personnel
2717 N Steves Bl
Flagstaff, AZ 86004
(602) 526-1010
Specialty: G
Personnel Consultant/Recruiter

Office Manager
Delcor Technical Placements
2526 E University Dr
Phoenix, AZ 85034
(602) 273-7754
Specialty: G
Employment Agency/Recruiter

Barbara J Hinches, Manager
DES-Job Service
232 London Bridge Rd
Lake Havasu City, AZ 86403
(602) 680-6005
(602) 680-6010 FAX
Specialty: G
Employment Agency/Recruiter

Evie Kay CPC
Dorado Employment
5024 N Oracle Rd
Tucson, AZ 85704
(602) 888-3900
Specialty: G
Personnel Consultant/Recruiter

Office Manager
Dynamic Science Inc
8433 N Black Canyon Hwy
Phoenix, AZ 85021
(602) 995-3700
Specialty: G
Employment Agency/Recruiter

Office Manager
EAI Medical Personnel Services
777 W Southern Ave
Mesa, AZ 85210
(602) 649-9260
Specialty: H
Employment Agency/Recruiter

Ellen B Echales, Owner/Operator
EAI Medical Personnel Services
5110 N Central Ave Ste 301
Phoenix, AZ 85012
(602) 266-5704
(602) 266-5772 FAX
Specialty: H
Employment Agency/Recruiter

Office Manager
Eleventh Hour Personnel
1550 E Missouri Ave
Phoenix, AZ 85014
(602) 234-3102
Specialty: G
Employment Agency/Recruiter

Martin Jacobs
Exec-2000
5251 N 16 Street
Phoenix, AZ 85016
(602) 246-7024
Specialty: H,S,Food,High Tech/Electronic,Legal,MIS, Physicians,Senior Management, Systems/Analysis
Personnel Consultant/Recruiter

Office Manager
Executemps In Of Phoenix
7330 N 16th St Ste 117
Phoenix, AZ 85020
(602) 861-1200
Specialty: G
Employment Agency/Recruiter

Office Manager
Far Western Placement Service
8111 N 9th Ave
Phoenix, AZ 85021
(602) 943-5026
Specialty: G
Employment Agency/Recruiter

Office Manager
First Choice Personnel Services
10301 N 92nd St Ste 216
Scottsdale, AZ 85258
(602) 661-1000
Specialty: G
Employment Agency/Recruiter

Office Manager
Foxie Temps & Advertising
2438 E McDowell Rd
Phoenix, AZ 85213
(602) 231-8766
Specialty: G
Employment Agency/Recruiter

Office Manager
General Employment
3443 N Central Ave
Phoenix, AZ 85012
(602) 265-7800
Specialty: G
Employment Agency/Recruiter

Office Manager
Healthcare Recruiters of Arizona
11811 N Tatum Blvd Ste 3031
Phoenix, AZ 85032
(602) 953-7760
Specialty: H
Employment Agency/Recruiter

Office Manager
Human Resource Network Medical
6060 E Thomas Rd
Scottsdale, AZ 85251
(602) 947-1993
Specialty: H
Employment Agency

Office Manager
Industrial Personnel Inc
1119 S Mesa Dr
Mesa, AZ 85210
(602) 835-5700
Specialty: G
Employment Agency/Recruiter

Office Manager
Insurance Personnel Consultants
4745 N 7th St
Phoenix, AZ 85014
(602) 266-3980
Specialty: I
Employment Agency/Recruiter

Carig Hallbourg
International Execusearch Ltd
6560 N Scottsdale Rd Ste J-102
Scottsdale, AZ 85253
(602) 991-5000
Specialty: G
Personnel Consultant/Recruiter

Office Manager
Job Service
301 Pine St
Kingman, AZ 86401
(602) 753-4333
Specialty: G
Employment Agency/Recruiter

Office Manager
JTPA Career Centers
412 E Oak St
Kingman, AZ 86401
(602) 753-0723
Specialty: G
Employment Agency/Recruiter

Office Manager
Kerry's Referrals
10240 N 31st Av Ste 220
Phoenix, AZ 85028
(602) 944-5595
Specialty: G
Employment Agency/Recruiter

Ronald R Regnier, Mg Agent
Key Personnel
1600 W Camelback Rd Ste 1-K
Phoenix, AZ 85015-3513
(602) 263-8356
Specialty: G
Employment Agency/Recruiter

James M Kingston
Kingston & Associates Inc
101 N Wilmot St Ste 210
Tucson, AZ 85711
(602) 745-3000
Specialty: G
Personnel Consultant/Recruiter

Office Manager
Labor Force
230 W Baseline Rd
Tempe AZ 85283
(602) 897-1409
Specialty: G
Employment Agency/Recruiter

Office Manager
Labor Profesionals Inc
654 W Camelback Rd
Phoenix, AZ 85013
(602) 234-1990
Specialty: G
Employment Agency/Recruiter

George Stebbings CPC
Legal Placement Services Inc
333 W Roosevelt
Phoenix, AZ 85003
(602) 257-4200
Specialty: L
Personnel Consultant/Recruiter

Office Manager
Magic Group The
5045 N 12th St Ste 130
Phoenix, AZ 85014
(602) 279-2800
Specialty: G
Employment Agency/Recruiter

Office Manager
Maricopa County Medical Society
326 E Coronado Rd
Phoenix, AZ 85004
(602) 252-3116
Specialty: H
Employment Agency/Recruiter

Office Manager
Mature Resources
9034 N 23rd Ave
Phoenix, AZ 85021
(602) 678-1900
Specialty: G
Employment Agency/Recruiter

Office Manager
Medical Society The
326 E Coronado
Phoenix, AZ 85004
(602) 252-3116
Specialty: H
Employment Agency/Recruiter

Office Manager
Network Personnel II Inc
3610 W 44th St
Phoenix, AZ 85018
(602) 468-1090
Specialty: G
Employment Agency/Recruiter

Office Manager
Norrell Health Care
4001 N 3rd St
Phoenix, AZ 85012
(602) 277-1996
Specialty: H
Employment Agency/Recruiter

Office Manager
Norrell Services Inc
2390 E Camelback Rd
Phoenix, AZ 85016
(602) 956-5844
Specialty: G
Employment Agency/Recruiter

Office Manager
North Phoenix Employment Training Center
225-227 W Hatcher Rd
Phoenix, AZ 85021
(602) 870-9655
Specialty: G
Employment Agency/Recruiter

Office Manager
Nursefinders of Phoenix Inc
950 W Indian School Rd
Phoenix, AZ 85013
(602) 274-0340
Specialty: H
Employment Agency/Recruiter

Kevin O'Connor, Owner
O'Connor & Associates
12601 N Cave Creek Rd Ste 109
Phoenix, AZ 85022
(602) 788-5890
(602) 788-5954 FAX
Specialty: Automotive
Employment Agency/Recruiter

Office Manager
Office World Personnel Inc
3737 N Seventh St
Phoenix, AZ 85014
(602) 234-2330
Specialty: O
Employment Agency/Recruiter

Office Manager
Officeteam
100 W Clarendon Ave
Phoenix, AZ 85013
(602) 285-9925
Specialty: O
Employment Agency/Recruiter

Office Manager
Ogden Aviation Services
3737 E Bonanea Way
Ski Harbor Int'l Airport
Phoenix, AZ 85219
(602) 225-5114
(602) 225-0741 FAX
Specialty: T(Commercial Airlines)
Employment Agency/Recruiter

Office Manager
OM5/Office Mates 5
6900 E Camelback Rd
Scottsdale, AZ 85251
(602) 941-5627
Specialty: O
Employment Agency/Recruiter

Office Manager
Orion Personnel Ltd
1500 E Bethany Home Rd
Phoenix, AZ 85014
(602) 266-0774
Specialty: G
Employment Agency/Recruiter

Chuck Bentley, Technical Rep
P D I Corp
1439 N 1st St
Phoenix, AZ 85004
(602) 252-0866
(602) 254-9309 FAX
Specialty: G
Employment Agency/Recruiter

Office Manager
Perry Placement Service
3146 E Windsor Ave
Phoenix, AZ 85008
(602) 957-9418
Specialty: G
Employment Agency/Recruiter

Office Manager
Personnel Resource Corp
3829 N 3rd St
Phoenix, AZ 85012
(602) 248-0010
Specialty: S
Employment Agency/Recruiter

Office Manager
Plus-50 Placement Center Inc
1256 W Chandler Bl
Chandler, AZ 85224
(602) 899-4822
Specialty: G
Employment Agency/Recruiter

Office Manager
Plus-50 Placement Center Inc
7116 N 56th Ave
Glendale, AZ 85301
(602) 939-5698
Specialty: G
Employment Agency/Recruiter

Office Manager
Plus-50 Placement Center Inc
247 N MacDonald St
Mesa, AZ 85201
(602) 962-5612
Specialty: G
Employment Agency/Recruiter

Office Manager
Plus-50 Placement Center Inc
5119 N 19th Ave
Phoenix, AZ 85015
(602) 246-0260
Specialty: G
Employment Agency/Recruiter

Office Manager
Plus-50 Placement Center Inc
7375 E 2nd St
Scottsdale, AZ 85251
(602) 994-2714
Specialty: G
Employment Agency/Recruiter

Office Manager
Plus-50 Placement Center Inc
2150 E Orange
Tempe, AZ 85281
(602) 968-3425
Specialty: G
Employment Agency/Recruiter

Office Manager
Prestige Support 2000/PPS Inc
5251 N 16th St Ste 310
Phoenix, AZ 85016
(602) 279-6424
Specialty: G
Employment Agency/Recruiter

Office Manager
Professional Career Consultants
7501 E McCormick Parkway
Ste 110
Scottsdale, AZ 85258
(602) 274-6666
Specialty: G
Employment Agency/Recruiter

Office Manager
Professional Nursing Services
2001 W Camelback Ste 346
Phoenix, AZ 85015
(602) 249-0991
Specialty: H
Employment Agency/Recruiter

Office Manager
Professional Perspectives
11811 N Tatum Bl Ste 1050
Phoenix, AZ 85028
(602) 953-1969
Specialty: G
Employment Agency/Recruiter

Wayne Calhoun CPC
Professional Placement Inc
2400 W Dunlap Ste 155
Phoenix, AZ 85021
(602) 870-4191
Specialty: G
Personnel Consultant/Recruiter

Office Manager
Professional Placements Inc
3900 E Camelback Rd
Phoenix, AZ 85018
(602) 955-0870
Specialty: G
Employment Agency/Recruiter

Office Manager
Professional Placements Inc
250 W Baseline Rd
Tempe, AZ 85283
(602) 820-4360
Specialty: G
Employment Agency/Recruiter

Office Manager
Professional Placements Inc
2030 E Broadway Blvd
Tucson, AZ 85719
(602) 792-0382
Specialty: G
Employment Agency/Recruiter

Office Manager
Quantum Associates Inc
64 E Broadway Rd
Tempe, AZ 85282
(602) 921-9313
Specialty: G
Employment Agency/Recruiter

Office Manager
R S I Search Division
4643 E Thomas Rd
Phoenix, AZ 85018
(602) 957-6308
Specialty: G
Employment Agency/Recruiter

Office Manager
Ray Rashkin Assocs Inc
10240 N 31st Ave
Phoenix, AZ 85051
(602) 678-1450
Specialty: G
Employment Agency/Recruiter

Office Manager
Rees Enterprises Inc
2010 E University Ste 12
Tempe, AZ 85281
(602) 968-0956
Specialty: G
Employment Agency/Recruiter

Stephen Silvas, Pres
Roberson And Company
1300 E Missouri Ste D-200
Phoenix, AZ 85014
(602) 264-1128
Specialty: G
Personnel Consultant/Recruiter

Office Manager
Robert Half International
1811 S Alma School Rd
Mesa, AZ 85210
(602) 820-4616
Specialty: B,C,F
Employment Agency/Recruiter

Office Manager
Robert Half International
100 W Clarendon Ave
Phoenix, AZ 85013
(602) 264-6488
Specialty: B,C,F
Employment Agency/Recruiter

Donna Johnson, Manager
Russell Group The
9699 N Hayden Rd Ste 108
Scottsdale, AZ 85258
(602) 998-3522
(602) 948-9654 FAX
Specialty: C,S,E(Software)
Employment Agency/Recruiter

Office Manager
Scottsdale Employment Agency
7220 1st Ave
Scottsdale, AZ 85251
(602) 947-7578
Specialty: G
Employment Agency/Recruiter

Office Manager
SER-Jobs for Progress
225 W Hather Rd
Phoenix, AZ 85021
(602) 249-0888
Specialty: G
Employment Agency/Recruiter

Office Manager
Snelling Personnel Services
3030 N Central Av Ste 808
Phoenix, AZ 85012
(602) 277-1818
Specialty: G
Employment Agency/Recruiter

Bob Rich
Source EDP
4722 N 24th St
Phoenix, AZ 85016
(602) 224-0014
Specialty: C,Information Technology,Systems Analysis & Integration
Employment Agency/Recruiter

John Kuzmick
Source Finance
4722 N 24th St
Phoenix, AZ 85016
(602) 955-1240
Specialty: F,G,Management
Employment Agency/Recruiter

Office Manager
Southwest Search Inc
4500 S Lakeshore Dr
Tempe, AZ 85282
(602) 838-0333
Specialty: C
Employment Agency/Recruiter

Office Manager
Southwest Semiconductor Specialists
628 E Grace Dr
Tempe, AZ 85281
(602) 947-5891
Specialty: C
Employment Agency/Recruiter

Ronni Anderson
Staff One Inc
2800 N 44th St Ste 340
Phoenix, AZ 85008
(602) 952-9060
Specialty: G
Personnel Consultant/Recruiter

Office Manager
Staffing Solutions of Arizona Inc
4802 E Betty Elyse Ln
Scottsdale, AZ 85254
(602) 788-5747
Specialty: G
Employment Agency/Recruiter

Office Manager
Sterling Enterprises Inc
1130 E University Dr
Tempe, AZ 85281
(602) 731-3600
Specialty: G
Employment Agency/Recruiter

Office Manager
Sun Health Corp
13180 N 103rd Dr
Sun City, AZ 85351
(602) 977-7211
Specialty: H
Employment Agency/Recruiter

Office Manager
Technical Search Service
1 E Camelback Rd
Phoenix, AZ 85012
(602) 230-1151
Specialty: Technical
Employment Agency/Recruiter

Office Manager
Thomas Laura
5125 SN 16th St
Phoenix, AZ 85016
(602) 277-0065
(602) 277-0527 Fax
Specialty: G
Employment Agency/Recruiter

Fran Sherman
Top Personnel
4647 N 16th St Ste 240
Phoenix, AZ 85016
(602) 263-9675
Specialty: G
Personnel Consultant/Recruiter

Office Manager
Twin Star Productions Inc
7345 E Evans Rd
Scottsdale, AZ 85260
(602) 951-6360
Specialty: G
Employment Agency/Recruiter

Office Manager
Valley Employment Agency
635 W Indian School Rd
Phoenix, AZ 85013
(602) 264-7325
Specialty: G
Employment Agency/Recruiter

Richard Chanick
VSP Personnel Service Inc
2111 E Highland Ste 148
Phoenix, AZ 85016
(602) 274-5627
Specialty: G
Personnel Consultant/Recruiter

Richard A Fishel
Western Personnel Associates
316 E Flower
Phoenix, AZ 85012
(602) 279-5301
Specialty: G
Personnel Consultant/Recruiter

Office Manager
Western Personnel Employment
10410 N 31st Ave
Phoenix, AZ 85051
(602) 993-8992
Specialty: G
Employment Agency/Recruiter

Office Manager
Western Personnel Employment Service
777 W Southern Av
Mesa, AZ 85210
(602) 833-4601
Specialty: G
Employment Agency/Recruiter

JOB SEEKERS SURVIVAL HINTS

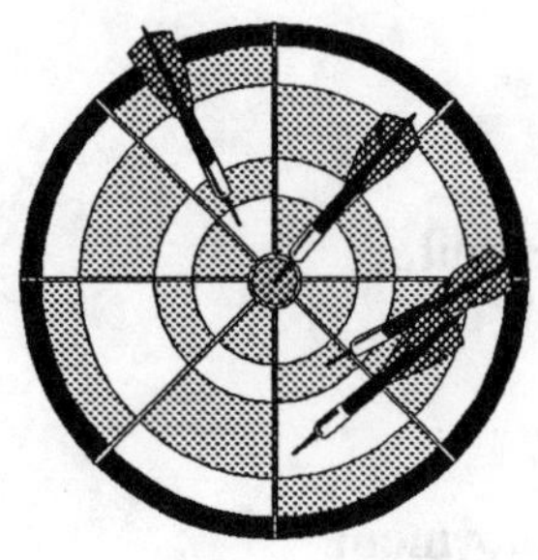

Target your contacts!

When pursuing a position within a particular industry, use your network to reach the hiring manager or person in authority within the department where your type of position is most often located.

Lacking contacts from your network, the next best approach is to be direct.

First, make a few phone calls to the targeted company to obtain the department manager's name and the name of the person in charge of Personnel. Another means of obtaining this type of information is through your local library. Many libraries today have computerized reference systems which provide quick access to names and titles of key individuals within targeted firms. Seek out the reference librarian for assistance.

Once the key individuals have been identified, write a letter direct to these individuals, highlighting your qualifications in relationship to possible needs within their company.

Finally, put them in your tickler file for a follow up telephone call ten days from the date that you sent out your letter.

Employment Agencies/Recruiters - New Mexico

The following pages contain the specialty cross-reference listings to an alphabetical list of active employment agencies/recruiters located in New Mexico.

The alphabetical listing is immediately after the cross-reference list.

INDEX CROSS REFERENCE BY SPECIALTY

Specialty: B
(Banking)

Robert Half International

Specialty: C
(Computers & Data Processing)

Robert Half International

Specialty: E
(Engineering)

ACC Corporation

Specialty: F
(Finance & Accounting)

Accountemps
Roadrunner Personnel
Robert Half International

Specialty: G
(General Applications)

Adia Personnel Services
Albuquerque Personnel Inc
Alliance Job Service
Applied Methods Inc
Butler Service Group
Career Placement Systems
EXCEL
Linda Porter Professional Sch
Marcia Owen Associates
New Mexico Personnel Inc
New Vistas
Owen-Peterson Marcia Employment Services
Proba Resources
Professional Personnel Placements
Sanderson Employment Svc Inc
Sandia Personnel Service
Santa Fe Jobs for Progress Inc
Santa Fe Services Inc
Snelling & Snelling
Snelling Personnel Svcs
Sue Wilson Personnel Svcs
Wilson-Richardson & Assoc

Specialty: H
(Healthcare)

Physician International

Specialty: L
(Legal)

ACC Corporation
Roadrunner Personnel

Specialty: O
(Office Administration)

OfficeTeam
Roadrunner Personnel

Specialty: S
(Sales & Marketing)

Roadrunner Personnel

Other Specific Specialties:

Specialty: Construction

Construction Services

Specialty: Technical

Ewing Technical Design Inc
Tad Technical Services

Office Manager
ACC Corporation
1613 Stagecoach Rd SE
Albuquerque, NM 87123
(505) 294-9701
Specialty: E,L
Employment Agency/Recruiter

Office Manager
Accountemps
2155 Louisiana Blvd NE
Albuquerque, NM 87110
(505) 884-4557
Specialty: F
Employment Agency/Recruiter

Office Manager
Adia Personnel Services
5505 Osuna Rd NE
Albuquerque, NM 87109
(505) 888-4545
Specialty: G
Employment Agency/Recruiter

Office Manager
Albuquerque Personnel Inc
5600-U McLeod Rd N E
Albuquerque, NM 87109
(505) 888-3555
Specialty: G
Employment Agency/Recruiter

Office Manager
Alliance Job Service
1200 4th St NW
Albuquerque, NM 87102
(505) 843-9797
Specialty: G
Employment Agency/Recruiter

Office Manager
Applied Methods Inc
1720 Louisiana Blvd NE
Albuquerque, NM 87110
(505) 255-5531
Specialty: G
Employment Agency/Recruiter

Office Manager
Butler Service Group
10211 Montgomery Blvd NE
Albuquerque, NM 87111
(505) 296-9553
Specialty: G
Employment Agency/Recruiter

Office Manager
Career Placement Systems
P O Box 1163
Corrales, NM 87048
(505) 898-1114
Specialty: G
Employment Agency/Recruiter

Office Manager
Construction Services
5101 Cooper Ave NE Ste 108
Albuquerque, NM 87108
(505) 262-2678
Specialty: Construction
Employment Agency/Recruiter

Office Manager
Ewing Technical Design Inc
1709 Moon St NE Ste 205
Albuquerque, NM 87112
(505) 291-5505
Specialty: Technical
Employment Agency/Recruiter

Office Manager
EXCEL
1700 Louisiana Blvd NE
Albuquerque, NM 87110
(505) 262-1871
Specialty: G
Employment Agency/Recruiter

Office Manager
Linda Porter Professional Sch
P O Box 87198
Albuquerque, NM 87198
(505) 255-6153
Specialty: G
Employment Agency/Recruiter

Office Manager
Marcia Owen Associates
128 Grant Ave
Santa Fe, NM 87501
(505) 983-7775
Specialty: G
Employment Agency/Recruiter

Office Manager
New Mexico Personnel Inc
6605 Uptown Blvd NE Ste 390
Albuquerque, NM 87110
(505) 888-3888
Specialty: G
Employment Agency/Recruiter

Office Manager
New Vistas
2890 Trades West Rd
Santa Fe, NM 87501
(505) 473-2123
Specialty: G
Employment Agency/Recruiter

Office Manager
OfficeTeam
2155 Louisiana Blvd N E
Albuquerque, NM 87110
(505) 888-4002
Specialty: O
Employment Agency/Recruiter

Office Manager
Owen-Peterson Marcia Employment Services
128 Grant Ave
Santa Fe, NM 87501
(505) 983-1454
Specialty: G
Employment Agency/Recruiter

Office Manager
Physician International
1040 Montano Rd N W
Albuquerque, NM 87107
(505) 344-7832
Specialty: H
Employment Agency/Recruiter

Office Manager
Proba Resources
2509 Vermont St N E Ste D
Albuquerque, NM 87110
(505) 271-1860
Specialty: G
Employment Agency/Recruiter

Office Manager
Professional Personnel Placements
4205 Glen Arbor Ct N W
Albuquerque, NM 87107
(505) 345-6661
Specialty: G
Employment Agency/Recruiter

Doug Elliott, Owner
Roadrunner Personnel
4015 Carlisle Blvd NE Ste C
Albuquerque, NM 87107
(505) 881-1994
(505) 881-8749 FAX
Specialty: F,L,O,S
Employment Agency/Recruiter

Office Manager
Robert Half International
2155 Louisiana Blvd N E
Albuquerque, NM 87110
(505) 884-4557
Specialty: B,C,F
Employment Agency/Recruiter

Office Manager
Sanderson Employment Svc Inc
1610 San Pedro Dr NE
Albuquerque, NM 87110
(505) 265-8827
Specialty: G
Employment Agency/Recruiter

Office Manager
Sandia Personnel Service
2438 San Mateo Pl N E
Albuquerque, NM 87110
(505) 881-1500
Specialty: G
Employment Agency/Recruiter

Office Manager
Snelling Personnel Svcs
2601 Wyoming Blvd N E
Albuquerque, NM 87112
(505) 293-7800
Specialty: G
Employment Agency/Recruiter

Office Manager
Snelling Personnel Svcs
1482-B St Francis Dr
Santa Fe, NM 87501
(505) 982-5757
Specialty: G
Employment Agency/Recruiter

Pat Murphy, Owner
Snelling & Snelling
2400 Louisiana Blvd NE Ste 580
Albuquerque, NM 87110
(505) 293-9800
(505) 881-2624 FAX
Specialty: G
Employment Agency/Recruiter

Office Manager
Santa Fe Jobs for Progress Inc
P O Box 2471
Santa Fe, NM 87504
(505) 984-1454
Specialty: G
Employment Agency/Recruiter

Office Manager
Santa Fe Services Inc
142 Lincoln Ave Ste 205
Santa Fe, NM 87501
(505) 984-8511
Specialty: G
Employment Agency/Recruiter

Office Manager
Sue Wilson Personnel Svcs
1717 Louisiana Blvd N E
Albuquerque, NM 87110
(505) 268-1905
Specialty: G
Employment Agency/Recruiter

Office Manager
Tad Technical Services
2701 San Pedro Dr N E Ste D
Albuquerque, NM 87110
(505) 889-9397
Specialty: Technical
Employment Agency/Recruiter

Office Manager
Wilson-Richardson & Assoc
2509 Vermont St N E Ste D
Albuquerque, NM 87110
(505) 271-1860
Specialty: G
Employment Agency/Recruiter

JOB SEEKERS SURVIVAL HINTS

The old saying that the early bird gets the worm certainly applies to the task of job hunting.

Stay ahead of the pack by doing the following:

- Review Sunday's paper as soon as it is out on the news stands. Check for any new job openings for which you are qualified and respond the same day by mail with a tailored cover letter and resume.

- Call the first thing Monday morning on all offers with a phone number to announce your interest and to let the employer know that a resume is on its way. Work to qualify the job offer and create an interest on their behalf. If the employer appears interested, then try to set up a time for an interview.

- Get the morning paper each day and send your responses out by noon on any new job openings.

- Maintain a log of all ads responded to so that you have a record of the cover letter sent, date/time of the ad, source of the ad, and the date/time of your response. Cross reference this log to new job openings to prevent a duplication of effort on your part.

Employment Agencies/Recruiters - Oklahoma

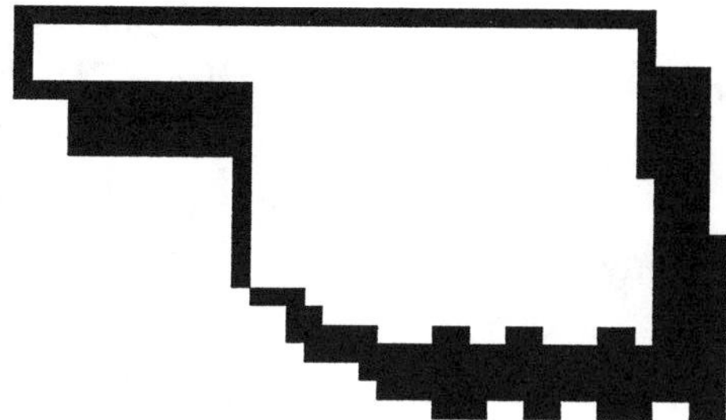

The following pages contain the specialty cross-reference listings to an alphabetical list of active employment agencies/recruiters located in Oklahoma.

The alphabetical listing is immediately after the cross-reference list.

INDEX CROSS REFERENCE BY SPECIALTY

Specialty: B
(Banking)

Robert Half International

Specialty: C
(Computers & Data Processing)

Bullock And Company Inc
Dunhill of N Oklahoma City
Dunhill Personnel of Northeast Tulsa Inc
Robert Half International

Specialty: E
(Engineering)

Sumner Ray Technical Resources

Specialty: F
(Finance & Accounting)

Bullock And Company Inc
Dunhill of N Oklahoma City
Dunhill Personnel of Northeast Tulsa Inc
Robert Half International
Sooner Placement Service

Specialty: G
(General Applications)

A A Personnel Inc
A-Plus Associates Inc
AC Personnel Services Inc
Alpha Omega Personnel
American Careers Inc
AmeriResource Group Inc
Ann Canode And Associates Inc
Bar Belles
Bonnie Smalley Personnel
Bunt Carter Personnel
Canode Ann & Associates
Career Consultants
Career Employmemt Service Inc
Career Futures Inc
Career Lifestyles
Career Management Services
Career Point Business School
Career Visions
Dawson & Pratt
Dunhill of N Oklahoma City
Dunhill Personnel Tulsa
Employment Resources Inc
Energy Search Consultants
Esquire Personnel of OKC Inc
Executive Resources Group Inc
Express Personnel Service
Express Services
Ford Recruiters
Freedom Personnel Inc
Frew Susan & Company
Genie Personnel Service Inc
High Tech
Jean Kelley Personnel

Job Service
Labor Source Inc
Lloyd Richards Personnel Services
Management Consultants of OKC
Management Recruiters
Management Recruiters of OKC
Neese Terry Personnel Svcs
Officeteam
Oklahoma Employment Service
Oklahoma Junior College
Oklahoma State Employment Svc
Oklahoma Tribal Assistance Program
Oklahoma-State of Employment Security Commission
PAB Personnel Agency Inc
PAB Personnel Agency Inc
Private Industry Training
Quality Staffing
Reality Group
Refugee Center
Roth Young Personnel
Senior Community Service
Shirley's Employment Svc
Sooner Placement Service
T P C Consultants
T S S Jobs
Tuck S & Associates
Tulsa Oklahoma Personnel Inc
Wright Business School
Wylie John Assoiciates Inc

Specialty: H (Healthcare)

Dunhill of N Oklahoma City
Health Specialities
Healthcare Resources Group
Maxwell/Healthcare Inc

Specialty: I (Insurance)

Dunhill Personnel of Northeast Tulsa Inc

Specialty: L (Legal)

Legal Placement Service
Sooner Placement Service
Tulsa County Bar Association

Specialty: M (Manufacturing)

Dunhill of N Oklahoma City
Gifford J Inc
Sumner Ray Technical Resources

Specialty: O (Office Administration)

Healthcare Resources Group
Sooner Placement Service

Specialty: P (Personnel & Human Resources)

Dunhill Personnel of Northeast Tulsa Inc

Specialty: S (Sales & Marketing)

Dunhill of N Oklahoma City
Healthcare Resources Group
Sales Careers
Sales Consultants
Sales Recruiters
Sooner Placement Service

Other Specific Specialities:

Specialty: Drafting

Sumner Ray Technical Resources

Specialty: Energy/Utilities

Gifford J Inc

Specialty: Inventory Management

Healthcare Resources Group

Specialty: Management /Management Consultants

Dunhill Personnel of Northeast Tulsa Inc
Healthcare Resources Group

Specialty: Purchasing

Healthcare Resources Group

Specialty: Technical

Sumner Ray Technical Resources

Earl N Neese
A A Personnel Inc
2709 N West 39th Expressway
Oklahoma City, OK 73112
(405) 942-8551
Specialty: G
Employment Agency/Recruiter

Office Manager
American Careers Inc
1015 Waterwood Pkwy Ste E
Oklahoma City, OK 73132
(405) 341-7004
Specialty: G
Employment Agency/Recruiter

Office Manager
A-Plus Associates Inc
3333 NW 63
Oklahoma City, OK 73132
(405) 848-0044
Specialty: G
Employment Agency/Recruiter

Office Manager
AmeriResource Group Inc
2525 NW Expressway St
Oklahoma City, OK 73112
(405) 842-5900
Specialty: G
Employment Agency/Recruiter

Office Manager
AC Personnel Services Inc
6213 N Meridian Ave
Oklahoma City, OK 73112
(405) 728-3503
Specialty: G
Employment Agency/Recruiter

Ann Canode
Ann Canode And Associates Inc
6600 S Yale Ste 520
Tulsa, OK 74136
(918) 491-9900
Specialty: G
Employment Agency/Recruiter

Office Manager
Alpha Omega Personnel
4504 E 67th St
Tulsa, OK 74136
(918) 494-3888
Specialty: G
Employment Agency/Recruiter

Office Manager
Bar Belles
324 Main Mall
Tulsa, OK 74103
(918) 584-1097
Specialty: G
Employment Agency/Recruiter

Office Manager
Bonnie Smalley Personnel
8548 E 41st St
Tulsa, OK 74145
(918) 663-5427
Specialty: G
Employment Agency/Recruiter

Janet D Bullock
Bullock And Company Inc
5800 East Skelly Drive Ste 712
Tulsa, OK 74135
(918) 665-0735
Specialty: C,F
Employment Agency/Recruiter

Office Manager
Bunt Carter Personnel
2121 S Columbia Ave
Tulsa, OK 74114
(918) 749-9511
Specialty: G
Employment Agency/Recruiter

Office Manager
Canode Ann & Associates
6600 S Yale Ave
Tulsa, OK 74136
(918) 491-9900
Specialty: G
Employment Agency/Recruiter

Office Manager
Career Consultants
5400 N Grand Blvd
Oklahoma City, OK 73112
(405) 942-3092
Specialty: G
Employment Agency/Recruiter

Carmen Stanton
Career Employmemt Service Inc
P O Box 2096
Bartlesville, OK 74005
(918) 336-4122
Specialty: G
Employment Agency/Recruiter

Office Manager
Career Futures Inc
3021 W Wilshire Blvd
Oklahoma City, OK 73132
(405) 848-7037
Specialty: G
Employment Agency/Recruiter

Office Manager
Career Lifestyles
4520 S Harvard Ave
Tulsa, OK 74135
(918) 749-3009
Specialty: G
Employment Agency/Recruiter

Office Manager
Career Management Services
4900 Richmond Square
Oklahoma City, OK 73118
(405) 840-5312
Specialty: G
Employment Agency/Recruiter

Office Manager
Career Point Business School
3138 S Garnett Rd
Tulsa, OK 74146
(918) 622-4100
Specialty: G
Employment Agency/Recruiter

Office Manager
Career Visions
5401 S Sheridan Rd
Tulsa, OK 74145
(918) 627-5656
Specialty: G
Employment Agency/Recruiter

Office Manager
Dawson & Pratt
P O Box 690304
Tulsa, OK 74169
(918) 583-0343
Specialty: G
Employment Agency/Recruiter

Office Manager
Dunhill of N Oklahoma City
1000 W Wilshire Blvd
Oklahoma City, OK 73132
(405) 843-8669
Specialty:F,G,H,M,S,Information Technology
Employment Agency/Recruiter

Judy Norfleet
Dunhill Personnel of Northeast Tulsa Inc
10159 E 11th St
Tulsa, OK 74128
(918) 832-8857
Specialty: F,I,P,Information Technology,Management, Management Consultants
Employment Agency/Recruiter

John H Maxwell, Jr CPC
Dunhill Personnel Tulsa
8221 East 63rd Place
Tulsa, OK 74133
(918) 252-9667
Specialty: G
Employment Agency/Recruiter

Office Manager
Employment Resources Inc
2526 E 71st St
Tulsa, OK 74136
(918) 493-1952
Specialty: G
Employment Agency/Recruiter

Office Manager
Energy Search Consultants
4425 E 31st St
Tulsa, OK 74135
(918) 743-4464
Specialty: G
Employment Agency/Recruiter

Office Manager
Esquire Personnel of OKC Inc
5100 N Brookline
Oklahoma City, OK 73112
(405) 943-0104
Specialty: G
Employment Agency/Recruiter

Office Manager
Executive Resources Group Inc
6051 N Brookline
Oklahoma City, OK 73112
(405) 843-8344
Specialty: G
Employment Agency/Recruiter

Art Atkinson
Express Personnel Service
6300 NW Expressway Ste 200
Oklahoma City, OK 73132
(405) 720-1000
Specialty: G
Employment Agency/Recruiter

Office Manager
Express Services
810 W Gore Blvd
Lawton, OK 73501
(405) 355-1132
Specialty: G
Employment Agency/Recruiter

Robert A Funk
Express Services
6300 NW Expressway Ste 200
Oklahoma City, OK 73132
(405) 840-5000
Specialty: G
Employment Agency/Recruiter

Office Manager
Express Services
4636 S Harvard Ave
Tulsa, OK 74135
(918) 663-4826
Specialty: G
Employment Agency/Recruiter

Office Manager
Express Services Temporary & Permanent Personnel
5909 NW Expressway St
Oklahoma City, OK 73132
(405) 720-1000
Specialty: G
Employment Agency/Recruiter

Office Manager
Ford Recruiters
5801 E 41st St
Tulsa, OK 74135
(918) 663-8916
Specialty: G
Employment Agency/Recruiter

Office Manager
Freedom Personnel Inc
5100 N Brookline
Oklahoma City, OK 73112
(405) 943-7677
Specialty: G
Employment Agency/Recruiter

Office Manager
Frew Susan & Company
3727 NW 63 St
Oklahoma City, OK 73132
(405) 842-6300
Specialty: G
Employment Agency/Recruiter

Jean Mercer
Genie Personnel Service Inc
P O Box 10777
Midwest City, OK 73140
(405) 737-6677
Specialty: G
Employment Agency/Recruiter

Kate Knappenberger
Genie Personnel Service Inc
3817 NW Expressway Ste 140
Oklahoma City, OK 73112
(405) 947-2222
Specialty: G
Employment Agency/Recruiter

James R Gifford
Gifford J Inc
5310 E 31st ST Ste 514
Tulsa, OK 74135
(918) 665-2626
Specialty: M,Energy/Utilities
Employment Agency/Recruiter

Office Manager
Health Specialities
5100 N Brookline
Oklahoma City, OK 73112
(405) 943-1231
Specialty: H
Employment Agency/Recruiter

Office Manager
Healthcare Resources Group
3000 United Founders Bl
Ste 225F
Oklahoma City, OK 73112
(405) 843-4287
Specialty: H,O,S,Middle Management,Purchasing, Inventory Management,
Employment Agency/Recruiter

Office Manager
High Tech
6120 S Yale Ave
Tulsa, OK 74136
(918) 481-8822
Specialty: G
Employment Agency/Recruiter

Jean Kelley
Jean Kelley Personnel
7030 S Yale Ste 601
Tulsa, OK 74136
(918) 496-9192
Specialty: G
Employment Agency/Recruiter

Office Manager
Job Service
3105 E Skelly Drive
Tulsa, OK 74105
(918) 749-6861
Specialty: G
Employment Agency/Recruiter

Office Manager
Labor Source Inc
1015 S Detroit Ave
Tulsa, OK 74120
(918) 582-1111
Specialty: G
Employment Agency/Recruiter

Office Manager
Legal Placement Service
119 N Robinson
Oklahoma City, OK 73102
(405) 235-4399
Specialty: L
Employment Agency/Recruiter

Lloyd Richards CPC
Lloyd Richards Personnel Services
507 South Main St Ste 502
Tulsa, OK 74103
(918) 582-5251
Specialty: G
Employment Agency/Recruiter

Office Manager
Management Consultants of OKC
5929 N May Ave
Oklahoma City, OK 73112
(405) 848-8880
Specialty: G
Employment Agency/Recruiter

Tony Wolters
Management Recruiters
5801 E 41st St Ste 440
Tulsa, OK 74135-5614
(918) 663-6744
Specialty: G
Employment Agency/Recruiter

David Orwig
Management Recruiters of OKC
2800 W Country Club Dr
Oklahoma City, OK 73116
(405) 842-3173
Specialty: G
Employment Agency/Recruiter

Murl Smith, Mgr
Oklahoma Employment Service
2120 S Broadway
Edmond, OK 73013
(405) 341-9000
Specialty: G
Employment Agency/Recruiter

Office Manager
Maxwell/Healthcare Inc
8221 E 63rd Pl
Tulsa, OK 74133
(918) 252-0808
Specialty: H
Employment Agency/Recruiter

Office Manager
Oklahoma Junior College
3232 NW 65th
Oklahoma City, OK 73132
(405) 848-3484
Specialty: G
Employment Agency/Recruiter

Office Manager
Neese Terry Personnel Svcs
2709 NW 39 St
Oklahoma City, OK 73112
(405) 942-8551
Specialty: G
Employment Agency/Recruiter

Office Manager
Oklahoma State Employment Svc
3105 E Skelly Dr
Tulsa, OK 74105
(918) 749-6861
Specialty: G
Employment Agency/Recruiter

Office Manager
Officeteam
1 W 3rd St
Tulsa, OK 74103
(918) 585-1500
Specialty: G
Employment Agency/Recruiter

Office Manager
Oklahoma State Employment Svc
567 E 36 N St
Tulsa, OK 74106
(918) 428-3881
Specialty: G
Employment Agency/Recruiter

Office Manager
Oklahoma Tribal Assistance Program
1806 E 15th St
Tulsa, OK 74104
(918) 744-8866
Specialty: G
Employment Agency/Recruiter

Glenda Owen, Office Mgr
Oklahoma-State of Employment Security Commission
1711 SW 11th Street
Lawton, OK 73501
(405) 357-3500
(405) 357-9629 FAX
Specialty: G
Employment Agency/Recruiter

Jackie Crumrine, Mgr
PAB Personnel Agency Inc
121 S Santa Fe Suite A
Norman, OK 73069
(405) 329-1933
(405) 329-1967 FAX
Specialty: G
Employment Agency/Recruiter

Office Manager
PAB Personnel Agency Inc
119 S Santa Fe Ave
Norman, OK 73069
(405) 329-1933
Specialty: G
Employment Agency/Recruiter

Office Manager
Private Industry Training
110 S Hartford Ave
Tulsa, OK 74120
(918) 596-7679
Specialty: G
Employment Agency/Recruiter

Office Manager
Quality Staffing
3617 N Meridian
Oklahoma City, OK 73112
(405) 946-2800
Specialty: G
Employment Agency/Recruiter

Office Manager
Reality Group
5100 E Skelly Dr
Tulsa, OK 74135
(918) 622-0228
Specialty: G
Employment Agency/Recruiter

Office Manager
Refugee Center
3121 N Classen Blvd
Oklahoma City, OK 73118
(405) 524-2947
Specialty: G
Employment Agency/Recruiter

Office Manager
Robert Half International
119 N Robinson Ave
Oklahoma City, OK 73102
(405) 236-0880
Specialty: B,C,F
Employment Agency/Recruiter

Office Manager
Robert Half International
1 W Third St
Tulsa, OK 74103
(918) 585-1700
Specialty: B,C,F
Employment Agency/Recruiter

Office Manager
Roth Young Personnel
2000 Classen Blvd N
Oklahoma City, OK 73106
(405) 524-0600
Specialty: G
Employment Agency/Recruiter

Office Manager
Sales Careers
5929 N May Avenue
Oklahoma City, OK 73112
(405) 848-6858
Specialty: S
Employment Agency/Recruiter

Tony Wolters
Sales Consultants
5801 E 41st St Ste 440
Tulsa, OK 74135-5610
(918) 663-6744
Specialty: S
Employment Agency/Recruiter

Office Manager
Sales Recruiters
3037 N W 63
Oklahoma City, OK 73132
(405) 848-1536
Specialty: S
Employment Agency/Recruiter

Office Manager
Senior Community Service
1344 E 11th St
Tulsa, OK 74120
(918) 582-7442
Specialty: G
Employment Agency/Recruiter

Office Manager
Shirley's Employment Svc
6336 E Admiral Pl
Tulsa, OK 74115
(918) 838-7722
Specialty: G
Employment Agency/Recruiter

Louis Borgman, Owner
Peggy Borgman, Owner
Sooner Placement Service
4001 N Classen Ste 210
Oklahoma City, OK 73118
(405) 528-2501
(405) 524-8046 FAX
Specialty: F,G,L,O,S
Employment Agency/Recruiter

Dee Ray, Pres
Sumner Ray Technical Resources
4500 S Garnett Rd Ste 612
Tulsa, OK 74146
(918) 665-8686
(918) 665-8693 FAX
Specialty:E,M,Drafting,Technical
Permanent & Temporary
Employment Agency/Recruiter

Office Manager
T P C Consultants
4606 E 67th St
Tulsa, OK 74136
(918) 496-9696
Specialty: G
Employment Agency/Recruiter

Office Manager
T S S Jobs
1700-1/2 S Sheridan Rd
Tulsa, OK 74112
(918) 832-0900
Specialty: G
Employment Agency/Recruiter

Office Manager
Tuck S & Associates
1718 E 15th St
Tulsa, OK 74104
(918) 745-2195
Specialty: G
Employment Agency/Recruiter

Office Manager
Tulsa County Bar Association
1446 S Boston
Tulsa, OK 74119
(918) 584-5483
Specialty: L
Employment Agency/Recruiter

Tony Santiago CPC
Tulsa Oklahoma Personnel Inc
5314 South Yale Park Tower
Ste 315
Tulsa, OK 74134
(918) 492-2676
Specialty: G
Employment Agency/Recruiter

Office Manager
Wright Business School
2219 SW 74th St
Oklahoma City, OK 73159
(405) 681-2300
Specialty: G
Employment Agency/Recruiter

Office Manager
Wylie John Assoiciates Inc
1727 E 71st St
Tulsa, OK 74136
(918) 496-2100
Specialty: G
Employment Agency/Recruiter

JOB SEEKERS SURVIVAL HINTS

Don't let your job search efforts get out of control.

Get organized and stay organized right from the start. Perform the following tasks to assist you in this area:

- Create a log book of potential leads.
- Track all cover letters and interviews.
- Build a set of cover letters tailored to fit the needs of the companies contacted.
- Put your resume together and have it professionally printed.
- Keep a supply of resumes on hand.

Employment Agencies/Recruiters - Texas

The following pages contain the specialty cross-reference listings to an alphabetical list of active employment agencies/recruiters located in Texas.

The alphabetical listing is immediately after the cross-reference list.

INDEX CROSS REFERENCE BY SPECIALTY

Specialty: A
(Advertising)

Adia Personnel Services
Evins Personnel Consultants
M David Lowe Personnel Services

Specialty: B
(Banking)

Accountemps
Evins Personnel Consultants
Gordon Roberts Inc
M David Lowe Personnel Services
Marilyn Austin CPC & Assoc
Mortgage Bankers Consultants
Mortgage Recruiting Consultants
Robert Half Inc
Robert Half International
Robert Half of Dallas

Specialty: C
(Computers & Data Processing)

Accountemps
Adia Personnel Services
Annco Consultants
Babich & Associates Inc
Career Resources
Computer Career Advancement
Computer Professionals Unlimited
Continental Personnel Service
Dallas Business Automation Consultants
Data Management Search Inc
Data Masters
Data Processing Careers Inc
DataPro Personnel Consultants
Dave Davidson Data Processing Recruiting
Dunhill of Arlington
E D P Computer Services
E D P Personnel
Emjay Computer Careers
Employers Registry
Evins Personnel Consultants
Execsource
General Employment Personnel Consultants
Information Search Group
Insight Personnel Group Inc
International Data Search
Keypeople Resources Inc
King Computersearch Inc
Linn-Truett Inc
M David Lowe Personnel Services
Marilyn Austin CPC & Assoc
Morson International Inc
National Prosource Inc
OmniSearch
Opportunity Unlimited Inc
P & S Datapro
Prestige Recruiters Inc
Pro Fit EDP
Robert George & Associates
Robert Half Inc

Robert Half International
Robert Half of Dallas
S & W Technical Services Inc
Snelling And Snelling
Source EDP
Suburban Services
Superior Programming Services

Specialty: E
(Engineering)

Babich & Associates Inc
Bott & Associates Inc
Engineering Employment
Channel Personnel Services
Continental Personnel Service
Engineering Technical Recruiters
Experienced Personnel Services
M David Lowe Personnel Services
MegaSearch Inc
Morson International Inc
Opportunity Unlimited Inc
Robert George & Associates
S & W Technical Services Inc
Seegers Estes & Associates Inc
Singleton Associates
Snelling And Snelling
Source Engineering
Technical Staff Recruiters
ValPers Inc

Specialty: F
(Finance & Accounting)

Abacus Accouting Personnel
Accountants Executive Search
Accountants On Call
Accountemps
Accounting Action Personnel
Accounting Connection The
Accounting Edge
Accounting Resource Group
Adia Personnel Services
Annco Consultants
Babich & Associates Inc
Beyer Sharon & Associates
BTI
Business Women of Dallas
Carlton Accounting Services
Continental Personnel Service
Dunhill of Arlington
Eagle Personnel Services Inc
Ellis & Associates Inc
Evins Personnel Consultants
Feldt Personnel
Financial Staff Recruiters
Financial Staffing Centre
General Sales & Search
Kane & Company
M David Lowe Personnel Services
Marilyn Austin CPC & Assoc
Mortgage Bankers Consultants
Mortgage Recruiting Consultants
Personnel One
Robert Half Inc
Robert Half International
Robert Half of Dallas
Snelling And Snelling

Snelling Personnel Services
Source Finance
Stephens Little & Assocs Inc
Sterling Personnel
The Roberts Group

Specialty: G
(General Applications)

AAA Personnel Agency
Abilities Unlimited
Accolade Inc Personnel Svcs
Accountabilities PersonnelServices
AccountSource Personnel Inc
Adia Personnel Services
Administrative Personnel Associates of Houston
Administrative Resources Inc
Adstaff Personnel Services Inc
Advanced Systems Consulting
Agape Personnel Agency
Alco Consultants
Arrington A & Associates
Associated Personnel Services Inc
Austin Career Consultants Inc
Aware Affiliates Personnel Service
B & B Personnel Service of Austin Inc
B & M Associates
Babich & Associates
Bailey Personnel Services
Baker Street Group Inc
Bay Area Personnel
Benum Michele Associates
Best Personnel Staffing
Boss Company Consulting Inc
Bowman K Personnel Service
Boyd Ronnie And Associates
Brabo Labor Agency
Brooks Linda Gay Personnel Consultant
Brooks Robert & Associates
Bruco Inc
Bruco Personnel Services Inc
Bullock Personnel of S A
Burnett Personnel Consultants
Burnett's Southwest Personnel Services Inc
Burrell & Associates
Campos Permanent & Temporary Personnel Services
Career Counseling Center
Career Marketing Inc
Career Path Inc
Career Personnel Centre
Career Placement Service Inc
Career Point Business School
Carltech
Cendrick Personnel
Christopher Matthew Group
Citizen Development Assn
Claire Fontaine & Assoc
Clayton Personnel
Cochran Personnel Services
Cockrell Hull
Consultant's & Designers Inc
Continental Personnel Service
Corporate Accountant Staffing
Corporate Consultants Professional Search
Corporate Staff Recruiters
Corporate Staff Recruiters
Crossroad Personnel

Cypress Creek Employment Consultants
Daher & Associates Insurance Search Specialists
Daisy's Employment Service
Dallas Employment Service
Data-Quest Research Inc
Davis Gail Personnel
DeGeorge & Associates
Delta Dallas Personnel
DFM & Associates
Diversied Human Resource Group
Diversified Human Resources
Dixco Enterprises Inc
Donovan & Watkins
Duncanville Employment Agency
Dunhill of Arlington
Dunhill of Cypress Inc
Dunhill Professional Search of Post Oak
Dunhill West Houston-Executive Search Consultant
Ehrich Enterprises
El Paso Employment Service
Ellis & Associates Inc
Emde Marji Personnel
Employment Systems Incorporated
Enertech Resource
Evins Personnel Consultants
Exchange Personnel
Express Services Temporary & Permanent Personnel
FJD Services
Force Employment Agency
FrontLine Search
Fults K B Inc
Future Prospects
Future's Unlimited
Gail Darling Temporaries
Gail Davis Personnel
General Services
Gibson & Associates
Global Career Services Inc
Global Dynamics
Goehring Personnel
Gordon Roberts Inc
Gresham & Gresham
Griggs Pamela Hunter Personnel Services
Grove Employment Services Inc
Gulf States Personnel Consultants
H L Yoh Company
Harper Sylvia & Associates
Harris J Co Personnel Services
Harrison Personnel Services Inc
Hay Darlene & Associates
Help Employment Agency
Hennessy Search Associates
Hilbert Companies
Hill Ted & Associates
Hill Wanda Pesonnel
Hospitality Personnel
Hotelier Inc The
Houston City Personnel Corp
Houston International Placement
Howard E Loftin Employment Specialist
IBC In-Bond Central Inc
Impact Personnel
Insight Personnel Group Inc
Interim Personnel
J D And Associates
J Pittman Raye

Jo Gunter Selective Employment
Job Placement Specialist
Job Services Inc
Jobs For Handicapped
Johnson Career Consultants Inc
Johnson Consultants
Jordan Employment Services
Joyce Polasek K
Just Le-Gals
K International Overseas Jobs
Kane & Company
Kathleen Ater Personnel
Keegan & Keegan
Kehrer Sylvia Personnel Inc
Kern Kenneth C Personnel Svcs
Kingwood Personnel
Koym Employment & Counseling
La Barge & Associates
Labor Force
Laffer & Associates Inc
Lancaster Melodie
Lancaster Resources
Lawrence James Associates
Leadership Resources
Leaseway Personnel Corp
Lee's Personnel Service Inc
Legend Marine Inc
Leigh Personnel
Lengston Corporation & Assoc
Leslie Corporation
Lewisville-Regional Personnel Agency
Liberty Personnel/Executive Search
Link Personnel Services
Lone Star Personnel Inc
Lonergran Farrar & Associates
Lucas Associates Inc
Lusk & Associates Personnel Services Inc
Lyndian Inc
M David Lowe Personnel Services
Management Alliance Group
Management Personnel Service
Management Recruiters
Management Recruiters of Fort Worth Southwest
Management Recruiters of Plano
Management Recruiters-Addison
Management Recruiters-Worth-Arlington
Marilyn Austin CPC & Assoc
Marksbury Jaye
Marshall Career Service Inc
Martin-Ericson
Mary Green's Employment Finders
Massarini Pete & Assocs Inc
Matchmaker Personnel Consulting
McGhee And Asociates
McNeff Judith & Associates
McSearch Personnel Consultants
Meador-Brady Personnel Services
Meador-Wright & Associates
MegaSearch Inc
Memorial City Personnel
Meridien Speciality Personnel Service Inc
Met Inc
Metro Personnel
MetroCareer Inc
Metropolitan Employment Resources

Michael James & Associates
Milam Design Services Inc
Miller Personnel Inc
Miya Personnel
Morgan Barnett & Associates Inc
MSI International
National Staffing Services
Net-Com Interim Staffing Inc
North American Nanny Network & Institute Inc
Now Personnel Service Inc
NR Skillmaster
O'Keefe & Associates
Odell & Associates
Officemates 5
Officeteam
Overcomer Marketing Group
Pate Resources Group
Performance Group The
Performance Recruiters of Dallas
Permanent Success Personnel Services
Personnel Connection Inc
Personnel One
Personnel Pool
Phoenix Group The
Placement Resource The
Placement Resources
PRC-Professional Recruiting Consultants
Prestige Personnel Consultants
Primary Service
Printing Industries Assn of Texas
Private Industry Council Admin
Pro Staff Personnel Service
Professional Career Associate
Professional Placement Inc
Professional Recruiting Consultants
Professional Staff Recruiters
Professional Staffing Assocs
Profiles
Profiles of Houston
Quad Employment Agency
Quest Personnel Resources
Quiles Employment Service
Quinet Personnel Services Inc
R J Myers Consulting Services
Rangers Consultants
Ray Rashkin Associates Inc
Realtime Staffing Inc
Recruiting Specialists
Recruitment International
Referral Service
Regal Personnel Inc
Relief Services Inc
Rellstab Associates
Richard Wayne & Roberts
Robinson Margo Personnel
Roth Young
Rozelle Anne & Associates Employment Consultants
S E R-Jobs for Progress Inc
S L Fults & Associates
Saber Consultants
Sasseen Co-Career Opportunities
Schmidt Ron Companies
Search & Recruit International
Select Personnel
Senior Community Service Employment Program
SER Employment
SER-Jobs For Progress of the Texas Coast Inc

Serivicious Personales
Sheila Smith & Associates Inc
Sides & Associates
Silver & Associates
Singleton Associates
SLS Servies
Smith-Bennett & Associates
Snelling & Snelling Employment Service-Campbell Centre
Snelling Personnel Recruiting Division
Snelling Personnel Services
Source Finance
Southwest Resource
Development Placement
SP Associates/VIP Personnel
SPS Group Inc
Staff Benefits Inc
Staff Source
Staffingers Personnel
Steele Juanell & Associates Personnel Service
Steitz & Corbett Personnel Group Inc
Sterling Enterprises
Steverson & Company
Stone Joyce & Associates
Storb Stockton Hillenburg & Associates
Strain R Lee
Suburban Services
Summit Consulting Group Inc
Summit Employment Agency
Superior Employment Services
Systems Source Corporations
T M T Manpower Corporation
Talent Southwest
Talent Tree Personnel Services
Southwestern Companies
Talent Tree Personnel Svcs
Task Masters Inc
Tekwork
Texas Career Services
Texas Employment Commission
Texas State of Employment Commission
Texstaf-Texas Staffing Corp
The Chester Group Inc
The Jackson Employment Agency
The Michael's Group
Townsend Associates
Trakit Resource Management Inc
Tri-Starr Personnel
Tri-Starr Personnel of San Antonio
Turner Dehavilland Inc
U S Staffing of Texas
Upper Rio Grande Private Industry Council
Valley Job Placement Agency
ValPers Inc
VIP Personnel Service
Vivian Martin Employment Svc
Vocational Support Services
Walker Personnel & Associates
Wanda's Personnel Service
Warwick Search Group
Whitaker Fellows & Associates
White & Associates
Williams Pat & Associates Personnel
Williams R L & Associates
Wimberly James K & Associates
Windsor Consultants Inc

Withers Thomas D
Woodlands Executive Employment Service
Work Connection Inc The

Specialty: H
(Heath Care)

Career Advancement Opportunities
Continental Personnel Service
Cooksey & Associates
Dallas Business Automation Consultants
Dental Assistance Associates
Dental Assistance Personnel
Dental Auxilary Service Inc
Dental Resource Management
Dr Personnel Medical Dental Employment Service
DR Personnel
EAI Medical Personnel Services
Evins Personnel Consultants
Experienced Personnel Services
General Employment Personnel Consultants
Health Care Resources Group
Healthcare Personnel Int'l Inc
Healthcare Recruiters International
Healthcare Staff Resources
Heathcare Recruiters of Houston
International Health Care Provider
JWS Health Consultants Inc
Kane & Company
M David Lowe Personnel Services
Marilyn Austin CPC & Assoc
Medical Personnel Service
Medical Professional Placements
Medical Technocrats Inc
Medlaw Recruiters
Omni Health Services Inc
S & W Technical Services Inc
Snelling And Snelling
Snelling Personnel Services
Texas Doctor's Group
The Health Instructor Network
Whitaker Fellows & Associates

Specialty: I
(Insurance)

Adia Personnel Services
Austin Insurance Recruiters
Besinger Group The
Continental Personnel Service
Ellis & Associates Inc
Evins Personnel Consultants
Insurance Personnel Unlimited
Kelly Group Insurance Search Consultants
M David Lowe Personnel Services
Management Recruiters-Addison
Marilyn Austin CPC & Assoc
Summit Search Specialists

Specialty: L
(Legal)

Adia Personnel Services
Attorney Resource
Briggs Legal Staffing
Career Advancement Opportunities
Ellis & Associates Inc
Evins Personnel Consultants
Kane & Company
L A W Personnel Inc
Legal Staffing Inc
M David Lowe Personnel Services
Marilyn Austin CPC & Assoc
Medlaw Recruiters
Snelling Personnel Services
Whitaker Fellows & Associates

Specialty: M
(Manufacturing)

Dunhill of Arlington
Evie Kreisler And Associates
Kelly McBride Associates Employment Consultants
M David Lowe Personnel Services
Marilyn Austin CPC & Assoc
Priority Search Inc
Singleton Associates
Snelling And Snelling
Snelling Personnel Services
Teamsource
ValPers Inc

Specialty: O
(Office Administration)

Accounting Action Personnel
Andrews-Carter Personnel
B & B Personnel Service of Austin Inc
Babich & Associates Inc
Beyer Sharon & Associates
Business Women of Dallas
Career Advancement Opportunities
Carrollton Employment Service
Continental Personnel Service
Dallas Business Automation Consultants
Data Personnel Service
Data Staffing Centre
DataWay Resources
Eagle Personnel Services Inc
Ellis & Associates Inc
Evins Personnel Consultants
General Employment Personnel Consultants
Insight Personnel Group Inc
Kane & Company
KCB Personnel Consultants
Lee's Personnel Service Inc
M David Lowe Personnel Services
Officeteam
Personnel One
Quinby Personnel Services
Secretarial Contracting Services
Secretaries of Dallas
Secretary Inc The Tempower
Snelling Personnel Services
Sterling Personnel

Suburban Services
The Personnel Source
The Roberts Group

Specialty: P
(Personnel/Human Resources)

M David Lowe Personnel Services
Management Recruiters-Addison
Singleton Associates
Snelling Personnel Services

Specialty: R
(Research & Development)

M David Lowe Personnel Services
ValPers Inc

Specialty: S
(Sales & Marketing)

Andrews-Carter Personnel
Babich & Associates Inc
Career Advancement Opportunities
Continental Personnel Service
Dunhill of Arlington
Evins Personnel Consultants
Experienced Personnel Services
General Employment Personnel Consultants
Kane & Company
Kelly McBride Associates Employment Consultants
M David Lowe Personnel Services
Personnel One
Singleton Associates
Snelling And Snelling
Snelling Personnel Services
The Roberts Group
ValPers Inc

Specialty: T
(Travel & Hospitality)

Andrews-Carter Personnel
Evins Personnel Consultants
Hospitality Personnel
M David Lowe Personnel Services
MegaSearch Inc
Restaurant Recruiters Inc
Travel Placement Specialists
Travel Staffers

Other Specific Specialties:

Specialty: Administrative

Babich & Associates Inc

Specialty: Architecture

Architectural Career Network

Specialty: Chemicals

Seegers Estes & Associates Inc
Whitaker Fellows & Associates

Specialty: Computer Training & Placement for the Economically Deprived

Cherier Business School

Specialty: Consulting

Superior Programming Services

Specialty: Consumer Products

The Urban Placement Service

Specialty: Cosmetology

Cosmetology Employment & Placement Services

Specialty: Domestics

Dallas Domestic Employment Agency
River Oaks Domestic Agency

Specialty: Electronics

J Robert Thompson Companies

Specialty: Employment/Training for income eligible-dislocated workers

Austin/Travis County Private Industry Council

Specialty: Environmental

Stanton/Schoen Professionals

Specialty: Executive

Babich & Associates Inc

Specialty: International Recruitment

ARA International Inc
Gulco International Recruiting

Specialty: Labor

Industrial Labor Service

Specialty: Light Industrial

Eagle Personnel Services Inc
Express Services Temporary & Permanent Personnel
The Personnel Source

Specialty: Management

Continental Personnel Service
Experienced Personnel Services
Kelly McBride Associates Employment Consultants
Personnel One
Source Finance

Specialty: Mangement Trainees/ Recent Grads

Continental Personnel Service

Specialty: Minorities

The Urban Placement Service

Specialty: Oil & Gas

Insight Personnel Group Inc
The Urban Placement Service

Specialty: Packaging

Kelly McBride Associates Employment Consultants

Specialty: Pharmaceutical

The Urban Placement Service

Specialty: Plastics

Whitaker Fellows & Associates

Specialty: Retail

Evie Kreisler And Associates

Specialty: Salons

Salon Employment Datalink Corp

Specialty: Science Professionals

Babich & Associates Inc
Lab Support Inc
Stanton/Schoen Professionals

Specialty: Technical

Aacme High Tech Services
Computer Professionals Unlimited
Contech Resources
Engineering Technical Recruiters
Express Services Temporary & Permanent Personnel
Olsten Technical Services
Personnel One

Pro Staff Personnel Services
Technical Division
S & W Technical Services Inc
Snelling And Snelling
Stanton/Schoen Professionals
Superior Technical Specialist
Taci/Technical Assistance Co Inc
Technical Careers of Houston
Technical Careers
Technical Search Inc
Technical Staff Recruiters

Office Manager
Aacme High Tech Services
14001 Goldmark Drive
Dallas, TX 75240
(214) 437-5739
Specialty: Technical
Employment Agency/Recruiter

Office Manager
AAA Personnel Agency
4311 N 10th St
McAllen, TX 78504
(210) 687-7766
Specialty: G
Employment Agency/Recruiter

Office Manager
Abacus Accouting Personnel
5177 Richmond Ave
Houston, TX 77060
(713) 875-5700
Specialty: F
Employment Agency/Recruiter

Office Manager
Abilities Unlimited
P O Box 90991
Houston, TX 77290
(713) 580-1777
Specialty: G
Employment Agency/Recruiter

Office Manager
Accolade Inc Personnel Svcs
2537 S Gessner
Houston, TX 77063
(713) 975-8814
Specialty: G
Employment Agency/Recruiter

Office Manager
Accountabilities Personnel Services
1980 Post Oak Blvd
Houston, TX 77056
(713) 961-5803
Specialty: G
Employment Agency/Recruiter

Office Manager
Accountants Executive Search
300 Crescent Ct Ste 930
Dallas, TX 75201
(214) 979-9001
Specialty: F
Employment Agency/Recruiter

Brett Schaeger, Mgr
Accountants Executive Search
5520 L B J Frwy Ste 150
Dallas, TX 75240
(214) 980-4184
(214) 980-2359 FAX
Specialty: F
Employment Agency/Recruiter

Stacy Selbo
Accountants On Call
2001 Ross Ave Ste 360
Dallas, TX 75201
(214) 214-979-9001
Specialty: F
Employment Agency/Recruiter

Stacy Selbo
Accountants On Call
5520 LBJ Freeway Ste 10
Dallas, TX 75240
(214) 980-4184
Specialty: F
Employment Agency/Recruiter

Phyllis Eriksen
Accountants On Call
1980 Post Oak Bl Ste 1300
Houston, TX 77056
(713) 961-5603
Specialty: F
Employment Agency/Recruiter

Jana Fichtner, VP
Accountemps
1360 Post Oak Blvd Ste 1470
Houston, TX 77056
(713) 623-8367
Specialty: B,C,F
Employment Agency/Recruiter

Office Manager
Accounting Action Personnel
3010 LBJ Frwy
Dallas, TX 75234
(214) 241-1543
Specialty: F,O
Employment Agency/Recruiter

Office Manager
Accounting Connection The
12012 Wickchester Ln
Houston, TX 77079
(713) 493-3699
Specialty: F
Employment Agency/Recruiter

Office Manager
Accounting Edge
12655 N Central Expwy
Dallas, TX 75243
(214) 991-3330
Specialty: F
Employment Agency/Recruiter

Office Manager
Accounting Resource Group
5001 Spring Valley Road
Dallas, TX 75244
(214) 386-5714
Specialty: F
Employment Agency/Recruiter

Office Manager
Accounting Resource Group
3040 Post Oak Ste 440
Houston, TX 77056
(713) 960-1747
Specialty: F
Employment Agency/Recruiter

Office Manager
Adia Personnel Services
4100 Spring Valley Road
Dallas, TX 75244
(214) 661-1356
Specialty: A,C,F,I,L,
Employment Agency/Recruiter

Office Manager
AccountSource Personnel Inc
1250 NE Loop 410
San Antonio, TX 78209
(512) 826-1558
Specialty: G
Employment Agency/Recruiter

Office Manager
Adia Personnel Services
5433 Westheimer Rd
Houston, TX 77056
(713) 961-7551
Specialty: G
Employment Agency/Recruiter

Office Manager
Adia Personnel Services
1106 Clayton Ln
Austin, TX 78723
(512) 454-5211
Specialty: G
Employment Agency/Recruiter

Office Manager
Adia Personnel Services
1010 Lamar
Houston, TX 77002
(713) 654-5075
Specialty: G
Employment Agency/Recruiter

Debbie Steiner
Adia Personnel Services
600 N Pearl St
Dallas, TX 75201
(214) 754-7117
Specialty: A,C,F,I,L,
Employment Agency/Recruiter

Office Manager
Adia Personnel Services
4950 N O'Connor Road
Irving, TX 75062
(214) 541-0770
Specialty: A,C,F,I,L,
Employment Agency/Recruiter

Office Manager
Adia Personnel Services
301 W Parker
Plano, TX 75023
(214) 424-1788
Specialty: G
Employment Agency/Recruiter

Office Manager
Adia Personnel Services
7330 San Pedro Ave
San Antonio, TX 78216
(512) 349-4499
Specialty: G
Employment Agency/Recruiter

Office Manager
Administrative Personnel Associates of Houston
3355 W Alabama St
Houston, TX 77098
(713) 622-1560
Specialty: G
Employment Agency/Recruiter

Office Manager
Administrative Resources Inc
1726 Augusta Dr
Houston, TX 77057
(713) 974-9044
Specialty: G
Employment Agency/Recruiter

Office Manager
Adstaff Personnel Services Inc
4635 Southwest Frwy
Houston, TX 77027
(713) 552-1010
Specialty: G
Employment Agency/Recruiter

Office Manager
Advanced Systems Consulting
5001 Spring Valley Road
Dallas, TX 75244
(214) 239-6572
Specialty: G
Employment Agency/Recruiter

Billy J Deweese, Owner
Agape Personnel Agency
8200 C Nashville Ave Ste 109
Lubbock, TX 79423
(806) 794-5511
Specialty: G
Employment Agency/Recruiter

Sheila Hansen CPC
Alco Consultants
2401 Fountain Veiw Dr Ste 930
Houston, TX 77057
(713) 977-0808
Specialty: G
Employment Agency/Recruiter

Leann Andrews CPC, Owner
Andrews-Carter Personnel
13140 Coit Road Ste 519
Dallas, TX 75240
(214) 680-9484
Specialty: O,S,T(Restaurant Mangement)
Employment Agency/Recruiter

Office Manager
Annco Consultants
2730 S Stemmons Fwy Ste 609
West Tower
Dallas, TX 75207
(214) 630-7101
Specialty: C,F
Employment Agency/Recruiter

Rodney J Gullo, Pres
ARA International Inc
15710 John F Kennedy Blvd
Ste 110
Houston, TX 77032
(713) 590-1453
(713) 590-1503 FAX
Specialty: International Recruitment
Employment Agency

Office Manager
Architectural Career Network
5252 Westchester Ste 275
Houston, TX 77005
(713) 663-5873
Specialty: Architecture
Employment Agency/Recruiter

Office Manager
Arrington A & Associates
5050 Quorum Drive
Dallas, TX 75240
(214) 701-9430
Specialty: G
Employment Agency/Recruiter

Office Manager
Associated Personnel Services Inc
15006 Welcome Lane
Houston, TX 77014
(713) 440-4333
Specialty: G
Employment Agency/Recruiter

Office Manager
Attorney Resource
2301 Cedar Springs Road
Dallas, TX 75201
(214) 922-8050
Specialty: L
Employment Agency/Recruiter

Patricia Goodwin CPC
Austin Career Consultants Inc
3624 North Hills Dr Ste B-205
Austin, TX 78731
(512) 346-6660
Specialty: G
Employment Agency/Recruiter

Joe Ellis
Austin Insurance Recruiters
1250 Capital of TX Hwy
Building 3 Ste 620
Austin, TX 78746
(512) 329-8815
Specialty: I
Employment Agency/Recruiter

Office Manager
Austin/Travis County Private Industry Council
2211 S I-H 35
Austin, TX 78741
(512) 448-8800
(512) 448-8818
Specialty: A-X Employment and Training for income eligible and dislocated workers
Employment Agency/Recruiter

Office Manager
Aware Affiliates Personnel Svc
3004 W Lancaster Avenue
Fort Worth, TX 76107
(817) 870-2590
Specialty: G
Employment Agency/Recruiter

Nicole Russell, Account Exec
B & B Personnel Service of Austin Inc
2301 W Anderson Lane Ste 200
Austin, TX 78757
(512) 454-2345
(512) 452-9069 FAX
Specialty: G,O
Employment Agency/Recruiter

Office Manager
B & M Associates
9535 Forest Lane
Dallas, TX 75243
(214) 437-3188
Specialty: G
Employment Agency/Recruiter

Anthony Beshara
Babich & Associates
602 Malick Tower One
Summit Avenue
Ft Worth, TX 76102
(817) 336-7261
Specialty: G
Employment Agency/Recruiter

Anthony Beshara
Babich & Associates
6060 N Central Expressway
Twin Sixties Tower
Dallas, TX 75206
(214) 361-5735
Specialty: G
Employment Agency/Recruiter

Office Manager
Babich & Associates Inc
6060 N Central Expwy Ste 544
Dallas, TX 75206
(214) 361-5735
(214) 263-7585 FAX
Specialty: C,E,F,O,S,Scientific, Administrative,Executive
Employment Agency/Recruiter

John Waters
Bailey Personnel Services
510 N Valley Mills Dr STe 504
Waco, TX 76710
(817) 776-0230
Specialty: G
Employment Agency/Recruiter

Office Manager
Baker Street Group Inc
5718 Westheimer
Houston, TX 77057
(713) 952-8181
Specialty: G
Employment Agency/Recruiter

Office Manager
Bay Area Personnel
1000 Bay Area Blvd
Houston, TX 77058
(713) 488-1888
Specialty: G
Employment Agency/Recruiter

Office Manager
Benum Michele Associates
3939 Belt Line Road
Dallas, TX 75244
(214) 247-7110
Specialty: G
Employment Agency/Recruiter

Office Manager
Benum Michele Associates
2828 Forest Lane
Dallas, TX 75234
(214) 241-9645
Specialty: G
Employment Agency/Recruiter

Office Manager
Besinger Group The
1700 West Loop South Ste 365
Houston, TX 77027
(713) 622-7728
Specialty: I
Employment Agency/Recruiter

Office Manager
Best Personnel Staffing
4151 S W Freeway Ste 650
Houston, TX 77027
(713) 623-6466
Specialty: G
Employment Agency/Recruiter

Office Manager
Beyer Sharon & Associates
5215 N O'Connor Blvd
Irving, TX 75062
(214) 401-3367
Specialty: F,O
Employment Agency/Recruiter

Office Manager
Boss Company Consulting Inc
5025 Arapaho Road
Dallas, TX 75248
(214) 458-1141
Specialty: G
Employment Agency/Recruiter

Office Manager
Bott & Associates Inc
Engineering Employment
10550 Richmond Ave
Houston, TX 77042
(713) 782-9814
Specialty: E
Employment Agency/Recruiter

Office Manager
Bowman K Personnel Service
10301 NW Frwy Ste 206
Houston, TX 77092
(713) 682-4875
Specialty: G
Employment Agency/Recruiter

Office Manager
Boyd Ronnie And Associates
2401 Fountain View Dr
Houston, TX 77057
(713) 783-5550
Specialty: G
Employment Agency/Recruiter

Office Manager
Brabo Labor Agency
1418 Beech St
McAllen, TX 78501
(210) 682-1611
Specialty: G
Employment Agency/Recruiter

Kellie K Collier, VP
Briggs Legal Staffing
1100 Milam Bldg Ste 2070
Houston, TX 77002
(713) 650-8195
(713) 650-6748 FAX
Specialty: L(Permanent & Temporary)
Employment Agency/Recruiter

Office Manager
Brooks Linda Gay
Personnel Consultant
2400 Augusta Dr
Houston, TX 77057
(713) 783-3533
Specialty: G
Employment Agency/Recruiter

Office Manager
Brooks Robert & Associates
5757 Alpha Road
Dallas, TX 75240
(214) 387-3300
Specialty: G
Employment Agency/Recruiter

Office Manager
Bruco Inc
500 E Harris
Houston, TX 77020
(713) 473-9251
Specialty: G
Employment Agency/Recruiter

Stella Walters CPC
Bruco Personnel Services Inc
P O Box 1214
Pasadena, TX 77501
(713) 473-9251
Specialty: G
Employment Agency/Recruiter

Office Manager
BTI
5323 Spring Valley Road
Dallas, TX 75240
(800) 243-8448
Specialty: F
Employment Agency/Recruiter

Betty Bullock
Bullock Personnel of S A
1020 NE Loop 410 Ste 650
San Antonio, TX 655-0090
(512) 655-0090
Specialty: G
Employment Agency/Recruiter

Sue Burnett CPC
Burnett Personnel Consultants
9800 Richmond Ave Ste 800
Houston, TX 77042
(713) 977-4777
Specialty: G
Employment Agency/Recruiter

Office Manager
Burnett Personnel Services
9442 N Capital of TX Hwy
Austin, TX 78759
(512) 794-0077
Specialty: G
Employment Agency/Recruiter

Office Manager
Burnett Personnel Services
13105 NW Frwy Ste 1290
Houston, TX 77040
(713) 462-6868
Specialty: G
Employment Agency/Recruiter

Office Manager
Burnett Personnel Services
1111 Bagby Ste 2060
Houston, TX 77002
(713) 759-9933
Specialty: G
Employment Agency/Recruiter

Paul Burnett
Burnett's Southwest Personnel Services Inc
2710 Avenue E East
Arlington, TX 76011
(817) 649-7000
Specialty: G
Employment Agency/Recruiter

Office Manager
Burrell & Associates
15851 Dallas Pkwy
Dallas, TX 75248
(214) 702-9000
Specialty: G
Employment Agency/Recruiter

Office Manager
Business Women of Dallas
1341 W Mockingbird Lane
Dallas, TX 75247
(214) 630-8411
Specialty: F,O
Employment Agency/Recruiter

Office Manager
Campos Permanent & Temporary Personnel Services
722 Morgan Blvd
Harlingen, TX 78550
(210) 428-5627
Specialty: G
Employment Agency/Recruiter

Office Manager
Career Advancement Opportunities
5728 LBJ Frwy
Dallas, TX 75240
(214) 991-9876
Specialty: H,L,O,S
Employment Agency/Recruiter

Office Manager
Career Counseling Center
617 Pecan Blvd
McAllen, TX 78501
(210) 687-9288
Specialty: G
Employment Agency/Recruiter

Office Manager
Career Marketing Inc
2603 Augusta Dr
Houston, TX 77057
(713) 780-3555
Specialty: G
Employment Agency/Recruiter

Office Manager
Career Point Business School
485 Spencer Lane
San Antonio, TX 78201
(512) 732-3000
Specialty: G
Employment Agency/Recruiter

Pat Blackman
Career Path Inc
4410 N Midkiff Ste D-200
Midland, TX 79705-4223
(915) 967-6710
Specialty: G
Employment Agency/Recruiter

Diana Scott, Mgr
Career Resources
600 E Las Colinas Blvd Ste 1650
Irving, TX 75039
(214) 402-0110
(214) 869-1945 FAX
Specialty: C
Employment Agency/Recruiter

Office Manager
Career Personnel Centre
5599 San Felipe
Houston, TX 77056
(713) 965-9975
Specialty: G
Employment Agency/Recruiter

Office Manager
Carltech
24 E Greenway Plz
Houston, TX 77046
(713) 629-5700
Specialty: G
Employment Agency/Recruiter

Office Manager
Career Placement Service Inc
4444 Richmond
Houston, TX 77027
(713) 621-8880
Specialty: G
Employment Agency/Recruiter

Office Manager
Carlton Accounting Services
24 Greenway Plaza
Houston, TX 77046
(713) 629-1700
Specialty: F
Employment Agency/Recruiter

Office Manager
Carrollton Employment Service Inc
1925 E Belt Line Road
Carrollton, TX 75006
(214) 416-8708
Specialty: O
Employment Agency/Recruiter

Office Manager
Cendrick Personnel
9898 Bissonnet
Houston, TX 77036
(713) 771-4210
Specialty: G
Employment Agency/Recruiter

Vera Stephens
Channel Personnel Services
7007 Gulf Freeway Ste 214
Houston, TX 77087
(713) 643-8001
Specialty: E
Employment Agency/Recruiter

Office Manager
Cherier Business School Job Skills Placement
4200 South Freeway SL 102
Fort Worth, TX 76115
(817) 926-5627
Specialty: Computer Training & Placement for the Economically Deprived
Employment Agency/Recruiter

Office Manager
Christopher Matthew Group
2825 Wilcrest Dr
Houston, TX 77042
(713) 789-2901
Specialty: G
Employment Agency/Recruiter

Office Manager
Citizen Development Assn
3233 Hadley St
Houston, TX 77004
(713) 659-7753
Specialty: G
Employment Agency/Recruiter

Office Manager
Claire Fontaine & Assoc
701 Brazos St
Austin, TX 78701
(512) 320-9188
Specialty: G
Employment Agency/Recruiter

Office Manager
Clayton Personnel
480 N Sam Houston Pkwy E
Houston, TX 77060
(713) 999-3080
Specialty: G
Employment Agency/Recruiter

Dot Cochran
Cochran Personnel Services
3031 Allen Ste 208
Dallas, TX 74204
(214) 855-0840
Specialty: G
Employment Agency/Recruiter

Office Manager
Cockrell Hull
P O Box 797002
Dallas, TX 75379
(214) 387-0206
Specialty: G
Employment Agency/Recruiter

Julian Adams, VP
Computer Career Advancement
4306 Creekbend Dr
Houston, TX 77035
(713) 952-2500
(713) 783-7500 FAX
Specialty: C
Employment Agency/Recruiter

Mark Allen
Computer Professionals Unlimited
13612 Midway Road Ste 333
Dallas, TX 75244
(214) 233-1773
Specialty: C,Technical
Employment Agency/Recruiter

Office Manager
Consultant's & Designers Inc
10500 Richmond Ave
Houston, TX 77042
(713) 784-3696
Specialty: G
Employment Agency/Recruiter

Office Manager
Contech Resources
2925 LBJ Frwy
Dallas, TX 75234
(214) 484-9400
Specialty: Technical
Employment Agency/Recruiter

Office Manager
Continental Personnel Service
6060 N Central Expwy
Dallas, TX 75206
(214) 363-5296
Specialty: C,E,F,H, I,O,S,Management,Mangement Trainees, Recent Grads
Employment Agency/Recruiter

Office Manager
Continental Personnel Service
8700 Stemons Fwy
Dallas, TX 75247
(214) 630-8912
Specialty: G
Employment Agency/Recruiter

Office Manager
Continental Personnel Service
14505 Torrey Chase Blvd
Houston, TX 77014
(713) 587-1700
Specialty: G
Employment Agency/Recruiter

J Mitchell CPC
Continental Personnel Service
P O Box 740134
Houston, TX 77274
(713) 771-7181
Specialty: G
Employment Agency/Recruiter

Office Manager
Continental Personnel Service
400 N Sam Houston Pkwy E
Houston, TX 77060
(713) 820-1470
Specialty: G
Employment Agency/Recruiter

Office Manager
Continental Personnel Service
3000 Weslayan
Houston, TX 77027
(713) 626-8770
Specialty: G
Employment Agency/Recruiter

Office Manager
Continental Personnel Service
626 Uvalde
Houston, TX 77015
(713) 453-7293
Specialty: G
Employment Agency/Recruiter

Office Manager
Continental Personnel Service
6671 Southwest Frwy
Houston, TX 77074
(713) 771-7181
Specialty: G
Employment Agency/Recruiter

Office Manager
Cooksey & Associates
6419 Mimms
Dallas, TX 75252
(214) 248-2676
Specialty: H
Employment Agency/Recruiter

Office Manager
Corporate Accountant Staffing
800 Wilcrest DR
Houston, TX 77042
(713) 789-1522
(713) 789-1523
Specialty: G
Employment Agency/Recruiter

Office Manager
Corporate Consultants Professional Search
4201 W FM 1960
Houston, TX 77068
(713) 580-6480
Specialty: G
Employment Agency/Recruiter

Office Manager
Corporate Staff Recruiters
2915 LBJ Frwy
Dallas, TX 75234
(214) 243-3114
Specialty: G
Employment Agency/Recruiter

Office Manager
Corporate Staff Recruiters
5001 Spring Valley Road
Dallas, TX 75244
(214) 458-9588
Specialty: G
Employment Agency/Recruiter

Office Manager
Cosmetology Employment & Placement Services
2157 W FM 1960
Houston, TX 77090
(713) 893-7374
Specialty: Cosmetology
Employment Agency/Recruiter

Office Manager
Crossroad Personnel
3336 Richmond Ave
Houston, TX 77098
(713) 529-8367
Specialty: G
Employment Agency/Recruiter

Charles H Waites, Owner
Cypress Creek Employment Consultants
13131 Champions Dr Ste 202
Houston, TX 77069
(713) 893-1130
(713) 893-8433 FAX
Specialty: G
Employment Agency/Recruiter

Office Manager
Daher & Associates Insurance Search Specialists
5311 Kirby Dr
Houston, TX 77005
(713) 529-8261
Specialty: G
Employment Agency/Recruiter

Office Manager
Daisy's Employment Service
106 W 5 St
Fort Worth, TX 76102
(817) 335-6205
Specialty: G
Employment Agency/Recruiter

Office Manager
Dallas Business Automation Consultants
3015 Harlee Drive
Dallas, TX 75234
(214) 406-1231
Specialty: C,H,O
Employment Agency/Recruiter

Office Manager
Dallas Domestic Employment Agency
6116 N Central Expwy
Dallas, TX 75206
(214) 361-0888
Specialty: Domestics
Employment Agency/Recruiter

Kenneth D Sutton CPC
Dallas Employment Service
1505 Elm Ste 1525
Dallas, TX 75201
(214) 954-0700
Specialty: G
Employment Agency/Recruiter

Charles Fox
Data Management Search Inc
340 Providence Towers E
LBJ 5001 Spring Vlly
Dallas, TX 75244-3910
(214) 490-0505
Specialty: C
Employment Agency/Recruiter

Michael L Wilson, Pres
Data Masters
2825 Wilcrest Ste 100
Houston, TX 77042
(713) 975-9900
Specialty: C
Employment Agency/Recruiter

Office Manager
Data Personnel Service
1202 Peveto
Houston, TX 77019
(713) 529-9776
Specialty: O
Employment Agency/Recruiter

Office Manager
Data Processing Careers Inc
2720 N Stemmons Frwy
Dallas, TX 75207
(214) 637-6360
Specialty: C
Employment Agency/Recruiter

Office Manager
Data Processing Careers Inc
1200 Sumit Avenue Ste 442
Fort Worth, TX 76102
(817) 336-4565
Specialty: C
24 Years Employment Agency/Recruiter

Office Manager
Data Staffing Centre
5910 N Central Expwy
Dallas, TX 75206
(214) 891-6888
Specialty: O
Employment Agency/Recruiter

Office Manager
Data-Quest Research Inc
2500 Tanglewilde St
Houston, TX 77063
(713) 977-4150
Specialty: G
Employment Agency/Recruiter

Jack Kallison, CPC
DataPro Personnel Consultants
13355 Noel Rd Ste 2001
Dallas, TX 75240
(214) 661-8600
Specialty: C
Employment Agency/Recruiter

Office Manager
DataPro Personnel Consultants
13355 Noel Road
Dallas, TX 75240
(214) 661-8600
Specialty: C
Employment Agency/Recruiter

Office Manager
DataWay Resources
4141 Blue Lake Cir
Dallas, TX 75244
(214) 392-9246
Specialty: O
Employment Agency/Recruiter

Office Manager
Dave Davidson Data Processing Recruiting
204 W Bedford Euless Road
Fort Worth, TX 76180
(817) 268-6820
Specialty: C
Employment Agency/Recruiter

Office Manager
Davis Gail Personnel
18333 Egret Bay Blvd
Houston, TX 77058
(713) 333-2330
Specialty: G
Employment Agency/Recruiter

Office Manager
DeGeorge & Associates
10301 Northwest Frwy
Houston, TX 77092
(713) 956-9797
Specialty: G
Employment Agency/Recruiter

Office Manager
Delta Dallas Personnel
14001 Dallas Pwky
Dallas, TX 75240
(214) 788-2300
Specialty: G
Employment Agency/Recruiter

Office Manager
Dental Assistance Associates
8462 San Fernando Way
Dallas, TX 75218
(214) 324-9109
Specialty: H
Employment Agency/Recruiter

Office Manager
Dental Assistance Personnel
6776 Southwest Frwy
Houston, TX 77074
(713) 953-9500
Specialty: H
Employment Agency/Recruiter

Office Manager
Dental Auxilary Service Inc
4424 Southern
Dallas, TX 75205
(214) 522-2008
Specialty: H
Employment Agency/Recruiter

Office Manager
Dental Resource Management
1946 S IH 35
Austin, TX 78704
(512) 462-2959
Specialty: H
Employment Agency/Recruiter

Office Manager
DFM & Associates
4201 Spring Valley Road
Dallas, TX 75244
(214) 991-7227
Specialty: G
Employment Agency/Recruiter

Joy Perkins CPC
Diversied Human Resource Group
5001 Spring Valley Rd Ste 900
Dallas, TX 75244-3910
(214) 458-8500
Specialty: G
Employment Agency/Recruiter

Annette Guinsburg
Diversified Human Resources
900 Providence Towers E LB5
5001 Spring Valley
Dallas, TX 75244
(214) 387-1910
Specialty: G
Employment Agency/Recruiter

Suzanne Porter
Diversified Human Resources Group Inc
5599 San Felipe Ste 830
Houston, TX 77056
(713) 965-0946
(713) 965-0155(Fax)
Specialty: G
Employment Agency/Recruiter

Office Manager
Dixco Enterprises Inc
1306 Clay St
Houston, TX 77002
(713) 650-8905
Specialty: G
Employment Agency/Recruiter

Office Manager
Donovan & Watkins
1100 Louisiana
Houston, TX 77002
(713) 951-0777
Specialty: G
Employment Agency/Recruiter

Office Manager
Dr Personnel Medical Dental Employment Service
5282 Medical Dr
San Antonio, TX 78229
(512) 614-3886
Specialty: H
Employment Agency/Recruiter

Office Manager
DR Personnel
5900 Memorial Dr
Houston, TX 77007
(713) 880-8080
Specialty: H
Employment Agency/Recruiter

Office Manager
Duncanville Employment Agency
431 W Wheatland Road
Dallas, TX 75232
(214) 298-3400
Specialty: G
Employment Agency/Recruiter

Office Manager
Dunhill of Arlington
1301 S Bowen Road
Arlington, TX 76013
(817) 265-2291
Specialty: F,G,M,S,Information Technology
Employment Agency/Recruiter

Office Manager
Dunhill of Cypress Inc
6555 Harbor Town Dr
Houston, TX 77036
(713) 271-0271
Specialty: G
Employment Agency/Recruiter

Office Manager
Dunhill Professional Search of Post Oak
2500 Tanglewilde St
Houston, TX 77063
(713) 974-3490
Specialty: G
Employment Agency/Recruiter

Office Manager
Dunhill West Houston-Executive Search Consultant
11507 Piping Rock Ln
Houston, TX 77077
(713) 589-1291
Specialty: G
Employment Agency/Recruiter

Office Manager
E D P Computer Services
1201 Louisiana
Houston, TX 77002
(713) 759-1000
Specialty: C
Employment Agency/Recruiter

Office Manager
E D P Personnel
505 Woodway
Houston, TX 77056
(713) 629-1107
(713) 629-1106 (Fax)
Specialty: C
Employment Agency/Recruiter

Office Manager
Eagle Personnel Services Inc
222 W Las Colinas Blvd
Irving, TX 75039
(214) 869-3488
Specialty: F,O,Light Industrial
Employment Agency/Recruiter

Jennifer Dean, Mgr
EAI Medical Personnel Services
3120 Southwest Frwy Ste 215
Houston, TX 77098
(713) 529-1001
(713) 529-9589 FAX
Specialty: H
Employment Agency/Recruiter

Office Manager
Ehrich Enterprises
14011 Whispering Palms
Houston, TX 77066
(713) 537-8297
Specialty: G
Employment Agency/Recruiter

Office Manager
El Paso Employment Service
5959 Gateway Blvd West
El Paso, TX 79925
(915) 778-8899
Specialty: G
Employment Agency/Recruiter

Joe Ellis, Principal
Ellis & Associates Inc
1250 Capital of TX Hwy S
Building 3 Ste 620
Austin, TX 78746
(512) 328-5067
(512) 328-5069 FAX
Specialty: F,G,I,L,O
Employment Agency/Recruiter

Office Manager
Employment Systems Incorporated
7701 Stemmons Frwy
Dallas, TX 75247
(214) 638-8776
Specialty: G
Employment Agency/Recruiter

Office Manager
Emde Marji Personnel
1700 West Loop South
Houston, TX 77054
(713) 621-1177
Specialty: G
Employment Agency/Recruiter

Office Manager
Enertech Resource
13810 Champion Forest Dr
Houston, TX 77069
(713) 566-9074
Specialty: G
Employment Agency/Recruiter

Emma Jacobs
Emjay Computer Careers
1824 Portsmouth
Houston, TX 77098-4302
(713) 259-5000
Specialty: C
Employment Agency/Recruiter

Office Manager
Engineering Technical Recruiters
5001 Spring Valley Road
Dallas, TX 75244
(214) 991-7569
Specialty: E,Technical
Employment Agency/Recruiter

S Katz, Mgr
Employers Registry
9898 Bissonnet Street Ste 520
Houston, TX 77036
(713) 272-7377
(713) 272-6039 FAX
Specialty: C
Employment Agency/Recruiter

Office Manager
Evie Kreisler And Associates
2720 N Stemmons Frwy
Dallas, TX 75207
(214) 631-8994
Specialty: M,Retail
Employment Agency/Recruiter

Howard Wilkinson CPC, Owner
Evins Personnel Consultants
206 W Avenue B Ste 2
Killeen, TX 76541
(817) 526-4161
Specialty: A,B,C,F,G,H,I,L,O,S,T
Employment Agency/Recruiter

Office Manager
Evins Personnel Consultants Inc
2013 W Anderson Ln
Austin, TX 78757
(512) 454-9561
Specialty: G
Employment Agency/Recruiter

Office Manager
Exchange Personnel
3300 W Mockingbird Lane
Dallas, TX 75205
(214) 357-6281
Specialty: G
Employment Agency/Recruiter

Office Manager
Execsource
2501 Avenue J Ste 110
Arlington, TX 76006
(817) 649-3000
Specialty: C
Employment Agency/Recruiter

Office Manager
Experienced Personnel Services
703 McKinney Avenue
Dallas, TX 75202
(214) 954-0654
Specialty: E,H,S,Management
Employment Agency/Recruiter

Office Manager
Express Services Temporary & Permanent Personnel
7940 Shoal Creek Blvd
Austin, TX 78758
(512) 453-3836
Specialty: G
Employment Agency/Recruiter

Office Manager
Express Services Temporary & Permanent Personnel
256 N Sam Houston Pkwy E
Houston, TX 77060
(713) 931-7100
Specialty: G
Employment Agency/Recruiter

Office Manager
Express Services Temporary & Permanent Personnel
2025 N Mays Ct
Round Rock, TX 78664
(512) 255-2525
Specialty: G
Employment Agency/Recruiter

Vasu Radia, Mgr
Express Services Temporary & Permanent Personnel
7800 W IH 10 Ste 123
San Antonio, TX 78230
(210) 340-3939
Specialty: G,Light Industrial,Technical
Employment Agency/Recruiter

Marcia Feldt, Owner
Feldt Personnel
10101 Southwest Frwy Ste 340
Houston, TX 77074
(713) 981-0167
(713) 988-5627 FAX
Specialty: F
Employment Agency/Recruiter

Office Manager
Financial Staff Recruiters
5001 Spring Valley Road
Dallas, TX 75244
(214) 458-0090
Specialty: F
Employment Agency/Recruiter

Office Manager
Financial Staffing Centre
5910 N Central Expwy
Dallas, TX 75206
(214) 891-6680
Specialty: F
Employment Agency/Recruiter

Office Manager
FJD Services
3505 Boca Chica Blvd
Brownsville, TX 78521
(210) 548-2160
Specialty: G
Employment Agency/Recruiter

Office Manager
Force Employment Agency
6601 Hillcroft
Houston, TX 77081
(713) 541-4536
Specialty: G
Employment Agency/Recruiter

Office Manager
FrontLine Search
8018 Fair Oaks Avenue
Dallas, TX 75231
(214) 341-6096
Specialty: G
Employment Agency/Recruiter

Office Manager
Fults K B Inc
4100 Spring Valley Road
Dallas, TX 75244
(214) 661-3079
Specialty: G
Employment Agency/Recruiter

Office Manager
Future Prospects
7600 W Tidwell Rd
Houston, TX 77040
(713) 690-0871
Specialty: G
Employment Agency/Recruiter

Office Manager
Future's Unlimited
6070 Gateway Blvd East
El Paso, TX 79905
(915) 772-9242
Specialty: G
Employment Agency/Recruiter

Office Manager
Gail Darling Temporaries
1790 Lee Trevino Ste 202
El Paso, TX 79936
(915) 598-9900
(915) 598-9832 FAX
Specialty: G
Temporary Service

Office Manager
Gail Davis Personnel
18333 Egret Bay Blvd
Nassau Bay, TX 77058
(713) 486-5112
Specialty: G
Employment Agency/Recruiter

Office Manager
General Employment Personnel Consultants
2603 Augusta Dr Ste 850
Houston, TX 77057
(713) 952-0400
Specialty: C,H,S,O
Employment Agency/Recruiter

Mike Roth, Pres
General Sales & Search
P O Box 690172
Houston, TX 77269-0172
(713) 370-0414
(713) 370-2919 FAX
Specialty: F(Oil & Gas Accounting & Financial)
Recruiter

Office Manager
General Services
419 S Main Ave
San Antonio, TX 78204
(512) 227-4833
Specialty: G
Employment Agency/Recruiter

Yahne Gibson
Gibson & Associates
550 Westcott Ste 290
Houston, TX 77007
(713) 869-3600
Specialty: G
Employment Agency/Recruiter

Office Manager
Global Career Services Inc
8119 Bo Jack Dr
Houston, TX 77040
(713) 466-5555
Specialty: G
Employment Agency/Recruiter

Office Manager
Global Dynamics
4100 Amon Carter Blvd
Fort Worth, TX 76155
(817) 540-3163
Specialty: G
Employment Agency/Recruiter

Office Manager
Goehring Personnel
15150 Preston Road
Dallas, TX 75248
(214) 404-8282
Specialty: G
Employment Agency/Recruiter

Office Manager
Gordon Roberts Inc
7557 Rambler Road Ste 750
Dallas, TX 75231
(214) 691-8500
Specialty: B,G,S
Employment Agency/Recruiter

Office Manager
Gresham & Gresham
P O Box 820888
Houston, TX 77282
(713) 780-1000
Specialty: G
Employment Agency/Recruiter

Office Manager
Griggs Pamela Hunter
Personnel Services
1700 West Loop South
Houston, TX 77027
(713) 961-4976
Specialty: G
Employment Agency/Recruiter

Office Manager
Grove Employment Services Inc
5000 Quorum Drive
Dallas, TX 75240
(214) 661-0242
Specialty: G
Employment Agency/Recruiter

Rodney J Gullo, Pres
Gulco International Recruiting
15710 John F Kennedy Blvd
Ste 110
Houston, TX 77032
(713) 590-9001
(713) 590-1503 FAX
Specialty: International
Employment
Recruiter

Office Manager
Gulf States Personnel Consultants
650 N Sam Houston Pkwy E
Houston, TX 77060
(713) 999-0051
Specialty: G
Employment Agency/Recruiter

Office Manager
H L Yoh Company
6420 Richmond Ave
Houston, TX 77057
(713) 974-1717
Specialty: G
Employment Agency/Recruiter

Office Manager
Harper Sylvia & Associates
2500 Wilcrest Dr Ste 300
Houston, TX 77042
(713) 954-4820
Specialty: G
Employment Agency/Recruiter

Office Manager
Harris J Co Personnel Services
10210 N Central Pkwy
Dallas, TX 75231
(214) 369-9545
Specialty: G
Employment Agency/Recruiter

Office Manager
Harrison Personnel Services Inc
1800 St James Place
Houston, TX 77056
(713) 960-9006
Specialty: G
Employment Agency/Recruiter

Office Manager
Hay Darlene & Associates
2400 Augusta Dr
Houston, TX 77057
(713) 789-0486
Specialty: G
Employment Agency/Recruiter

Office Manager
Health Care Resources Group Inc
5001 Spring Valley Road
Dallas, TX 75244
(214) 404-8460
Specialty: H
Employment Agency/Recruiter

Office Manager
Healthcare Personnel Int'l Inc
13231 Champion Forest Dr
Houston, TX 77069
(713) 580-7700
Specialty: H
Employment Agency/Recruiter

Frank Cooksey
Healthcare Recruiters International
5420 LBJ Freeway Ste 575
Dallas, TX 75240
(214) 770-2020
Specialty: H
Employment Agency/Recruiter

Bettye A Rodgers
Healthcare Staff Resources
222 B Hawk Rd
Roanoke, TX 76262
(817) 430-3388
Specialty: H
Employment Agency/Recruiter

Office Manager
Heathcare Recruiters of Houston
9301 Southwest Frwy
Houston, TX 77074
(713) 771-7344
Specialty: H
Employment Agency/Recruiter

Office Manager
Help Employment Agency
6006 Bellaire Blvd
Houston, TX 77081
(713) 432-0415
Specialty: G
Employment Agency/Recruiter

Office Manager
Hennessy Search Associates
12607 Blackfoot Tr
Austin, TX 78729
(512) 331-7144
Specialty: G
Employment Agency/Recruiter

Office Manager
Hilbert Companies
7004 Bee Caves Rd
Austin, TX 78746
(512) 328-1555
Specialty: G
Employment Agency/Recruiter

Office Manager
Hill Ted & Associates
14614 Falling Creek
Houston, TX 77068
(713) 444-2489
Specialty: G
Employment Agency/Recruiter

Office Manager
Hill Wanda Pesonnel
3010 LBJ Frwy
Dallas, TX 75234
(214) 888-6040
Specialty: G
Employment Agency/Recruiter

Office Manager
Hospitality Personnel
2101 S IH 35
Austin, TX 78741
(512) 443-0101
Specialty: G,T
Employment Agency/Recruiter

Office Manager
Hotelier Inc The
6776 Southwest Frwy
Houston, TX 77074
(713) 785-2335
Specialty: G
Employment Agency/Recruiter

Office Manager
Houston City Personnel Corp
6060 Richmond Ave
Houston, TX 77057
(713) 704-0656
Specialty: G
Employment Agency/Recruiter

Office Manager
Houston City Personnel Corp
10260 Westheimer
Houston, TX 77042
(713) 765-2173
Specialty: G
Employment Agency/Recruiter

Office Manager
Houston International Placement
2616 South Loop West
Houston, TX 77054
(713) 660-7440
Specialty: G
Employment Agency/Recruiter

Office Manager
Howard E Loftin Employment Specialist
1125 Lawrence
Houston, TX 77008
(713) 864-0729
Specialty: G
Employment Agency/Recruiter

Office Manager
IBC In-Bond Central Inc
4150 Rio Bravo St
El Paso, TX 79902
(915) 533-9191
Specialty: G
Employment Agency/Recruiter

Office Manager
Impact Personnel
1700 West Loop South
Houston, TX 77027
(713) 965-9665
Specialty: G
Employment Agency/Recruiter

Office Manager
Industrial Labor Service
1212 Fredericksburg
San Antonio, TX 78201
(512) 525-1444
Specialty: Labor
Employment Agency/Recruiter

Bill Inglehart CPC
Information Search Group
701 N Post Oak Rd Ste 130
Houston, TX 77024-3810
(713) 681-6677
(713) 681-6690 FAX
Specialty: C
Employment Agency/Recruiter

David Richards, Recruiter
Insight Personnel Group Inc
2100 West Loop South Ste 800
Houston, TX 77027
(713) 850-7292
(713) 439-0641 FAX
Specialty: C,G,O,S,Coil & Gas
Employment Agency/Recruiter

Office Manager
Insurance Personnel Unlimited
2911 Turtle Breek Blvd
Dallas, TX 75219
(214) 522-8352
Specialty: I
Employment Agency/Recruiter

Office Manager
Interim Personnel
9525 Katy Frwy
Houston, TX 77024
(713) 932-6633
Specialty: G
Employment Agency/Recruiter

Office Manager
International Data Search
2700 Post Oak Blvd
Houston, TX 77056
(713) 965-0979
Specialty: C
Employment Agency/Recruiter

Office Manager
International Health Care Provider
909 Dairy Ashford
Houston, TX 77079
(713) 870-0190
Specialty: H
Employment Agency/Recruiter

Terri Smith
J D And Associates
700 W Highlander Blvd
Arlington, TX 76015
(817) 467-7714
Specialty: G
Employment Agency/Recruiter

Office Manager
J Pittman Raye
6300 La Calma Dr
Austin, TX 78752
(512) 458-8868
Specialty: G
Employment Agency/Recruiter

J Robert Thompson, Pres
J Robert Thompson Companies Inc
2200 W Loop South Ste 800
Houston, TX 77027
(713) 627-1940
(713) 627-1871 FAX
Specialty: Electronics
Electronics Search

Office Manager
Jo Gunter Selective Employment
1635 NE Loop 410
San Antonio, TX 78209
(512) 824-8544
Specialty: G
Employment Agency/Recruiter

Office Manager
Job Placement Specialist
P O Box 30115
Houston, TX 77249
(713) 635-8550
Specialty: G
Employment Agency/Recruiter

Office Manager
Job Services Inc
6404 Callaghan Rd
San Antonio, TX 78229
(512) 344-3444
Specialty: G
Employment Agency/Recruiter

Office Manager
Jobs For Handicapped
4525 Lemmon Avenue
Dallas, TX 75219
(214) 521-4895
Specialty: G
Employment Agency/Recruiter

Office Manager
Johnson Career Consultants Inc
9601 McAllister Frwy
San Antonio, TX 78216
(512) 344-7692
Specialty: G
Employment Agency/Recruiter

Office Manager
Johnson Consultants
7887 San Felipe
Houston, TX 77063
(713) 977-9300
Specialty: G
Employment Agency/Recruiter

Melvin K Jordan
Jordan Employment Services
1605 A Judson Road
Longview, TX 75601
(214) 753-4493
Specialty: G
Employment Agency/Recruiter

Office Manager
K International Overseas Jobs
12414 Nacogdoches
San Antonio, TX 78217
(512) 657-9334
Specialty: G
Employment Agency/Recruiter

Office Manager
Joyce Polasek K
2400 Augusta Dr
Houston, TX 77057
(713) 785-0044
Specialty: G
Employment Agency/Recruiter

John Kane, Partner
Kane & Company
2100 West Loop South Ste 800
Houston, TX 77027
(713) 621-2280
(713) 297-8864 FAX
Specialty: F,G,H,L,O,S
Employment Agency/Recruiter

Office Manager
Just Le-Gals
3626 N Hall Street
Dallas, TX 75219
(214) 520-8367
Specialty: G
Employment Agency/Recruiter

Office Manager
Kathleen Ater Personnel
6776 Southwest Frwy
Houston, TX 77074
(713) 978-6916
Specialty: G
Employment Agency/Recruiter

Office Manager
JWS Health Consultants Inc
3730 Kirby Dr
Houston, TX 77098
(713) 522-5355
Specialty: H
Employment Agency/Recruiter

Kathleen Barker CPC, Recruiter
KCB Personnel Consultants
12900 Preston Rd Ste 715
Dallas, TX 75230
(214) 386-0456
Specialty: O
Employment Agency/Recruiter

Office Manager
Keegan & Keegan
11821 East Frwy
Houston, TX 77029
(713) 455-4200
Specialty: G
Employment Agency/Recruiter

Office Manager
Kehrer Sylvia Personnel Inc
1616 West Loop South
Houston, TX 77027
(713) 621-1095
Specialty: G
Employment Agency/Recruiter

Office Manager
Kelly Group Insurance Search Consultants
4607 Merwin
Houston, TX 77027
(713) 439-1917
Specialty: I
Employment Agency/Recruiter

A Kelly McBride Jr CPC, Owner
Kelly McBride Associates Employment Consultants
P O Box 440294
Houston, TX 77244-0294
(713) 584-0098
Specialty: M,S,Packaging, Management
Recruiter

Office Manager
Kern Kenneth C Personnel Svcs
4444 Richmond Ave
Houston, TX 77027
(713) 621-8010
Specialty: G
Employment Agency/Recruiter

D V (Jean) Long, Pres
Keypeople Resources Inc
2100 West Loop South
Houston, TX 77027
(713) 877-1427
(713) 877-1826 FAX
Specialty: C
Employment Agency/Recruiter

Sally King CPC
King Computersearch Inc
9221 Lbj Freeway Ste 208
Dallas, TX 75243
(214) 238-1021
Specialty: C
Employment Agency/Recruiter

Carol M McCord
Kingwood Personnel
One Kingwood Place Ste 101
Kingwood, TX 77339
(713) 358-2018
Specialty: G
Employment Agency/Recruiter

Office Manager
Koym Employment & Counseling
4139 Gardendale
San Antonio, TX 78229
(512) 692-9731
Specialty: G
Employment Agency/Recruiter

Office Manager
L A W Personnel Inc
6110 E Mockingbird Lane
Dallas, TX 75214
(214) 828-2828
Specialty: L
Employment Agency/Recruiter

Office Manager
La Barge & Associates
12770 Coit Road Ste 900
Dallas, TX 75251
(214) 991-7713
Specialty: G
Employment Agency/Recruiter

Office Manager
Lab Support Inc
1900 West Loop South
Houston, TX 77027
(713) 621-0502
Specialty: Science Professionals
Employment Agency/Recruiter

Andrea Graham, Acct Mgr
LAB Support Inc
3003 LBJ Fwy Ste 132
Dallas, TX 75234
(214) 243-6897
(214) 243-1309 FAX
Specialty: Science Professionals
Temporary Employment Agency

Office Manager
Labor Force
1005 S Josey Lane
Dallas, TX 75234
(214) 418-0069
Specialty: G
Employment Agency/Recruiter

Office Manager
Labor Force
2182 Jackson-Keller Rd
San Antonio, TX 78213
(512) 341-9898
Specialty: G
Employment Agency/Recruiter

Office Manager
Laffer & Associates Inc
2995 LBJ Frwy
Dallas, TX 75234
(214) 484-9675
Specialty: G
Employment Agency/Recruiter

Office Manager
Lancaster Melodie
2000 S Dairy Ashford
Houston, TX 77077
(713) 589-2109
Specialty: G
Employment Agency/Recruiter

Office Manager
Lancaster Resources
2000 S Dairy Ashford
Houston, TX 77077
(713) 589-9500: 589-9519
Specialty: G
Employment Agency/Recruiter

Office Manager
Lawrence James Associates
9550 Skillman Street
Dallas, TX 75243
(214) 343-1110
Specialty: G
Employment Agency/Recruiter

Office Manager
Leadership Resources
222 W Las Colinas Blvd
Arlington, TX 75039
(214) 869-2262
Specialty: G
Employment Agency/Recruiter

Office Manager
Leaseway Personnel Corp
520 Avenue H East
Arlington, TX 76011
(214) 817 640-1343
Specialty: G
Employment Agency/Recruiter

Office Manager
Leaseway Personnel Corp
1341-A Lomaland Dr
El Paso, TX 79935
(915) 594-9142
Specialty: G
Employment Agency/Recruiter

Office Manager
Lee's Personnel Service Inc
15603 Kuykendahl Road Ste 332
Houston, TX 77090-3656
(713) 591-0090
Specialty: G,O,Temporary, Contract & Permanent
Employment Agency/Recruiter

Office Manager
Legal Staffing Inc
2121 San Jacinto St
Dallas, TX 75201
(214) 754-2940
Specialty: L
Employment Agency/Recruiter

Dean Clark, Pres
Legend Marine Inc
9894 Bissonnet Ste 860
Houston, TX 77036-8229
(713) 776-1000
(713) 776-1058 FAX
Specialty: G
Employment Agency/Recruiter

Office Manager
Leigh Personnel
2401 Fountain View Dr
Houston, TX 77057
(713) 784-4323
Specialty: G
Employment Agency/Recruiter

Office Manager
Lengston Corporation & Assoc Co
1111 Fannin
Houston, TX 77002
(713) 757-1331
Specialty: G
Employment Agency/Recruiter

Office Manager
Leslie Corporation
10700 North Frwy
Houston, TX 77037
(713) 591-0915
Specialty: G
Employment Agency/Recruiter

Office Manager
Lewisville-Regional Personnel Agency
522 Edmonds
Lewisville TX 75067
(214) 436-3541
Specialty: G
Employment Agency/Recruiter

Kenneth J Bohan CPC
Liberty Personnel/Executive Search
2100 W Loop South Ste 1300
Houston, TX 77027
(713) 961-7666
Specialty: G
Employment Agency/Recruiter

Office Manager
Link Personnel Services
2910 Crawford St
Houston, TX 77004
(713) 655-0344
Specialty: G
Employment Agency/Recruiter

Office Manager
Link Personnel Services
1 West Loop South
Houston, TX 77027
(713) 622-7488
Specialty: G
Employment Agency/Recruiter

Office Manager
Link Personnel Services
1066 Federal Rd
Houston, TX 77015
(713) 455-6700
Specialty: G
Employment Agency/Recruiter

Office Manager
Link Personnel Services
1219-1/2 Bay Area Blvd
Houston, TX 77058
(713) 486-1901
Specialty: G
Employment Agency/Recruiter

Office Manager
Link Personnel Services
3701 W Alabama
Houston, TX 77027
(713) 961-5465
Specialty: G
Employment Agency/Recruiter

Office Manager
Link Personnel Services
10103 Hammerly Blvd
Houston, TX 77080
(713) 935-0090
Specialty: G
Employment Agency/Recruiter

Hal Sullivant, Pres
Linn-Truett Inc
7800 I H 10 West Ste 512
San Antonio, TX 78230
(210) 340-3690
(210) 340-2158 FAX
Specialty: C
Employment Agency/Recruiter

Office Manager
Lone Star Personnel Inc
6800 Park Ten Blvd
San Antonio, TX 78213
(512) 732-5466
Specialty: G
Employment Agency/Recruiter

Office Manager
Lonergran Farrar & Associates Inc
363 N Sam Houston Pkwy E
Houston, TX 77060
(713) 999-0181
Specialty: G
Employment Agency/Recruiter

Office Manager
Lucas Associates Inc
12655 N Central Expwy
Dallas, TX 75243
(214) 980-4666
Specialty: G
Employment Agency/Recruiter

Office Manager
Lusk & Associates Personnel Services Inc
8950 N Central Expwy
Dallas, TX 75231
(214) 696-6997
Specialty: G
Employment Agency/Recruiter

Office Manager
Lyndian Inc
7322 Southwest Frwy
Houston, TX 77074
(713) 777-4334
Specialty: G
Employment Agency/Recruiter

Cheryl Proctor, Mgr
M David Lowe Personnel Services
1100 Milam Ste 2860
Houston, TX 77002
(713) 951-9339
(713) 951-9480 FAX
Specialty: A,B,C,E,F,G,H,I,L,M,O,P,R,S,T
Employment Agency/Recruiter

Judith Bretthauer, Mgr
M David Lowe Personnel Services
12555 Gulf Freeway
Houston, TX 77034
(713) 484-5500
(713) 481-2444 FAX
Specialty: A,B,C,E,F,G,H,I,L,M,O,P,R,S,T
Employment Agency/Recruiter

Ruth Reading, Mgr
M David Lowe Personnel Services
820 Gessner Ste 1400
Houston, TX 77024
(713) 468-0440
(713) 468-6855 FAX
Specialty: A,B,C,E,F,G,H,I,L,M,O,P,R,S,T
Employment Agency/Recruiter

M David Lowe, Pres/Ceo
M David Lowe Personnel Services
6117 Richmond Ave
Houston, TX 77057
(713) 784-4226
(713) 784-3880
(713) 784-7709 FAX
Specialty: A,B,C,E,F,G,H,I,L,M,O,P,R,S,T
Employment Agency/Recruiter

Office Manager
Management Alliance Group
3040 Post Oak Blvd
Houston, TX 77056
(713) 960-1747
(713) 960-8706(Fax)
Specialty: G
Employment Agency/Recruiter

Office Manager
Management Alliance Group
5599 San Felipe
Houston, TX 77056
(713) 629-5800
Specialty: G
Employment Agency/Recruiter

Office Manager
Management Personnel Service
5001 Spring Valley Rd
Dallas, TX 75244
(214) 991-7527
Specialty: G
Employment Agency/Recruiter

Office Manager
Management Recruiters
2161 NW Military Hwy
San Antonio, TX 78213
(512) 525-1800
Specialty: G
Employment Agency/Recruiter

William B Anderson, Mgr
Management Recruiters of Fort Worth Southwest
1701 River Run Rd
Fort Worth, TX 76107-6530
(817) 338-0066
Specialty: G
Employment Agency/Recruiter

Office Manager
Management Recruiters of Plano
101 E Park Blvd
Plano, TX 75074
(214) 424-3339
Specialty: G
Employment Agency/Recruiter

Office Manager
Management Recruiters-Addison
15400 Knoll Trail Dr
Dallas, TX 75248
(214) 960-1291
Specialty: G,I,P
Employment Agency/Recruiter

Office Manager
Management Recruiters-Worth-Arlington
1009 W Randol Mill Rd
Arlington, TX 76012
(817) 469-6161
Specialty: G
Employment Agency/Recruiter

Tammy Rinaldi, Pres
Marilyn Austin CPC & Assoc
11999 Katy Frwy Ste 150
Houston, TX 77079
(713) 493-5706
(713) 493-2682 FAX
Specialty: B,C,F,G,H,I,L,M,O
Employment Agency/Recruiter

Office Manager
Mary Green's Employment Finders
6044 Gateway Blvd East
El Paso, TX 79905
(915) 779-3770
Specialty: G
Employment Agency/Recruiter

Office Manager
Marksbury Jaye
6809 Clearhaven Drive
Dallas, TX 75248
(214) 934-3222
Specialty: G
Employment Agency/Recruiter

Office Manager
Massarini Pete & Assocs Inc
2630 Fountain View
Houston, TX 77057
(713) 977-0789
Specialty: G
Employment Agency/Recruiter

Office Manager
Marshall Career Service Inc
6500 West Frwy
Fort Worth, TX 76116
(817) 737-2645
Specialty: G
Employment Agency/Recruiter

Kathy Hancock, Owner
Matchmaker Personnel Consulting
9900 Weir Loop
Austin, TX 78736
(512) 288-6133
(512) 288-2544 FAX
Specialty: G
Employment Agency/Recruiter

Office Manager
Martin-Ericson
6604 Locke Avnue
Fort Worth, TX 76116
(817) 732-4484
Specialty: G
Employment Agency/Recruiter

Office Manager
McGhee And Asociates
8222 Douglas Ave
Dallas, TX 75225
(214) 691-9471
Specialty: G
Employment Agency/Recruiter

Office Manager
McNeff Judith & Associates
12900 Preston Rd
Dallas, TX 75230
(214) 458-1335
Specialty: G
Employment Agency/Recruiter

Linda McLaughlin CPC
McSearch Personnel Consultants
11300 N Central Exp Ste 100
Dallas, TX 75243
(214) 373-1171
Specialty: G
Employment Agency/Recruiter

Ben F Meador
Meador-Brady Personnel Services Inc
P O Box 2001
Pasadena, TX 77501-2001
(713) 941-0616
Specialty: G
Employment Agency/Recruiter

Office Manager
Meador-Brady Personnel Srv Inc
17000 El Camino Real
Houston, TX 77058
(713) 486-1700
Specialty: G
Employment Agency/Recruiter

Henry C Wright Jr
Meador-Wright & Associates
6211 W Northwest Hwy C-261
Dallas, TX 75225
(214) 691-3485
Specialty: G
Employment Agency/Recruiter

Dawn Hiner
Medical Personnel Service
4801 Woodway Ste 333 West
Houston, TX 77056
(713) 623-2200
(713) 623-6733
Specialty: H
Employment Agency/Recruiter

Donna Herschleb RN CPC
Medical Professional Placements
8007 Raintree Place
Austin, TX 78759
(512) 343-2145
Specialty: H
Employment Agency/Recruiter

Office Manager
Medical Technocrats Inc
10520 Plano Rd
Dallas, TX 75238
(214) 340-6450
Specialty: H
Employment Agency/Recruiter

Mark Schnitzer, Owner
Medlaw Recruiters
8323 Southwest Frwy Ste 800
Houston, TX 77074
(713) 988-0945
Specialty: H,L
Employment Agency/Recruiter

Kevin D Page, Principal
MegaSearch Inc
15425 North Frwy Ste 330
Houston, TX 77090
(713) 872-7800
(713) 872-7810 FAX
Specialty: E,G,T
Employment Agency/Recruiter

Office Manager
Memorial City Personnel
1700 West Loop South
Houston, TX 77054
(713) 622-9122
Specialty: G
Employment Agency/Recruiter

Office Manager
Meridien Speciality Personnel Service Inc
16800 Imperial Valley Dr
Houston, TX 77060
(713) 448-7900
Specialty: G
Employment Agency/Recruiter

Office Manager
Met Inc
5415 Maple Ave
Dallas, TX 75235
(214) 630-3265
Specialty: G
Employment Agency/Recruiter

Office Manager
Metro Personnel
12700 Hillcrest Rd
Dallas, TX 75230
(214) 934-1095
Specialty: G
Employment Agency/Recruiter

Office Manager
MetroCareer Inc
10777 Westheimer Rd
Houston, TX 77042
(713) 781-7215
Specialty: G
Employment Agency/Recruiter

Office Manager
Metropolitan Employment Resources
8800 S Braeswood Blvd
Houston, TX 77031
(713) 270-5627
Specialty: G
Employment Agency/Recruiter

Office Manager
Michael James & Associates
4340 Spring Valley Rd
Dallas, TX 75244
(214) 386-0547
Specialty: G
Employment Agency/Recruiter

Office Manager
Milam Design Services Inc
7748 W Hwy 290
Austin, TX 78736
(512) 288-7747
Specialty: G
Employment Agency/Recruiter

Office Manager
Milam Design Services Inc
1730 Blalock Rd
Houston, TX 77080
(713) 461-9178
Specialty: G
Employment Agency/Recruiter

Office Manager
Miller Personnel Inc
4006 Belt Line Road
Dallas, TX 75244
(214) 702-9891
Specialty: G
Employment Agency/Recruiter

Office Manager
Miya Personnel
6010 Waggoner Dr
Dallas, TX 75230
(214) 692-6555
Specialty: G
Employment Agency/Recruiter

Office Manager
Morgan Barnett & Associates Inc
3050 Post Oak Blvd
Houston, TX 77056
(713) 993-9990
Specialty: G
Employment Agency/Recruiter

William J Cherney, Br Mgr
Morson International Inc
400 N Sam Houston Pkwy E
Ste 307
Houston, TX 77060-3737
(713) 445-4450
(713) 445-4475 FAX
Specialty: C,E,P,R
Employment Agency/Recruiter

Office Manager
Mortgage Bankers Consultants
2515 McKinney Avenue Ste 1600
Dallas, TX 75201-1945
(214) 520-1324
Specialty: B,F
Employment Agency/Recruiter

Debbie Bowman, Br Mgr
Mortgage Recruiting Consultants
5728 L B J Freeway
Dallas, TX 458-7880
(214) 458-7880
(214) 458-0465 FAX
Specialty: B,F
Employment Agency/Recruiter

Office Manager
Mortgage Recruiting Consultants Inc
8701 Bedford Euless Road
Fort Worth, TX 76180
(817) 589-1334
Specialty: F
Employment Agency/Recruiter

Elizabeth Grinslade
MSI International
5215 N O'Connor Blvd Ste 1875
Irving, TX 75039
(214) 869-3939
Specialty: G
Employment Agency/Recruiter

Trish Davis, Recruiter
National Prosource Inc
9301 Southwest Frwy Ste 250
Houston, TX 77074
(713) 242-1896
Specialty: C
Employment Agency/Recruiter

Office Manager
National Staffing Services
5001 Spring Valley Rd Ste 350 W
Dallas, TX 75244
(214) 661-3733
Specialty: G
Employment Agency/Recruiter

Office Manager
Net-Com Interim Staffing Inc
10575 Katy Frwy Ste 230
Houston, TX 77024
(713) 468-5790
Specialty: G
Employment Agency/Recruiter

Office Manager
North American Nanny Network & Institute Inc
8845 Long Point Rd
Houston, TX 77055
(713) 464-0978
Specialty: G
Employment Agency/Recruiter

Office Manager
Now Personnel Service Inc
10700 Richmond Ave
Houston, TX 77042
(713) 974-3203
Specialty: G
Employment Agency/Recruiter

Office Manager
NR Skillmaster
5353 W Alabama
Houston, TX 77056
(713) 871-5200
Specialty: G
Employment Agency/Recruiter

Office Manager
O'Keefe & Associates
3420 Executive Center Dr
Austin, TX 78731
(512) 343-1134
Specialty: G
Employment Agency/Recruiter

Office Manager
Odell & Associates
12700 Park Central Dr
Dallas, TX 75251
(214) 458-7900
Specialty: G
Employment Agency/Recruiter

Office Manager
Officemates 5
1250 S Capital of TX Hwy
Austin, TX 78746
(512) 327-8292
Specialty: G
Employment Agency/Recruiter

Sharon Rice, Br Mgr
Officeteam
1360 Post Oak Blvd Ste 1400
Houston, TX 77056
(713) 623-4060
Specialty: G,O
Employment Agency/Recruiter

Office Manager
Olsten Technical Services
10550 Northwest Frwy
Houston, TX 77092
(713) 688-1955
Specialty: Technical
Employment Agency/Recruiter

Office Manager
Omni Health Services Inc
2600 N Gessner
Houston, TX 77080
(713) 690-1971
Specialty: H
Employment Agency/Recruiter

Office Manager
OmniSearch
2350 Airport Freeway Ste 100
Bedford, TX 76022-6026
(817) 545-4851
(817) 545-3363 FAX
Specialty: C
Employment Agency/Recruiter

John Kearley, Mgr
Opportunity Unlimited Inc
2720 W Mockingbird Ln
Dallas, TX 75235
(214) 357-9196
Specialty: C,E
Employment Agency/Recruiter

Office Manager
Overcomer Marketing Group
1621 Pine Drive Ste A
Dickinson, TAX 77539
(713) 337-4827
Specialty: G
Employment Agency/Recruiter

Office Manager
P & S Datapro
2401 E Randol Mill Rd Ste 141
Arlington, TX 76011
(817) 640-8131
Specialty: C
Employment Agency/Recruiter

Office Manager
Pate Resources Group
11200 Westheimer Rd
Houston, TX 77042
(713) 783-3999
Specialty: G
Employment Agency/Recruiter

Office Manager
Performance Group The
2825 Wilcrest Dr
Houston, TX 77042
(713) 975-9900
Specialty: G
Employment Agency/Recruiter

Office Manager
Performance Recruiters of Dallas
8080 N Central Expressway
Dallas, TX 75206
(214) 891-8277
Specialty: G
Employment Agency/Recruiter

Office Manager
Permanent Success Personnel Services
800 W Airport Freeway
Irving, TX 75062
(214) 445-1255
Specialty: G
Employment Agency/Recruiter

Penny Peters
Personnel Connection Inc
14951 Dallas Pkwy Ste 110
Dallas, TX 75240
(214) 934-1200
Specialty: G
Employment Agency/Recruiter

Karen O'Keefe
Personnel Connection Inc
613 N W Loop 410 Ste 150
San Antonio, TX 78216
(512) 342-8868
Specialty: G
Employment Agency/Recruiter

Office Manager
Personnel One
4158 S Cooper St
Arlington, TX 76015
(817) 468-3900
Specialty: G
Employment Agency/Recruiter

Office Manager
Personnel One
6110 Greenville Avenue Ste 500
Dallas, TX 75206
(214) 361-6000
Specialty: F,O,S,Management
Technical
Employment Agency/Recruiter

Office Manager
Personnel One
13525 Montfort Drive
Dallas, TX 75240
(214) 392-0900
Specialty: F,O,S,Management
Technical
Employment Agency/Recruiter

Office Manager
Personnel One
2107 N O'Connor Rd
Irving, TX 75061
(214) 554-1100
Specialty: G
Employment Agency/Recruiter

Office Manager
Personnel Pool
8303 N Mo-Pac Expwy
Austin, TX 78759
(512) 338-9675
Specialty: G
Employment Agency/Recruiter

Office Manager
Phoenix Group The
5260 Memorial Dr
Houston, TX 77007
(713) 863-7577
Specialty: G
Employment Agency/Recruiter

Office Manager
Placement Resource The
105 Biltmore
San Antonio, TX 78213
(512) 525-1993
Specialty: G
Employment Agency/Recruiter

Office Manager
Placement Resources
7277 Regency Sq Blvd
Houston, TX 77036
(713) 783-5830
Specialty: G
Employment Agency/Recruiter

Office Manager
PRC-Professional Recruiting Consultants
45 NE Loop 410
San Antonio, TX 78216
(512) 349-7801
Specialty: G
Employment Agency/Recruiter

Judy Arnold CPC
Prestige Personnel Consultants
4608 Summerhill Rd
Texarkana, TX 75503
(214) 794-1411
Specialty: G
Employment Agency/Recruiter

Donna Greer, Owner
Prestige Recruiters Inc
1543 Green Oaks Place Ste 200
Kingwood, TX 77339
(713) 359-2525
Specialty: C
Recruiter

Office Manager
Primary Service
520 Post Oak Blvd
Houston, TX 77027
(713) 850-7010
Specialty: G
Employment Agency/Recruiter

Office Manager
Printing Industries Assn of Texas
910 W Mockingbird Ln
Dallas, TX 75247
(214) 630-8871
Specialty: G
Employment Agency/Recruiter

Nellie Cuaron, Partner
Rachel Varnell, Partner
Priority Search Inc
444 Executive Center Blvd
Ste 233
El Paso, TX 79902
(915) 534-4457
(915) 544-5368 FAX
Specialty: M
Employment Agency/Recruiter

Office Manager
Private Industry Council Admin
285 Kings Hwy
Brownsville, TX 78521
(210) 548-6743
Specialty: G
Employment Agency/Recruiter

Cynthie Rosendale
Pro Fit EDP
11918 Meadowdale
Stafford, TX 77477
(713) 879-0848
Specialty: C
Employment Agency/Recruiter

Office Manager
Pro Staff Personnel Service
10777 Westheimer Rd
Houston, TX 77042
(713) 953-9993
Specialty: G
Employment Agency/Recruiter

Office Manager
Pro Staff Personnel Services
8080 N Central Expressway
Dallas, TX 75206
(214) 891-8110
Specialty: G
Employment Agency/Recruiter

Office Manager
Pro Staff Personnel Services Technical Division
4141 Blue Lake Circle Ste 141
Dallas, TX 75244
(214) 416-3900
Specialty: Technical
Employment Agency/Recruiter

Office Manager
Pro Staff Personnel Services Temporary Division
115 Executive Way
DeSoto, TX 75115
(214) 709-0076
Specialty: G
Employment Agency/Recruiter

Office Manager
Professional Career Associates
9430 Research Blvd
Austin, TX 78759
(512) 338-9144
Specialty: G
Employment Agency/Recruiter

Office Manager
Professional Placement Inc
4120 Rio Bravo St
El Paso, TX 79902
(915) 532-2996
Specialty: G
Employment Agency/Recruiter

Wes Looney
Professional Recruiting Consultants
45 N E Loop Ste 410 Ste 850
San Antonio, TX 78216
(512) 349-7801
Specialty: G
Employment Agency/Recruiter

Office Manager
Professional Staff Recruiters
5910 N Central Expressway
Dallas, TX 75206
(214) 891-6660
Specialty: G
Employment Agency/Recruiter

Office Manager
Professional Staffing Assocs
10935 Estates Lane
Dallas, TX 75238
(214) 340-3737
Specialty: G
Employment Agency/Recruiter

Office Manager
Profiles
2220 Brazos St
Houston, TX 77002
(713) 522-9192
Specialty: G
Employment Agency/Recruiter

Office Manager
Profiles of Houston
1618 W Sam Houston Pkwy N
Houston, TX 77043
(713) 467-8378
Specialty: G
Employment Agency/Recruiter

Office Manager
Quad Employment Agency
5514 Royal Ln
Dallas, TX 75229
(214) 692-6903
Specialty: G
Employment Agency/Recruiter

Sharon Seligman
Quest Personnel Resources
50 Briar Hollow Lane
Ste 510 East
Houston, TX 77027
(713) 961-0605
Specialty: G
Employment Agency/Recruiter

Office Manager
Quiles Employment Service
6655 Hillcroft
Houston, TX 77081
(713) 981-1207
Specialty: G
Employment Agency/Recruiter

Office Manager
Quiles Employment Service
6633 Hillcroft
Houston, TX 77081
(713) 981-8824
Specialty: G
Employment Agency/Recruiter

Debbie Gregory, Br Mgr
Quinby Personnel Services
1001 E Southmore Ave Ste 1012
Pasadena, TX 77502
(713) 920-1283
(713) 920-1287 FAX
Specialty: O
Employment Agency/Recruiter

Office Manager
Rangers Consultants
5930 Lockhill Rd
San Antonio, TX 78240
(512) 691-8955
Specialty: G
Employment Agency/Recruiter

Office Manager
Quinet Personnel Services Inc
6776 Southwest Frwy
Houston, TX 77074
(713) 977-7733
Specialty: G
Employment Agency/Recruiter

Office Manager
Ray Rashkin Associates Inc
2437 Bay Area Blvd
Houston, TX 77058
(713) 480-8114
Specialty: G
Employment Agency/Recruiter

Roberta Delius, Pres
R J Myers Consulting Services
1011 Richmond Ste 670
Houston, TX 77042
(713) 266-8094
(713) 266-8102 FAX
Specialty: G
Employment Agency/Recruiter

Office Manager
Realtime Staffing Inc
5430 L B J Freeway
Dallas, TX 75240
(214) 770-2323
Specialty: G
Employment Agency/Recruiter

Roberta Delius, Pres
R J Myers Consulting Services
1777 NE Loop 410
San Antonio, TX 78217
(512) 820-2648
Specialty: G
Employment Agency/Recruiter

Office Manager
Recruiting Specialists
5930 L B J Freeway
Dallas, TX 75240
(214) 233-9749
Specialty: G
Employment Agency/Recruiter

Office Manager
Recruitment International
2401 Fountain View Dr
Houston, TX 77057
(713) 977-1167
Specialty: G
Employment Agency/Recruiter

Office Manager
Referral Service
1029 Alabama St
Houston, TX 77004
(713) 524-2883
Specialty: G
Employment Agency/Recruiter

Office Manager
Regal Personnel Inc
13740 Midway Rd Ste 600
Dallas, TX 75244
(214) 788-0355
Specialty: G
Employment Agency/Recruiter

Office Manager
Relief Services Inc
12860 Hillcrest Rd Ste 203
Dallas, TX 75230
(214) 701-9916
Specialty: G
Employment Agency/Recruiter

Al Rellstab
Rellstab Associates
7709 Long Point Dr
Austin, TX 78731
(512) 345-1684
Specialty: G
Employment Agency/Recruiter

Bill Troff, Sr Acct Exec
Restaurant Recruiters Inc
3701 Kirby Dr Ste 866
Houston, TX 77098
(713) 529-0123
Specialty: T
Employment Agency/Recruiter

J W Iden CPC
Richard Wayne & Roberts
24 Greenway Plaza Ste 1304
Houston, TX 77046
(713) 629-6681
Specialty: G
Employment Agency/Recruiter

Office Manager
River Oaks Domestic Agency
2727 Kirby Dr
Houston, TX 77098
(713) 523-2011
Specialty: Domestics
Employment Agency/Recruiter

Fred Krafcik CPC, Owner
Robert George & Associates
1303-103 W Buckingham Ste 232
Garland, TX 75040
(214) 495-1271
(214) 495-0697 FAX
Specialty: C,E
Employment Agency/Recruiter

Office Manager
Robert Half International
6243 Interstate Hwy 10 W
San Antonio, TX 78201
(512) 736-2467
Specialty: B,C,F
Employment Agency/Recruiter

Office Manager
Robert Half Inc
800 W Airport Freeway
Irving, TX 75062
(214) 721-0800
Specialty: B,C,F
Employment Agency/Recruiter

Roger Davidson
Robert Half of Dallas
3 Northpark East Ste 110
Dallas, TX 75231
(214) 363-3300
Specialty: B,C,F
Employment Agency/Recruiter

Office Manager
Robert Half International
12015 Park Thirty-Five Ctr
Austin, TX 78753
(512) 835-0883
Specialty: B,C,F
Employment Agency/Recruiter

Office Manager
Robinson Margo Personnel
1700 West Loop South
Houston, TX 77054
(713) 623-0574
Specialty: G
Employment Agency/Recruiter

Office Manager
Robert Half International
1300 Summit Ave
Fort Worth, TX 76102
(817) 870-1200
Specialty: B,C,F
Employment Agency/Recruiter

Office Manager
Roth Young
5344 Alpha Rd
Dallas, TX 75240
(214) 233-5000
Specialty: G
Employment Agency/Recruiter

Office Manager
Rozelle Anne & Associates Employment Consultants
2323 S Voss Rd
Houston, TX 77057
(713) 783-4740
Specialty: G
Employment Agency/Recruiter

Steven LeMay
Saber Consultants
5300 Hollister Ste 100
Houston, TX 77040
(713) 462-6900
Specialty: G
Employment Agency/Recruiter

Betty Aldridge, Per Spcl
S & W Technical Services Inc
8122 Datapoint Ste 326
San Antonio, TX 78229
(210) 614-1080
(210) 614-7085 FAX
Specialty: C,E,Technical,Medical Technicians
Employment Agency/Recruiter

Office Manager
Salon Employment Datalink Corp
12262 Inwood Road
Dallas, TX 75244
(214) 991-7686
Specialty: Salons
Employment Agency/Recruiter

Office Manager
S E R-Jobs for Progress Inc
525 Cupples Rd
San Antonio, TX 78237
(512) 434-9491
Specialty: G
Employment Agency/Recruiter

Office Manager
Sasseen Co-Career Opportunities
3113 S University Dr
Arlington, TX 76013
(817) 926-5627
Specialty: G
Employment Agency/Recruiter

Office Manager
S L Fults & Associates
9099 Katy Frwy
Houston, TX 77024
(713) 935-9797
Specialty: G
Employment Agency/Recruiter

Office Manager
Schmidt Ron Companies
8620 N New Braunfels
San Antonio, TX 78217
(512) 821-3705
Specialty: G
Employment Agency/Recruiter

Office Manager
Search & Recruit International
4538 Cantarview
San Antonio, TX 78228
(512) 735-9362
Specialty: G
Employment Agency/Recruiter

Office Manager
Secretarial Contracting Services
1402 Corinth St
Dallas, TX 75215
(214) 421-3491
Specialty: O
Employment Agency/Recruiter

Office Manager
Secretaries of Dallas
5001 Spring Valley Rd Ste 350 W
Dallas, TX 75244
(214) 661-3733
Specialty: O
Employment Agency/Recruiter

Catherine Hickey CPC
Secretaries of Dallas Inc
1700 Pacific Ave Ste 3880
Dallas, TX 75201
(214) 953-0605
Specialty: O
Employment Agency/Recruiter

Office Manager
Secretary Inc The Tempower
1 Sugar Creek Center Blvd
Sugar Land, TX 77448
(713) 242-2442
Specialty: O
Employment Agency/Recruiter

Dave Estes CPC, Pres
Seegers Estes & Associates Inc
2121 Sage Rd Ste 240
Houston, TX 77056
(713) 840-8765
(713) 840-8769 FAX
Specialty: E,Chemicals
Employment Agency/Recruiter

Office Manager
Select Personnel
1616 West Loop South
Houston, TX 77054
(713) 961-0111
Specialty: G
Employment Agency/Recruiter

Office Manager
Senior Community Service Employment Program Project
600 Chelsea St
El Paso, TX 79903
(915) 779-3588
Specialty: G
Employment Agency/Recruiter

Office Manager
SER Employment
4838 Montana Ave
El Paso, TX 79903
(915) 565-4888
Specialty: G
Employment Agency/Recruiter

Office Manager
SER-Jobs For Progress of the Texas Coast Inc
2150 W 18
Houston, TX 77008
(713) 868-1144
Specialty: G
Employment Agency/Recruiter

Office Manager
Serivicious Personales
5819 Bellaire Blvd
Houston, TX 77081
(713) 660-8946
Specialty: G
Employment Agency/Recruiter

Sheila Long CPC
Sheila Smith & Associates Inc
1615 Guadalupe Ste 203
Austin, TX 78701
(512) 472-1400
Specialty: G
Employment Agency/Recruiter

Office Manager
Sides & Associates
11511 Katy Frwy
Houston, TX 77079
(713) 870-1700
Specialty: G
Employment Agency/Recruiter

Office Manager
Silver & Associates
1331 Lamar
Houston, TX 77010
(713) 650-3055
Specialty: G
Employment Agency/Recruiter

Greg Singleton, Recruiter
Singleton Associates
1603 Babcock Rd Ste 175
San Antonio, TX 78251
(210) 342-1087
(210) 342-1191 FAX
Specialty: E,G.M,P,S
Employment Agency/Recruiter

Office Manager
SLS Servies
105 S Main St
Fort Worth, TX 76102
(817) 870-1200
Specialty: G
Employment Agency/Recruiter

Robert Bennett CPC
Smith-Bennett & Associates
13918 Preston Valley Pl
Dallas, TX 75240
(214) 429-0988
Specialty: G
Employment Agency/Recruiter

Office Manager
Snelling And Snelling
1420 W Mockingbird Lane
Ste 190
Dallas, TX 75247
(214) 637-6210
Specialty: C,E,F,H,M,S,Technical
Employment Agency/Recruiter

Office Manager
Snelling & Snelling Employment Service-Campbell Centre
8350 N Central Expressway
Dallas, TX 75206
(214) 363-8800
Specialty: G
Employment Agency/Recruiter

Office Manager
Snelling Personnel Recruiting Division
118 W Castellano Dr
El Paso, TX 79912
(915) 532-1981
Specialty: G
Employment Agency/Recruiter

Sharon Pratz
Snelling And Snelling
1000 Beltline Ste 100
Carrollton, TX 75006
(214) 242-8575
Specialty: C,E,F,H,M,S,Technical
Employment Agency/Recruiter

Office Manager
Snelling Personnel Services
9461 L B J Freeway
Dallas, TX 75243
(214) 235-0800
Specialty: G
Employment Agency/Recruiter

Office Manager
Snelling And Snelling
12801 N Central Expressway
Ste 215
Dallas, TX 75243
(214) 701-8080
Specialty: C,E,F,H,M,S,Technical
Employment Agency/Recruiter

Susan J Stone, Pres
Snelling Personnel Services
11811 North Frwy Ste 100
Houston, TX 77060
(713) 847-1700
(713) 847-2700 FAX
Specialty: G,O,P,S
Employment Agency/Recruiter

Office Manager
Snelling Personnel Services
200 10th St S
McAllen, TX 78501
(210) 687-8311
Specialty: G
Employment Agency/Recruiter

Office Manager
Snelling Personnel Services
8626 Tesoro Dr
San Antonio, TX 78217
(512) 822-8224
Specialty: G
Employment Agency/Recruiter

John H Johnson Jr
Snelling Personnel Services
1303 Walnut Hill Ste 103
Walnut Hill Center
Irving, TX 75038
(214) 258-5973
Specialty: F,H,L,M,O,S
Employment Agency/Recruiter

Mike Varrichio, Mgr Dir
Source EDP
6606 L B J Frwy Ste 148
Dallas, TX 75240
(214) 387-1600
(214) 387-0204 FAX
Specialty: C,Software,Information Technology,Systems Integration
Employment Agency/Recruiter

Audrianne Zachara, Director
Source Engineering
4545 Fuller Dr Ste 100
Irving, TX 75038
(214) 717-5005
(214) 717-0075 FAX
Specialty: E
Employment Agency/Recruiter

Robert DeVoe
Source Finance
2515 McKinney Ave
Dallas, TX 75201
(214) 754-0600
Specialty: F,G,Management
Employment Agency/Recruiter

Robert DeVoe, Mg Partner
Source Finance
6606 L B J Frwy Ste 148
Dallas, TX 75240
(214) 387-2200
(214) 387-0204 FAX
Specialty: F,
Employment Agency/Recruiter

Office Manager
Southwest Resource Development Placement
8700 Crownhill Blvd
San Antonio, TX 78209
(512) 821-5872
Specialty: G
Employment Agency/Recruiter

Michael Himoff
SP Associates/VIP Personnel
P O Box 40399
San Antonio, TX 78229-1399
(512) 340-2000
Specialty: G
Employment Agency/Recruiter

Office Manager
SPS Group Inc
2200 Post Oak Blvd
Houston, TX 77056
(713) 961-4903
Specialty: G
Employment Agency/Recruiter

Office Manager
Staff Benefits Inc
5307 E Mockingbird Lane
Dallas, TX 75206
(214) 821-9098
Specialty: G
Employment Agency/Recruiter

Office Manager
Staff Source
5757 Woodway
Houston, TX 77057
(713) 267-2700
Specialty: G
Employment Agency/Recruiter

Office Manager
Staffingers Personnel
16666 Northchase Dr
Houston, TX 77060
(713) 875-5680
Specialty: G
Employment Agency/Recruiter

Office Manager
Staffingers Personnel
5177 Richmond
Houston, TX 77056
(713) 850-9130
Specialty: G
Employment Agency/Recruiter

Leta S Schoen CPC
Stanton/Schoen Professionals
1800 E St James Place Ste 303
Houston, TX 77056
(713) 961-9970
Specialty: Scientific/Technical, Environmental
Employment Agency/Recruiter

Office Manager
Steele Juanell & Associates Personnel Service
9525 Katy Frwy
Houston, TX 77024
(713) 461-5823
Specialty: G
Employment Agency/Recruiter

Caroline Corbett
Steitz & Corbett Personnel Group Inc
3100 S Gessner Ste 600
Houston, TX 77057
(713) 974-3800
Specialty: G
Employment Agency/Recruiter

Office Manager
Sterling Personnel
12225 Greenville
Dallas, TX 75243
(214) 699-1595
Specialty: F,O
Employment Agency/Recruiter

Office Manager
Stephens Little & Assocs Inc
1341 W Mockingbird
Dallas, TX 75247
(214) 631-5588
Specialty: F
Employment Agency/Recruiter

Office Manager
Steverson & Company
10550 Richmond Ave
Houston, TX 77042
(713) 789-2299
Specialty: G
Employment Agency/Recruiter

Office Manager
Sterling Enterprises
400 E Anderson Ln Ste 101
Austin, TX 78752
(512) 339-8482
Specialty: G
Employment Agency/Recruiter

Office Manager
Steverson & Company Inc
16010 Barkers Point Ln
Houston, TX 77079
(713) 496-5313
Specialty: G
Employment Agency/Recruiter

Office Manager
Sterling Personnel
14180 Dallas Pkwy
Dallas, TX 75240
(214) 404-1595
Specialty: F,O
Employment Agency/Recruiter

Office Manager
Stone Joyce & Associates
5100 Westheimer
Houston, TX 77056
(713) 623-0073
Specialty: G
Employment Agency/Recruiter

Office Manager
Storb Stockton Hillenburg & Associates
908 Town & Country Blvd
Houston, TX 77024
(713) 461-3343
Specialty: G
Employment Agency/Recruiter

Office Manager
Strain R Lee
3200 Southwest Frwy
Houston, TX 77027
(713) 622-7750
Specialty: G
Employment Agency/Recruiter

Mary-Smith Williams
Suburban Services
4801 Woodway Ste 260 West
Houston, TX 77056-1805
(713) 626-9440
(713) 626-9442 FAX
Specialty: C,G,O
Employment Agency/Recruiter

Office Manager
Summit Consulting Group Inc
3301 Airport Frwy
Bedford, TX 76021
(214) 817-267-3461
Specialty: G
Employment Agency/Recruiter

Office Manager
Summit Employment Agency
4600 NW Loop 410
San Antonio, TX 78229
(512) 736-6512
Specialty: G
Employment Agency/Recruiter

Dave Bunce, Owner
Summit Search Specialists
14825 St Mary's Lane Ste 210
Houston, TX 77079
(713) 497-5840
(713) 493-3927 FAX
Specialty: I
Employment Agency/Recruiter

Office Manager
Superior Employment Services
1616 San Pedro Ave
San Antonio, TX 78212
(512) 734-9345
Specialty: G
Employment Agency/Recruiter

Tonya M Hughes, Sr Mkt Rep
Superior Programming Services Inc
2950 North Loop West Suite 130
Houston, TX 77092
(713) 956-0200
(713) 956-0258 FAX
Specialty: C,Consulting
Employment Agency/Recruiter

Office Manager
Superior Technical Specialist
1300 Post Oak Blvd
Houston, TX 77056
(713) 877-8577
Specialty: Technical
Employment Agency/Recruiter

Office Manager
Systems Source Corporations
11520 N Central Parkway
Dallas, TX 75243
(214) 349-4888
Specialty: G
Employment Agency/Recruiter

Office Manager
T M T Manpower Corporation
426 Menchaca
San Antonio, TX 78207
(512) 734-6615
Specialty: G
Employment Agency/Recruiter

Office Manager
Taci/Technical Assistance Co Inc
4702 W FM 1960
Houston, TX 77069
(713) 440-5627
Specialty: Technical
Employment Agency/Recruiter

Office Manager
Talent Southwest
6130 Montana Ave
El Paso, TX 79925
(915) 772-1474
Specialty: G
Employment Agency/Recruiter

William Caudell
Talent Tree Personnel Service-Houston
9703 Richmond Ave
P O Box 3506
Houston, TX 77253
(713) 974-0520
Specialty: G
Employment Agency/Recruiter

Bob Rule
Talent Tree Personnel Southwestern Companies
9703 Richmond Ave
Houston, TX 77042
(713) 789-1818
Specialty: G
Employment Agency/Recruiter

Office Manager
Talent Tree Personnel Services
45 NE Loop 410
San Antonio, TX 78216
(512) 341-7672
Specialty: G
Employment Agency/Recruiter

Office Manager
Talent Tree Personnel Svcs
1900 West Loop South
Houston, TX 77027
(713) 871-8777
Specialty: G
Employment Agency/Recruiter

Office Manager
Task Masters Inc
6800 Park Ten Blvd Ste 190 West
San Antonio, TX 78213
(512) 732-9616
Specialty: G
Employment Agency/Recruiter

Kendra Bounds, Admin Mgr
Teamsource
2320 Donley Drive Ste A
Austin, TX 78758
(512) 834-0585
(512) 834-9693 FAX
Specialty: M
Employment Agency/Recruiter

Office Manager
Technical Careers of Houston
5599 San Felipe
Houston, TX 77056
(713) 965-9461
Specialty: Technical
Employment Agency/Recruiter

Office Manager
Technical Careers
5001 Spring Valley Road
Dallas, TX 75244
(214) 991-9424
Specialty: Technical
Employment Agency/Recruiter

Office Manager
Technical Search Inc
6776 Southwest Frwy
Houston, TX 77074
(713) 343-1400
Specialty: Technical
Employment Agency/Recruiter

Michael Birch-Jones, Mgr
Technical Staff Recruiters
5910 N Central Expwy Ste 700
Dallas, TX 75206
(214) 891-6686
(214) 891-6672
Specialty: E
Employment Agency/Recruiter

Office Manager
Technical Staff Recruiters
2700 Post Oak Blvd
Houston, TX 77056
(713) 965-9305
Specialty: Technical
Employment Agency/Recruiter

Office Manager
Tekwork
2425 Sage Rd
Houston, TX 77056
(713) 622-9268
Specialty: G
Employment Agency/Recruiter

Office Manager
Texas Career Services
5600 Dye Drive
Arlington, TX 76013
(817) 429-9326
Specialty: G
Employment Agency/Recruiter

Office Manager
Texas Doctor's Group
702 Colorado
Austin, TX 78701
(512) 476-7129
Specialty: H
Employment Agency/Recruiter

Office Manager
Texas Employment Commission
2015 E University Dr
Edinburg, TX 78539
(210) 383-5621
Specialty: G
Employment Agency/Recruiter

Office Manager
Texas State of Employment Commission
851 Old Alice Rd
Brownsville, TX 78520
(210) 546-3141
Specialty: G
Employment Agency/Recruiter

Office Manager
Texas State of Employment Commission
301 W 13 St
Fort Worth, TX 76102
(817) 335-5111
Specialty: G
Employment Agency/Recruiter

Office Manager
Texas State of Employment Commission
202 W Hwy 303
Grand Prairie, TX 75051
(214) 263-4631
Specialty: G
Employment Agency/Recruiter

Office Manager
Texas State of Employment Commission
400 E Hackberry Ave
McAllen, TX 78501
(210) 686-8435
Specialty: G
Employment Agency/Recruiter

Office Manager
Texstaf-Texas Staffing Corp
15200 Trinity Blvd
Fort Worth, TX 76155
(817) 571-4249
Specialty: G
Employment Agency/Recruiter

Office Manager
The Chester Group Inc
13612 Midway Road
Dallas, TX 75244
(214) 239-7767
Specialty: G
Employment Agency/Recruiter

Office Manager
The Health Instructor Network
2932 Hollandale Lane
Dallas, TX 75234
(214) 243-2211
Specialty: H
Employment Agency/Recruiter

Office Manager
The Jackson Employment Agency
1505 Elm Street
Dallas, TX 75201
(214) 754-5918
Specialty: G
Employment Agency/Recruiter

Office Manager
The Michael's Group
7929 Walnut Hill Ln
Dallas, TX 75230
(214) 265-7172
Specialty: G
Employment Agency/Recruiter

Monica Porter, Client Ser Sup
The Personnel Source
595 Orleans Ste 707
Beaumont, TX 77701
(409) 833-0571
(409) 833-4646 FAX
Specialty: O, Light Industrial
Employment Agency/Recruiter

Peggy Sempa, Client Ser Sup
The Personnel Source
1301 Regents Park Ste 101
Houston, TX 77058
(713) 286-2700
(713) 286-8731 FAX
Specialty: O(Temporary)
Employment Agency/Recruiter

Office Manager
The Roberts Group
12655 N Central Expwy
Dallas, TX 75243
(214) 980-2333
Specialty: F,O,S
Employment Agency/Recruiter

Willie S Bright, Owner
The Urban Placement Service
602 Sawyer Ste 460
Houston, TX 77007
(713) 880-2211
(713) 880-5577 FAX
Specialty: Consumer Products, Pharmaceutical,Petro Chemical, Minorities
Employment Agency/Recruiter

Office Manager
Travel Staffers
800 Bering Dr
Houston, TX 77057
(713) 977-0322
Specialty: T
Employment Agency/Recruiter

Office Manager
Townsend Associates
4851 LBJ Frwy
Dallas, TX 75244
(214) 934-0777
Specialty: G
Employment Agency/Recruiter

Office Manager
Tri-Starr Personnel
10777 Northwest Frwy
Houston, TX 77092
(713) 683-9320
Specialty: G
Employment Agency/Recruiter

Office Manager
Trakit Resource Management Inc
16800 Imperial Valley Dr
Houston, TX 77060
(713) 931-9520
Specialty: G
Employment Agency/Recruiter

Kandi Pinkerton
Tri-Starr Personnel of San Antonio
8000 H 10 West Ste 160
San Antonio, TX 78230
(512) 342-7413
Specialty: G
Employment Agency/Recruiter

Pat Brown, Pres
Travel Placement Specialists
3311 Richmond Avenue Ste 230
Houston, TX 77098
(713) 942-0662
(713) 942-0665 FAX
Specialty: T,Travel Industry
Employment Agency/Recruiter

Office Manager
Turner Dehavilland Inc
1220 Augusta Dr
Houston, TX 77057
(713) 977-6542
Specialty: G
Employment Agency/Recruiter

Office Manager
U S Staffing of Texas
2630 Fountain View Dr
Houston, TX 77057
(713) 977-1855
Specialty: G
Employment Agency/Recruiter

Office Manager
Upper Rio Grande Private Industry Council
1155 Westmoreland St
El Paso, TX 79925
(915) 772-5627
Specialty: G
Employment Agency/Recruiter

Office Manager
Valley Job Placement Agency
413 Nolana Loop
McAllen, TX 78504
(210) 687-2527
Specialty: G
Employment Agency/Recruiter

Donald R Caffee, Pres
ValPers Inc
7324 Southwest Frwy Ste 880
Houston, TX 77074-2037
(713) 771-9420
(713) 771-7924 FAX
Specialty: E,G,M,R,S
Employment Agency/Recruiter

Office Manager
VIP Personnel Service
800 IH 10 West
San Antonio, TX 78230
(512) 349-2000
Specialty: G
Employment Agency/Recruiter

Office Manager
Vivian Martin Employment Svc
5401 N 10th St
McAllen, TX 78504
(210) 687-9404
Specialty: G
Employment Agency/Recruiter

Office Manager
Vocational Support Services
900 E Hwy 77
San Benito, TX 78586
(210) 361-3113
Specialty: G
Employment Agency/Recruiter

Office Manager
Walker Personnel & Associates
6065 Hillcroft
Houston, TX 77081
(713) 988-8828
Specialty: G
Employment Agency/Recruiter

Office Manager
Wanda's Personnel Service
4625 North Freeway
Houston, TX 77022
(713) 694-2000
Specialty: G
Employment Agency/Recruiter

Office Manager
Warwick Search Group
1000 Louisiana St
Houston, TX 77002
(713) 739-8100
Specialty: G
Employment Agency/Recruiter

Bruce Whitaker, CPC
Whitaker Fellows & Associates
820 Gessner Ste 1500
Houston, TX 77024
(713) 465-1500
Specialty: G,Chemicals,
Legal,Physicians,Plastics
Employment Agency/Recruiter

Office Manager
White & Associates
8080 N Central Expwy
Dallas, TX 75206
(214) 891-8116
Specialty: G
Employment Agency/Recruiter

Office Manager
Williams Pat & Associates Personnel
1700 West Loop South
Houston, TX 77054
(713) 621-0019
Specialty: G
Employment Agency/Recruiter

Office Manager
Williams R L & Associates
4131 N Central Pkwy
Dallas, TX 75204
(214) 526-9655
Specialty: G
Employment Agency/Recruiter

Office Manager
Wimberly James K & Associates
4100 Spring Valley Road
Dallas, TX 75244
(214) 386-7272
Specialty: G
Employment Agency/Recruiter

Office Manager
Windsor Consultants Inc
13939 Northwest Frwy
Houston, TX 77040
(713) 460-0586
Specialty: G
Employment Agency/Recruiter

Office Manager
Withers Thomas D
Loop 315 & Industrial Drive
Greenville, TX 75401
(214) 226-0222
Specialty: G
Employment Agency/Recruiter

F Carol Schneider
Woodlands Executive Employment Service
25025 North I-45 Ste 300
The Woodlands, TX 77387
(713) 367-3700
Specialty: G
Employment Agency/Recruiter

Office Manager
Work Connection Inc The
1222 N Main Ave
San Antonio, TX 78212
(512) 226-1468
Specialty: G
Employment Agency/Recruiter

DALLAS & THE SOUTH WEST JOB SEEKERS SOURCEBOOK

Section 5

Executive Recruiters

Executive Recruiters Defined

Executive Recruiters usually perform exclusive searches for positions that pay from $50,000 to several hundred thousand dollars per year. These firms are compensated by a hiring company to locate a person with specific qualifications to meet a predefined employment need.

The major executive search firms conduct searches for hiring companies on an exclusive retainer basis. This means that the search firm is paid for their efforts even if they are not successful in filling the position. Firms that work on a contingency basis are paid only if an acceptable candidate is found and hired by the hiring company.

Since many of the executive search firms work on a retainer basis, getting in to see one can sometimes be difficult. However, it is worth the effort to reach these firms since these industry specialists know the job market extremely well and can be helpful in providing advice as well as leads. An executive seeking total exposure should touch base with all executive search firms both contingency and retainer.

Neither type of firm should charge the individual; all fees are paid by the hiring company. Firms that charge fees to an individual are not typical and it is best to avoid them.

The value of an executive recruiter to a job seeker depends upon several things: the quality of the agency, the kind of work being sought, and your own level of experience. A good executive recruiter will help its candidates develop a strategy and prepare for personal interviews.

More and more executive recruiters are taking advantage of computer automation and professional affiliations to share both candidate and job order information with other recruiters, making such firms more beneficial to a both job seekers and hiring companies.

To assist you, we have filled the next few pages with important information which will be helpful in understanding how to:

- Select an Executive Recruiter
- Work with an Executive Recruiter

How to Select an Executive Recruiter

Finding the right executive recruiter to help you find a job or change jobs requires some careful research on your part.

This is an important process that cannot and should not be ignored. Also, this process is slightly different than the process used to select an employment agency, because for the most part executive recruiters are usually retained by hiring companies to fill specific management and staff positions that average salaries of over $50,000.

To maximize your chances of obtaining a job by contacting executive recruiters requires that you work hard to qualify and then select recruiters that want to represent you in your job search. To assist you in this selection process we've outlined some important selection criteria that should be useful.

Selection Criteria:

The selection of the right executive search firm to support your job search efforts should be based upon a combination of the following criteria:

Specialty — Does the firm specialize in making placements in your career field and industry?

If so, this firm is more likely to be able to help find you a new job. If it deals exclusively in your discipline, so much the better.

Proximity

Is the firm convenient for you to visit on a regular basis?

This is important when attempting to maintain high visibility with an individual recruiter.

Experience

How long has the firm and the recruiter been in the placement business? And how long has the firm been making placements for members of your profession?

It is best to select a recruiter who has at least three years experience specializing in your industry. These recruiters will already have established a network of contacts with a number of hiring companies and will be better sources for new job openings.

Personality

Does the recruiter like you and do you like the recruiter? Are you comfortable with the recruiter's business style and ability to represent you to hiring companies?

This is very important if you want to have a better shot at establishing and maintaining a good rapport with the recruiter on an ongoing basis.

Referrals

Was this firm referred to you by someone else in your field?

Added to the positive responses for the preceding qualifiers, a referral will give you an edge over other job seekers.

Quality — Does this recruiter have a good reputation and do they present themselves in a professional manner?

The best way to determine this is to talk to other job seekers and to visit the recruiter's office to obtain personal knowledge of the company image and how it works. If you're unhappy with what you see or find, keep looking.

Networks — Is this executive recruiter a member of a placement affiliation or shared database network?

If yes, then the chances are better that this firm will give you broader exposure to the employment market.

Most reputable firms belong to an organization titled the Association of Executive Recruiting Consultants (AERC).

Attitude — Does this executive recruiter demonstrate that he/she can be helpful in finding you a position?

If not, then continue to contact other executive recruiters until you find one who thinks that he/she can help you.

Questions to ask to qualify an executive recruiter:

1. How long have they been in the placement business?

   The longer a firm has been in the business, the more contacts they are likely to have, therefore the odds of the firm being able to help you are better.

2. How many client companies are they working with?

   While it is difficult to pinpoint an average number that would be about the right size to support you in your job search, if you correlate responses, the differences between firms will be apparent.

   Those firms attempting to handle a larger number of hiring companies per recruiter may be spreading their resources too thin, especially if the number of placements per recruiter is low.

3. How many job openings are they working on at any one time?

   Ten to fifteen per month is typical for a seasoned recruiter.

4. How many placements have they made (monthly/annually)?

   The average recruiter will make one to two per month.

5. Do they feel that they can help you?

   If not, then keep looking, but also ask the next question.

6. If they can't help you, can they recommend and refer you to someone else who could?

   Use this question to expand your network of contacts. If you can get a referral to another firm, then the odds are that you will increase your chances of getting an interview opportunity and personal attention of the other recruiter.

7. Do they accept resumes and how are the resumes reviewed and handled? Are there specific requirements for candidates?

   Many firms do not work with recent college grads, persons not currently employed, persons not in a specific field for a certain number of years or persons whose earnings don't meet their requirements. If this information is not known you can waste time and money on resumes and cover letters.

Working with an Executive Recruiter

To maximize your success of having an executive recruiter find you a job, you need to remember a few important axioms.

Executive recruiters normally are retained by a hiring company to find a specific type of individual to fill a specific job opening.

This means that unless you fill a current need, chances are recruiters may not be willing to spend too much time with you. First determine whether the firm specializes in positions that fit your background.

If the firm's area of expertise matches your background, then send the firm a current resume along with a targeted cover letter explaining the types of positions that you are qualified for.

Next, try to set an appointment to meet personally with a recruiter to sell yourself and establish a rapport. After this meeting, your next step is to do everything possible to help make the recruiter's job easier. This includes having a very good resume available for their use, and prepared and on time for any job interviews arranged.

Executive recruiters will quickly lose interest in a job applicant that continually turns down job offers.

To prevent problems, be specific with the executive recruiter as to what you are looking for in a company and a position. Do this during your first meeting. Give honest answers as to career goals and salary requirements.

If either the job offer, the position, or the company environment are not right, then by all means turn it down, but discuss it first with your recruiter so he/she understands your reasons. Just remember that you run the risk of losing their support if you turn down too many offers.

Executive recruiters prefer to have an exclusive commitment from a job seeker.

This means that if you are going to use multiple recruiters to speed up your job search, keep this information to yourself.

The level of interest executive recruiters have in helping you find a job drops to almost zero once they know that you are shopping around.

Executive recruiters see many people each day in addition to receiving a large number of resumes in the daily mail from job seekers.

This means that you must get noticed and stay noticed by them if you want them to help you. But this must be accomplished without becoming a pest. There are a variety of ways of doing this such as:

1. Hand deliver your resume and spend some time asking questions, answering questions, and establishing a rapport.

2. Call your contact on a weekly basis to update your status and ask for an update on the job market and your specific activity.

3. Send them a thank you note, after your initial meeting to thank them for taking an interest in helping you.

4. Drop by the office once every two weeks to spend a few quick moments with your contact. Avoid Mondays or Fridays, as these days are always their busiest.

5. From time to time, bring a small gift (ie. donuts, candy, etc.) with you when you drop in for a visit.

6. When you come across current articles in newspapers or magazines about company expansions or relocations that could be of interest to your recruiter, clip the article and send it to your recruiter along with a note.

The service executive recruiters provide to job seekers is free, but these recruiters need to make a living too.

Treat them with respect, and be thoughtful enough to at least notify them when you have taken a job offer from another source.

If you were extremely satisfied with their efforts, refer job openings to them as well as other good job seekers. This will allow you to maintain contact with them and keep your options open for some future date when you may need someone to again help you find a job in a timely manner.

If you really appreciated their efforts, send them a thank you card or a little gift to show your appreciation for their efforts. Next time, they'll welcome you with open arms.

Executive recruiters know their job, but they don't know you or how well you can perform your job.

This means that they need your help in getting to know you. Remember, you know your job qualifications and experiences better than anyone, so identify your strong points to them. Describe and classify the important features of previous accomplishments.

Furnish them with a means of measuring performance, such as a list of awards or reference letters.

Be honest about your background or problems. If you're not sure you want to change jobs, let your recruiter know about your uncertainty.

Questions to ask about job openings:

1. How long has the job opening been available?

   If just a short time and you've received an offer, the company involved can make decisions quickly. If the job has been open a long time, ask why, prior to making any acceptance decision.

2. Why wasn't the position filled from within the company?

   If you don't like the answer, then the odds for future promotions within the company may be slim.

3. Why is the job open?

   If someone retired or it's a new position, these are all positive signs. If someone left the company or was terminated, it would be helpful to understand the circumstances prior to making a long term commitment.

4. When does a decision have to be made?

   If the decision must be made immediately, then you know that they have a strong need and also a strong interest in you. Stall at least until the next day to allow yourself some time to sleep on it before giving your answer. Be comfortable with your decision or don't do it.

5. How many people have already been presented?

   If a large number, than the odds are that the hiring company has a backup candidate that will made an offer if you refuse or delay your own decision on the offer.

6. What is the long term opportunity for someone taking the position offered?

   Again, if you're looking for future growth, you need to be comfortable with the answer to this question.

Topics you should not discuss with recruiters:

1. Your knowledge about job openings in your field, until you have found and accepted a job yourself. Don't create unwanted competition for yourself.

2. Whether you are using other recruiters.

   To do so would reduce their interest in working with you.

If an executive search firm doesn't have the experience in your field or the placement industry, it isn't likely that this firm will be a source for your job search.

If they don't handle a large number or the right type of hiring companies or if they have an excessive number of job seekers on file, this firm may not a good choice for facilitating your job search.

Also, if they do not handle a large number of job openings, especially in your field, then chances are slim they will be of any meaningful help to you.

Remember, executive recruiters provide companies with a service first, supporting job seekers is secondary, so continue your job search elsewhere too.

INDEX CROSS REFERENCE BY SPECIALTY

Specialty: A
(Advertising)

Management Recruiters
of Austin
Orr Executive Search
R A Stone & Associates

Specialty: B
(Banking)

Bancselect Inc
Golden Charles Co The
John W Worsham & Associates
Marilyn Austin CPC & Assoc
Pate Resources Group
Robert Half
Robert Half International
Romac & Associates
T O Staton & Assoc Inc
The Executive Consulting Group
The Hiring Assistant
The Search Center Inc
Universal Search

Specialty: C
Computers & Data Processing)

Accounting Resources Int'l
Automated Resources
Baty R Gaines Associates
Comptime Inc
Computech Corporation
Cox Dodson & Story
D P Select
Damon & Associates Inc
Dick Van Vliet & Associates
Frankel & Adams
Harris Personnel Resources
International Search Division
of Entec Inc
J Gross & Assoc
Management Recruiters
of Austin
Marilyn Austin CPC & Assoc
Murphy Search Management
Opportunity Unlimited Inc
Pate Resources Group
Peter W Ambler Company
Professional Team Search
R Saxon & Associates
Robert George & Associates
Robert Half
Robert Half International
Roemer Bartlett & Kate
Russell Group The
Search Associates
Source EDP
Spectra International
The Personnel Office
Universal Search
Vick & Associates
Wardrup Associates Inc

Specialty: E
(Engineering)

Bartlett Bunn & Travis
Betty Tanner Professional Employment Service Inc
Bundy-Stewart Associates Inc
Champion Personnel Service
Computech Corporation
D P Select
Dick Van Vliet & Associates
Dunhill of Denton Inc
Dunhill Professional Search
Engineering Management Staff Recruiters
ExecuSource Int'l
Fortune Search Consultants
Frankel & Adams
Gullo R J & Associates
Harris Personnel Resources
Ideal Services
International Search Division of Entec Inc
J Gross & Assoc
John R Stephens & Associates
John Wylie Associates Inc
Kressenberg Associates
Lasky & Co
Loewenstein & Assoc
Lord & Albus Company
Management Recruiters
Management Recruiters of Austin
Management Recruiters of Clearlake
Management Recruiters of Dallas
Marvin L Silcott & Assoc Inc
Medical Executive Search Assoc
MegaSearch Inc
MicroSearch
Newman-Johnson-King Inc
Opportunity Unlimited Inc
Pate Resources Group
Peter W Ambler Company
Piper-Morgan Associates Personnel Consultants
Professional Executive Recruiters
Robert A Paul & Assoc
Robert George & Associates
Roemer Bartlett & Kate
Russell Group The
Sales Consultants of Austin
Search Consultants Int'l Inc
Source Engineering
Spectra International
Sumner Ray Technical Resources
The Hiring Assistant
The Personnel Office
The Realty Group
Trambley The Recruiter
Universal Search
Whitaker Fellows & Associates

Specialty: F
(Finance & Accounting)

Accounting Resources Int'l
Betty Tanner Professional Employment Service Inc
CFO Management Group
Dick Van Vliet & Associates
Ellis & Associates Inc
Ernst & Young
ExecuSource Int'l
Feldt Personnel
G Baldwin & Company
Ligon Paul Company
Marilyn Austin CPC & Assoc

Marvin L Silcott & Assoc Inc
Pate Resources Group
Peter W Ambler Company
Piper-Morgan Associates Personnel Consultants
Professional Team Search
Robert Half
Robert Half International
Romac & Associates
Search Associates
Source Finance
T O Staton & Assoc Inc
The Executive Consulting Group
Universal Search

Specialty: G (General Applications)

A H Justice & Assoc
AAAction Recruiting Services
Abacus Management Services Inc
Accusearch
Adams Ray & Associates Exec Search Consultants
Alexander Group The
Allen Consulting Associates Inc
Anderson Bradshaw Associates
Aragian Medical Int'l Inc
Arend & Associates
Ashen & Associates Inc
Ashley Personnel Service
Austin Group The
Austin Michaels Ltd
Baker John T & Associates Inc
Barclay Company
Baty R Gaines Associates
Beer & Associates Personnel
Best Associates Executive Search
Bigham Rhett & Associates
Biosearch Corp
Birnbach Martin & Associates
Bren Group The
Brennan Associates
Buff-Marshall & Associates
Burgeson Hospitality Search
Burns Dunnam & Whitehead
Career Concepts Personnel Svc
Career Consultants Inc
Career Consultants Professional Search Firm & Temp Svc
Carlin Associates
Catterton Inc
Cherbonnier Group The
Christopher Fredrick Executive Search
Clark Williams Corp
Coleman Patrick Inc
Corcoran Interests Inc
Corporate Search
Corporate Search Associates
Corporate Search Consultants
Countee J & Associates
Crown Recruiters Inc
Damon & Associates Inc
Danbrook Group
Davidson John & Associates
DHR International Inc
Dilworth & Wooldridge Inc
Dougan & McKinley Int'l Search Consultants
Dougan & McKinley Strain
Dragoset Group
Drake Beam Morin Inc
Eastman & Beaudine Inc

Ecosphere Systems Inc
Edwards B & Associates Legal Search
EFL Associates
Elliot Taylor & Assoc
Ellis & Associates Inc
Employment Access for Retirees
Energists The
Evans McDonnell
Excalibur Service Co
Excel of Aluquerque Inc
ExecuSearch
ExecuSource Int'l
Executive Search
Executive Search Consultants Ltd
Executive Search Personnel
Executive Staff Recruiters
Executives & Sales International
Financial Pros
Forty Plus of Dallas Inc
Fox Morris Associates Inc
Fults S L & Associates
Galbrath J B & Associates
Galloway James Inc
Gandin David L
Gillman & Associates Inc
Glover Tracy Company The
Group G
H S Group Inc
Halden & Associates
Hallmark Professional Search Inc
Halpin Personnel Services Inc
Hansar\Young International
Hardie James H
Health Care Recruiters Inc
Health Professionals of America Personnel Consultants
Healthcare Recruiters International
Hebel R W & Associates
Hedman Kent R & Associates
Heidrich And Struggles Inc
Henderson Taylor Consulting
Hero Janice Vickery
Hill John L & Associates
Hoffman Associates Inc
Interview Legal Search
J & B International Inc
J G Consultants
Jablo Partners
Jackman Financial Group Inc
Jackson & Coker
James Dean & Associates
James E Ticer Associates
James Group The
Jewett Gary
Joseph Chris & Associates
KDM Associates Inc
Kearney A T Inc
Kenton Associates
Kenzer Corp
King Computer Search Inc
Kingston & Associates
Klark & Associates
Korn/Ferry International
Kressenberg Associates
Kristan Associates Executive Search
Lamalie Associates Inc
Largent Parks & Partners Inc
Lea Randolph & Associates
Leadership Resources Inc
LeClair Sutton Assocs Inc
Lehman & Associates Inc
Lehman George Associates Inc

Len Oppenheimer & Associates
Leyendecker Douglas
Lineback Associates
Litchfield & Willis Inc
Lockland Associates Inc
Lucas Associates Inc
Lyn-Jay International Executive Search
M & M Associates
Management Recruiters
Management Recruiters of Santa Fe
Management Recruiters of Tucson
Management Recruiters-Dallas N
Marburger Ray & Associates Inc
Marilyn Austin CPC & Assoc
Marketing Resources Int'l
Marrs-McClane
Mauck Bill
MegaSearch Inc
Meredith J M & Assoc Inc
Merritt Hawkins & Assoc
Michaels W Root & Co
Miera Consultant International
Miller Karl Associates
Mitchell Jim & Associates Inc
Moerbe-Forman
Moore Thomas R Executive Sch
MSI Healthcare
Must Joanne Research Specialist
National Human Resource Group
Nenstiel William H & Assoc
Newman Arthur Assoc Inc
Newman-Johnson-King Inc
Nixon & Associates
O'Rourke John & Associates
Overseas Opportunities
Owens-Dallas Employment Services Corp
Page G S
Pan American Search Inc
Patson Ronald F
Pearson & Associates
Pencom Systems Inc
Peter W Ambler Company
Pool Henry & Partners
Powell's Executive Personnel -Search Inc
Preng & Associates
Pritchard & Associates Inc
ProCounsel
Professional Search
Prothero & Associates Inc
R L Scott Associates
Rand-Curtis Resources
Ray Paul & Carre Orban Int'l
Recruiters For Business & Industry
Resource Management Group
Resource Recruiters Inc
Resources Unlimited
Richard Earl & Associates
Robert Lowell International
Roddy Group Executive Search Consultants
Rodriguez RA & Associates
Rogers Carroll & Associates
Russell Reynold Associates Inc
RWS Partners in Search
S S & A Executive Search
Sacco Kevin P Executive Search
Salemi Stephen T Inc
Sales Consultants
Sales Consultants of Austin
Sales Resources Inc

Sandhurst Associates
Sanford Rose Assoc
Scannell & Hundley
Schwartz M S & Co Inc
Search Associates
Search Financial Inc
Search Network The
Sink C W & Co Inc
Southern Resources
Southwest Rehab Consultants
Sparks Thomas & Associates
Spencer Stuart & Associates
Spradley Legal Search
Stehouwer & Associates Inc
Steinfield & Associates
Stephens John R & Associates Exec Search Consutants
Steven A Williams & Associates
Surratt Travis
Talon Resources
Tarrant County Employment & Training & Private
Taylor & Associates
Taylor Carl J & Co
Technical Search Inc
Technifind
Telesolutions Of Arizona Inc
The Clements Frank Company
The Employment Assistance Group
The Hiring Assistant
Thomas Richardson Rundin & Co
Torrance Recruiting
Triad Associates
Trotman Wheat & Associates
Tucker Michael Associates
Tuttle Neidhart Semyan Inc
Universal Search
Unlimited Sources Inc
VanHorn Taylor & Assocs
Vernon Sage & Associates
Vincent Darryl & Associates
VRL & Associates
Walsh Denis P & Associates
Ward Howell Int'l Inc
Watkins & Associates Executive Search Consultants Inc
Watson Legal Search
Wesson Robert & Associates
Wheeler Moore & Co
White Pat & Associates
Wien & Associates
Winters Professional Recruiting
Witt Associates
Wood M & Associates
Wright Group The
Young & Co

Specialty: H (Healthcare)

Bartlett Bunn & Travis
BJB Medical Associates
D P Select
Damon & Associates Inc
Dunhill of Denton Inc
Dunhill Professional Search
Executive Health Care Recruiters
Gaudette & Company
Guidry East Barnes & Bono Inc
Healthcare Recruiters Inc
Healthcare Resources Group
Houtz • Strawn Associates Inc
HPR Health Staff

Kressenberg Associates
Lea Randolph & Associates
Managed Care Recruiters
Management Recruiters
Management Recruiters of Austin
Management Recruiters of Clearlake
Management Recruiters of Dallas
Marilyn Austin CPC & Assoc
Marjorie Starr & Associates
Medical Executive Search Assoc
Medical Results Inc
Odell & Associates Inc
Pate Resources Group
Peter W Ambler Company
Practice Dynamics Inc
Pro-Employer
Professions In Medicine
R L Scott Associates
Rodgers Ramsey Inc
Roth Young Dallas
Roth Young/Houston
Sales Consultants
Sales Consultants of Austin
Search Associates
Spectra International
Terry Stukalin Health Care
Management Services Inc The
The Rubicon Group
Universal Search
Vernon Sage & Associates
Whitaker Fellows & Associates

Specialty: I
(Insurance)

Bartlett Bunn & Travis
Ellis & Associates Inc
Fox Morris Associates Inc
Gaudette & Company
Kressenberg Associates
Ligon Paul Company
Managed Care Recruiters
Management Recruiters
Marilyn Austin CPC & Assoc
Rodgers Ramsey Inc
Sales Consultants
Spectra International
The Dawson Group
The Rubicon Group

Specialty: L
(Legal)

Bartlett Bunn & Travis
Baty R Gaines Associates
Carrie & Company Placement Service Inc
Ellis & Associates Inc
Major Wilson & Africa
Marilyn Austin CPC & Assoc
Marvin L Silcott & Assoc Inc
Odell & Associates Inc
Pate Resources Group
The Howard C Bloom Co
The Rubicon Group
Universal Search
Whitaker Fellows & Associates

Specialty: M (Manufacturing)

A H Justice & Assoc
Accounting Resources Int'l
Betty Tanner Professional Employment Service Inc
Brennan Associates
Bundy-Stewart Associates Inc
Champion Personnel Service
Charles P Aquavella & Assoc
Dick Van Vliet & Associates
ExecuSource Int'l
Fortune Search Consultants
Fox Morris Associates Inc
Frankel & Adams
Gullo R J & Associates
Harris Personnel Resources
International Search Division of Entec Inc
J Gross & Assoc
John Davidson & Assoc Inc
John Wylie Associates Inc
Kristan Associates Executive Search
Lasky & Co
Lord & Albus Company
Management Recruiters of Dallas
Marilyn Austin CPC & Assoc
Marvin L Silcott & Assoc Inc
Medical Executive Search Assoc
Murphy Search Management
Newman-Johnson-King Inc
Peter W Ambler Company
Professional Team Search
Roth Young Dallas
Search Masters Int'l
Summit Search
Sumner Ray Technical Resources
The Hiring Assistant
Trambley The Recruiter
Universal Search
Vernon Sage & Associates

Specialty: O (Office Administration)

Ellis & Associates Inc
Marilyn Austin CPC & Assoc
Spectra International
Universal Search

Specialty: P (Personnel & Human Resources)

Carrie & Company Placement Service Inc
Charles P Aquavella & Assoc
Employee Sources Inc
Frankel & Adams
G Baldwin & Company
Gonzalez Abel M & Assoc
Harris Personnel Resources
Lord & Albus Company
Pate Resources Group
Peter W Ambler Company
Piper-Morgan Associates Personnel Consultants
Professional Team Search
Roemer Bartlett & Kate
Roth Young Dallas
Search Associates
Spectra International
Staff Extension Inc

The Hiring Assistant
Universal Search

Specialty: R
(Research & Development)

ExecuSource Int'l
Fortune Search Consultants
John Wylie Associates Inc
Lasky & Co
Ligon Paul Company
Lord & Albus Company
Management Recruiters of Austin
Management Recruiters of Dallas
Management Recruiters of Northwest Austin
Marvin L Silcott & Assoc Inc
Medical Executive Search Assoc
Newman-Johnson-King Inc
Peter W Ambler Company
Sales Consultants of Austin
Search Masters Int'l
Spectra International
Trambley The Recruiter
Universal Search

Specialty: S
(Sales & Marketing)

Bartlett Bunn & Travis
Baty R Gaines Associates
Brennan Associates
Bundy-Stewart Associates Inc
Charles P Aquavella & Assoc
Corporate Search Group The
Damon & Associates Inc
Darryl Vincent & Associates
ExecuSource Int'l
Executives & Sales International
Frankel & Adams
Gaudette & Company
Harris Personnel Resources
Healthcare Resources Group
Kressenberg Associates
Kristan Associates Executive Search
Ligon Paul Company
Loewenstein & Assoc
Lord & Albus Company
Management Recruiters
Management Recruiters of Austin
Marjorie Starr & Associates
Medical Executive Search Assoc
Newman-Johnson-King Inc
Pate Resources Group
Peter W Ambler Company
Professional Team Search
Roth Young Dallas
Roth Young/Houston
Russell Group The
Sales Consultants
Sales Consultants of Austin
Search Associates
Search Masters Int'l
Spectra International
Universal Search
Wardrup Associates Inc
Wright Group The

Specialty: T (Travel,Food & Hospitality)

Charles P Aquavella & Assoc
J Gross & Assoc
Ligon Paul Company
MegaSearch Inc
Roth Young/Houston
Sales Consultants
Search America Consultants For Executive Selection

Other Specific Specialties:

Specialty: Agriculture

Management Search Inc

Specialty: Architecture

Loewenstein & Assoc

Specialty: Automotive

Automobile Franchise Consultants
Automotive Executive Search

Specialty: Benefits

Gaudette & Company

Specialty: BioTech

Lord & Albus Company
Marvin L Silcott & Assoc Inc
Management Recruiters of Northwest Austin
Medical Executive Search Assoc

Specialty: Building Products

Brennan Associates
Kristan Associates Executive Search

Specialty: Chemicals

Loewenstein & Assoc
Management Recruiters of Northwest Austin
Medical Executive Search Assoc
The Search Center Inc

Specialty: Communications

Ligon Paul Company

Specialty: Construction

Davian Construction Search Consultants
Fox Morris Associates Inc
John R Stephens & Associates
Professional Executive Recruiters
Robert A Paul & Assoc

Specialty: Corporate Executives

The Personnel Office

Specialty: Decision Support

Wright Group The

Specialty: Drafting

Sumner Ray Technical Resources

Specialty: Electronics

ESP III Consulting Services
ExecuSource Int'l

Specialty: Energy

Marvin L Silcott & Assoc Inc
Robert A Paul & Assoc
The Search Center Inc
The Energists

Specialty: Entertainment

R A Stone & Associates

Specialty: Environmental

Baty R Gaines Associates
Environmental Personnel Agency
Loewenstein & Assoc
Lord & Albus Company
Marvin L Silcott & Assoc Inc
Robert A Paul & Assoc
Sales Consultants of Austin
The Realty Group

Specialty: Hazardous Waste

Loewenstein & Assoc

Specialty: Hi-Tech

Cox Dodson & Story
ExecuSource Int'l
J Gross & Assoc
Shisler Axley & Associates
Wardrup Associates Inc

Specialty: Industrial Hygiene

The Realty Group

Specialty: Management

Baty R Gaines Associates
Gaudette & Company
J Gross & Assoc
Ligon Paul Company
Medical Executive Search Assoc
Romac & Associates

Specialty: Management Consultants

Accounting Resources Int'l

Specialty: Material Management

ExecuSource Int'l

Specialty: Media

R A Stone & Associates

Specialty: Medical/Medical Devices

Dunhill of Denton Inc
Sales Consultants of Austin

Specialty: Metal & Wood Fabrication

Brennan Associates

Specialty: Office Furnishings

Kristan Associates Executive Search

Specialty: Operations Research

R Saxon & Associates

Specialty: Petrochemicals

Gullo R J & Associates
Robert A Paul & Assoc

Specialty: Pharmaceutical

Management Recruiters of Northwest Austin
Medical Executive Search Assoc
Sales Consultants of Austin

Specialty: Pharmacy

Dunhill of Denton Inc

Specialty: Plant Management

Robert A Paul & Assoc

Specialty: Plastics

Dunhill of Denton Inc
Management Recruiters of Northwest Austin

Specialty: Primary Metal

A H Justice & Assoc

Specialty: Product Development

Wright Group The

Specialty: Pulp & Paper

John R Stephens & Associates

Specialty: Quality/Reliability

Fortune Search Consultants

Specialty: Regulatory Affairs

Fortune Search Consultants

Specialty: Retail

Carpenter & Associates Retail
Professional Search
Spectra International

Specialty: Rubber

Dunhill of Denton Inc

Specialty: Safety

The Realty Group

Specialty: Scientific

Loewenstein & Assoc

Specialty: Securities/ Stock Brokerage

Golden Charles Co The
Romac & Associates

Specialty: Security Systems

Sales Consultants of Austin

Specialty: Specialized Services

Accounting Resources Int'l
The Search Center Inc

Specialty: Supermarket

Roth Young/Houston

Specialty: Technical

Sumner Ray Technical Resources

Specialty: Transportation

A H Justice & Assoc
Fox Morris Associates Inc

Jack King, Pres
A H Justice & Assoc
P O Box 58345
Houston, TX 77258
(713) 474-7700
(713) 474-9382 FAX
Specialty: G,M,Primary Metal, Transportation,Bearings
Contingency/Retainer Search

Office Manager
AAAction Recruiting Services
16800 Imperial Valley Dr
Houston, TX 77060
(713) 999-3793
Specialty: G
Executive Search

Office Manager
Abacus Management Services Inc
5215 N O'Connor Ste 200
Irving, TX 75039
(214) 661-8366
Specialty: G
Executive Search

Dan Haller
Accounting Resources Int'l Inc
P O Box 890063
Houston, TX 77289
(713) 486-7037
Specialty: F,M,Information Tech, Specialized Services, Management Consultants
Executive Search

Office Manager
Accusearch
5959 Gateway West
El Paso, TX 79925
(915) 778-9312
Specialty: G
Executive Search

Office Manager
Adams Ray & Associates
Executive Search Consultants
11999 Katy Frwy
Houston, TX 496-1999
(713) 496-1999
Specialty: G
Executive Search

Office Manager
Alexander Group The
24 E Greenway Plz
Houston, TX 77046
(713) 961-7420
Specialty: G
Executive Search

Office Manager
Allen Consulting Associates Inc
6502 Brentfield Drive
Dallas, TX 75248
(214) 931-6208
Specialty: G
Executive Search

Office Manager
Anderson Bradshaw Associates Inc
1225 North Loop West
Houston, TX 77008
(713) 869-6789
Specialty: G
Executive Search

Office Manager
Aragian Medical Int'l Inc
5718 Westheimer Rd
Houston, TX 77057
(713) 975-9000
Specialty: G
Executive Search

Office Manager
Arend & Associates
13311 St Mary's Ln
Houston, TX 77079
(713) 827-7800
Specialty: G
Executive Search

Office Manager
Ashen & Associates Inc
7322 Southwest Frwy
Houston, TX 77074
(713) 271-1983
Specialty: G
Executive Search

Office Manager
Ashley Personnel Service
318 W Main St
Arlington, TX 76012
(817) 461-2991 633-2030
Specialty: G
Executive Search

Office Manager
Austin Group The
11511 Katy Frwy
Houston, TX 77079
(713) 497-8595
Specialty: G
Executive Search

Office Manager
Austin Michaels Ltd
7585 E Redfield Rd
Scottsdale, AZ 85260
(602) 483-5000
Specialty: G
Executive Search

Debbie Harding, Pres
Automated Resources
1639 Kingspoint
Carrollton, TX 75007
(214) 446-8745
(214) 960-0239 FAX
Specialty: C
Executive Search

Office Manager
Automobile Franchise Consultants
6666 Harwin Dr Ste 400
Houston, TX 77036
(713) 780-1242
Specialty: Automotive
Executive Search

Office Manager
Automotive Executive Search
2020 North Loop West
Houston, TX 77018
(713) 956-0995
Specialty: Automotive
Executive Search

Office Manager
Baker John T & Associates Inc
11757 Katy Frwy
Houston, TX 77079
(713) 556-1798
Specialty: G
Executive Search

Office Manager
Bancselect Inc
800 W Airport Frwy Ste 920
Irving, TX 75062
(214) 554-0011
Specialty: B
Executive Search

Office Manager
Barclay Company
4708 McKinney Avenue
Dallas, TX 75205
(214) 522-5221
Specialty: G
Executive Search

Ed Bunn, Managing Partner
Bartlett Bunn & Travis
6320 LBJ Freeway Ste 224
Dallas, TX 75240
(214) 980-0950
(214) 980-0160 FAX
Specialty: E,H,I,L,S
Contingency/Retainer Search

Office Manager
Baty R Gaines Associates
9400 N Central Expwy
Dallas, TX 75231
(214) 691-0531
Specialty: G,S,MIS,
Environmental,Legal,Middle
Management,
Executive Search

Office Manager
Beer & Associates Personnel
9330 LBJ Freeway Ste 900
Dallas, TX 75243
(214) 234-3344
Specialty: G
Executive Search

Office Manager
Best Associates Executive Search
520 Avenue H East
Arlington, TX 76011
(817) 649-0000
Specialty: G
Executive Search

Bruce W Tanner, Gen Mgr
Betty Tanner Professional Employment Service Inc
4150 Pinnacle Ste 116
El Paso, TX 79902
(915) 532-4447
(915) 532-4683 FAX
Specialty: E,F,M
Contingency/Retainer Search

Office Manager
Bigham Rhett & Associates
9801 Rhett & Associates
Houston, TX 77042
(713) 784-2482
Specialty: G
Executive Search

Office Manager
Biosearch Corp
4100 Spring Valley Road
Dallas, TX 75244
(214) 991-1898 732-0041
Specialty: G
Executive Search

Office Manager
Birnbach Martin & Associates
15150 Preston Road
Dallas, TX 75248
(214) 386-4431
Specialty: G
Executive Search

Office Manager
BJB Medical Associates
10245 E Via Linda St
Scottsdale, AZ 85258
(602) 451-0922
Specialty: H
Executive Search

Office Manager
Bren Group The
7610 E McDonald Dr
Scottsdale, AZ 85250
(602) 483-7656
Specialty: G
Executive Search

Jerry Brennan, Pres
Brennan Associates
P O Box 29026
Dallas, TX 75229
(214) 351-6005
(214) 351-6005 FAX
Specialty: G,M,S,Metal & Wood Fabrication,Building Products
Contingency/Retainer Search

Office Manager
Buff-Marshall & Associates
6500 West Frwy
Fort Worth, TX 76116
(817) 737-0516
Specialty: G
Executive Search

Carolyn Stewart, VP
Bundy-Stewart Associates Inc
12800 Hillcrest Ste 123
Dallas, TX 75230
(214) 458-0626
(214) 661-2670 FAX
Specialty: M,E,S
Contingency/Retainer Recruiter

Office Manager
Burgeson Hospitality Search
13300 Old Blanco Rd
San Antonio, TX 78216
(512) 493-1237
Specialty: G
Executive Search

Office Manager
Burns Dunnam & Whitehead
4151 Southwest Frwy
Houston, TX 77027
(713) 622-9299
Specialty: G
Executive Search

Office Manager
Career Concepts Personnel Svc
6070 Gateway East
El Paso, TX 79905
(915) 772-2200
Specialty: G
Executive Search

Office Manager
Career Consultants Inc
1980 Post Oak Blvd Ste 1950
Houston, TX 77056
(713) 626-4100
Specialty: G
Executive Search

Office Manager
Career Consultants Professional Search Firm & Temp Services
3624 North Hills Dr
Auston, TX 78731
(512) 346-6660
Specialty: G
Executive Search

Office Manager
Carlin Associates
16340 Park Ten Place
Houston, TX 77084
(713) 578-6215
Specialty: G
Executive Search

Office Manager
Carpenter & Associates Retail Professional Search
8333 Douglas Avenue
Dallas, TX 75225
(214) 691-6585
Specialty: Retail
Executive Search

Carrie L Kimmel, Pres
Carrie & Company Placement Service Inc
5910 N Central Expway Ste 1000
Dallas, TX 75206
(214) 741-4196
Specialty: L,P **ONLY**
Contingency Executive Search

Office Manager
Catterton Inc
2925 LBJ Frwy
Dallas, TX 75234
(214) 934-9000
Specialty: G
Executive Search

Office Manager
CFO Management Group
101 E Park Blvd Ste 600
Plano, TX 75074
(214) 516-3812
Specialty: F
Executive Search

Dolores D Jones, Pres
Champion Personnel Service
2640 Fountain View Ste 240
Houston, TX 77057
(713) 780-4640
(713) 780-4782 FAX
Specialty: E,M
Contingency Executive Search

Charles P Aquavella
Charles P Aquavella & Assoc
5925 Longo Dr
The Colony, TX 75056
(214) 370-1111
(214) 370-0022 FAX
Specialty: M,P,S,T
Executive Search
Human Resource Consulting

Office Manager
Cherbonnier Group The
1702 Rushbrook Dr
Houston, TX 77077
(713) 688-4701
Specialty: G
Executive Search

Office Manager
Christopher Fredrick Executive Search
12000 Westheimer Rd
Houston, TX 77077
(713) 496-9985
Specialty: G
Executive Search

Office Manager
Clark Williams Corp
3300 So Gessnor
Houston, TX 77063
(713) 784-8696
Specialty: G
Employment On Contract Basis

Office Manager
Coleman Patrick Inc
7752 E Foxmore Ln
Scottsdale, AZ 85258
(602) 951-1425
Specialty: G
Executive Search

John O'Keefe, Owner
Comptime Inc
3420 Executive Center Drive
Ste 114
Austin, TX 78731
(512) 343-1171
(512) 343-0142 FAX
Specialty: C
Contingency Executive Search

Bob Dirickson, Pres
Computech Corporation
4375 N 75th St
Scottsdale, AZ 85251
(602) 947-7534
(602) 947-7537 FAX
Specialty: C,E
Contingency/Retainer Search

Office Manager
Corcoran Interests Inc
15215 Beacham Dr
Houston, TX 77070
(713) 370-3841
Specialty: G
Executive Search

Office Manager
Corporate Search
2509 W Berry St
Fort Worth, TX 76109
(817) 429-1763
Specialty: G
Executive Search

Office Manager
Corporate Search Associates
4180 N Mesa St
El Paso, TX 79902
(915) 534-2583
(915) 534-2585 FAX
Specialty: G
Executive Search

Office Manager
Corporate Search Consultants
2900 Wilcrest Dr
Houston, TX 77042
(713) 977-1900
Specialty: G
Executive Search

Bruce Moore, Principal
Corporate Search Group The
3555 Timmons Lane Ste 1000
Houston, TX 77027
(713) 893-1719
(713) 622-5184
Specialty: S
Contingency/Retainer Search

Office Manager
Countee J & Associates
4950 W FM 1960
Houston, TX 77069
(713) 444-3535
Specialty: G
Executive Search

Office Manager
Cox Dodson & Story
16051 Addison Road Ste 204
Dallas, TX 75243
(214) ~~788-4644~~ 750 1067
Specialty: C, Hi-Tech
Executive Search

Office Manager
Crown Recruiters Inc
4809 Cole Avenue
Dallas, TX 75205
(214) 528-8555
Specialty: G
Executive Search

Michael Montanye, Gen Mgr
D P Select
9717 E 42nd St Ste 225
Tulsa, OK 74146
(918) 663-3847
(918) 663-0556 FAX
Specialty: C,E,H
Contingency/Retainer Search

H M Hailey, VP
Damon & Associates Inc
7515 Greenville Avenue Ste 900
Dallas, TX 75243
(214) 696-6990
(214) 696-6993 FAX
Specialty: C,G,H,S,Contract Furniture/Interiors,Medical, Office Products
Contingency/Retainer Recruiter

Office Manager
Danbrook Group
14180 Dallas Pkwy
Dallas, TX 75240
(214) 392-0057
Specialty: G
Executive Search

Darryl Vincent, Owner
Darryl Vincent & Associates
12651 Briar Forest Ste 165
Houston, TX 77077
(713) 494-5240
(713) 497-7945 FAX
Specialty: S(Cons Pkg Goods)
Contingency/Retainer Search

Office Manager
Davian Construction Search Consultants
952 Echo Lane Ste 200
Houston, TX 77024
(713) 468-6818
Specialty: Construction
Executive Search

Office Manager
Davidson John & Associates
3198 Royal Lane
Dallas, TX 75229
(214) 352-7800
Specialty: G
Executive Search

Jeff J Dandurand, VP
DHR International Inc
5215 N O'Connor Blvd Ste 200
Irving, TX 75062
(214) 556-1051
Specialty: G
Executive Search

Dick Van Vliet, Pres
Dick Van Vliet & Associates
2401 Fountain View Dr Ste 406
Houston, TX 77057
(713) 952-0371
Specialty: C,E,F,M
Contingency Executive Recruiter

Office Manager
Dilworth & Wooldridge Inc
5555 Morningside Dr
Houston, TX 77005
(713) 521-2800
Specialty: G
Executive Search

Office Manager
Dougan & McKinley Int'l Search Consultants
16800 Imperial Valley Dr
Houston, TX 77068
(713) 999-7209
Specialty: G
Executive Search

Office Manager
Dougan & McKinley Strain
3200 Southwest Frwy
Houston, TX 77027
(713) 623-6400
Specialty: G
Executive Search

Office Manager
Dragoset Group
1717 W Northern Ave
Phoenix, AZ 85021
(602) 870-7761
Specialty: G
Executive Search

Office Manager
Drake Beam Morin Inc
201 Main St
Fort Worth, TX 76102
(817) 870-1366
Specialty: G
Executive Search

Daniel J Pajak, Pres
Dunhill of Denton Inc
P O Box 50692
Dallas Drive
Denton, TX 76206
(817) 383-0700
Specialty: E,H,M,
Pharmacy,Plastics,
Rubber,Medical Devices
Contingency/Retainer Search

C Michael Dixon, Pres
Dunhill Professional Search
P O Box 293371
Lewisville, TX 75029
(214) 317-0608
(214) 317-0349 FAX
Specialty: E,H
Contingency/Retainer Search

Office Manager
Eastman & Beaudine Inc
13355 Noel Road
One Galleria Tower Suite 1370
Dallas, TX 75240
(214) 661-5520
Specialty: G
Executive Search

Office Manager
Ecosphere Systems Inc
6309 Washington Ave
Houston, TX 77007
(713) 861-8987
Specialty: G
Executive Search

Office Manager
Edwards B & Associates
Legal Search
1672 Beaconshire Rd
Houston, TX 77077
(713) 496-0930
Specialty: G
Executive Search

Office Manager
EFL Associates
8777 E Via De Ventura
Scottsdale, AZ 85258
(602) 483-0496
Specialty: G
Executive Search

Office Manager
Elliot Taylor & Assoc
1 Riverway Drive Ste 1700
Houston, TX 77056
(713) 840-1247
Specialty: G
Executive Search

Joe Ellis, Principal
Ellis & Associates Inc
1250 Capital of TX Hwy S
Building 3 Ste 620
Austin, TX 78746
(512) 328-5067
(512) 328-5069 FAX
Specialty: F,G,I,L,O
Executive Search

Erie E Calloway, Pres
Employee Sources Inc
1 Pinedale at Travis
Houston, TX 77006
(713) 520-7446
(713) 520-7518 FAX
Specialty: P
Executive/Professional
Search Firm

Office Manager
Employment Access for Retirees
9600 Great Hills Tr
Austin, TX 78759
(512) 345-8541
Specialty: G
Executive Search

Office Manager
Energists The
10260 Westheimer Rd
Houston, TX 77042
(713) 781-6881
Specialty: G
Executive Search

Office Manager
Engineering Management Staff Recruiters
5001 Spring Valley Road
Dallas, TX 75244
(214) 263-8582
Specialty: E
Executive Search

Bobby Robertson, Pres
Environmental Personnel Agency
5300 Hollister Ste 230
Houston, TX 77040
(713) 462-6832
(713) 462-1810 FAX
Specialty: Environmental
Contingency/Retainer Recruiter

Office Manager
Ernst & Young
2001 Ross Avenue Ste 2800
Dallas, TX 75201
(214) 979-1700
Specialty: F
Executive Search

L L Areaux CPC, Pres
ESP III Consulting Services
433 E Las Colinas Blvd Ste 940
Irving, TX 75039
(214) 869-0837
(817) 575-4597 (Fax Call)
Specialty: Electronics/Telecom
Retainer Only Executive Search

Office Manager
Evans McDonnell
17629 El Camino Real
Houston, TX 77058
(713) 286-7711
Specialty: G
Executive Search

John L Marshall
ExecuSource Int'l
4120 Rio Bravo Ste 106
El Paso, TX 79902-1012
(915) 542-4708
Specialty: F,G,M,S,R,High Tech/Electronic,Materials Mgt,Office Machinery,E(Production)
Executive Search

Office Manager
Excalibur Service Co
4615 Southwest Frwy
Houston, TX 77027
(713) 622-7200
Specialty: G
Executive Search

Office Manager
Executive Health Care Recruiters
12790 Merit Drive
Dallas, TX 75251
(214) 239-6960
Specialty: H
Executive Search

Office Manager
Excel of Aluquerque Inc
1700 Louisiana Blvd N E
Albuquerque, NM 87110
(505) 262-1871
Specialty: G
Executive Search

Office Manager
Executive Search
8100 Mountain Rd Pl N E
Albuquerque, NM 87110
(505) 268-3100
Specialty: G
Executive Search

Office Manager
ExecuSearch
6560 N Scottsdale Rd
Scottsdale, AZ 85250
(602) 991-5000
Specialty: G
Executive Search

Tobi Cox
4-16
Office Manager
Executive Search Consultants Ltd
7490 E Northwest Hwy
Dallas, TX 75238
(214) ~~349-0876~~ 394 4131
Specialty: G
Executive Search
3030 N Josey Ln 101
Carrollton 75007

Office Manager
Executive Search Personnel
5952 Royal Lane
Dallas, TX 75230
(214) 696-2201
Specialty: G
Executive Search

Office Manager
Executive Staff Recruiters
5910 N Central Expwy
Dallas, TX 75206
(214) 891-6676
Specialty: G
Executive Search

Office Manager
Executives & Sales International
5620 N Kolb Rd
Tucson, AZ 85715
(602) 299-5151
Specialty: G,S
Executive Search

Marcia Feldt, Owner
Feldt Personnel
10101 Southwest Frwy Ste 340
Houston, TX 77074
(713) 981-0167
(713) 988-5627 FAX
Specialty: F
Contingency Executive Search

Office Manager
Financial Pros
4100 Spring Valley Road
Dallas, TX 75244
(214) 239-1109
Specialty: G
Executive Search

Jim Morrisey, Pres
Fortune Search Consultants
10924 Vance Jackson Ste 303
San Antonio, TX 78230
(210) 690-9797
(210) 696-6909 FAX
Specialty: E,M,R,Quality/
Reliability,Regulatory Affairs
Executive Search

Office Manager
Forty Plus of Dallas Inc
13601 Preston Rd
Dallas, TX 75240
(214) 991-9917
Specialty: G
Executive Search

Office Manager
Fox Morris Associates Inc
14643 Dallas Pkwy
Dallas, TX 75240
(214) 404-8044
Specialty: G,I,M,Construction,
Services,Transportation
Executive Search

Howard Frankel, VP
Frankel & Adams
8834 Prichett Dr
Houston, TX 77096-2628
(713) 666-1001
(713) 666-1001 (Touch 33) FAX
Specialty: C,E,M,P,S
Contingency/Retainer Search

Office Manager
Fults S L & Associates
11811 Charles Rd
Houston, TX 77041
(713) 493-4918
Specialty: G
Executive Search

Gary Baldwin, Pres
G Baldwin & Company
2401 Fountainview Ste 210
Houston, TX 77057
(713) 977-2300
(713) 953-1820 FAX
Specialty: F,P
Contingency/Retainer Search

Office Manager
Galbrath J B & Associates
2311 Roosevelt Dr
Arlington, TX 460-1007
(817) 460-1007
Specialty: G
Executive Search

Office Manager
Galloway James Inc
14755 Preston Rd
Dallas, TX 75240
(214) 934-1181
Specialty: G
Executive Search

Office Manager
Gandin David L
6619 Browne Campbell St
Houston, TX 77086
(713) 448-4700
Specialty: G
Executive Search

Charles L Gaudette, Pres
Gaudette & Company
980 W Paseo Del Cilantro
Green Valley, AZ 85614
(602) 648-1963
Specialty: H,I,S,Benefits,Senior & Middle Management,
Executive Search

Office Manager
Gillman & Associates Inc
2603 Oak Lawn Ave
Dallas, TX 75219
(214) 522-9460
Specialty: G
Executive Search

Office Manager
Glover Tracy Company The
7557 Rambler Rd
Dallas, TX 75231
(214) 361-1071
Specialty: G
Executive Search

Office Manager
Golden Charles Co The
777 S Central Expressway Ste 103
Richardson, TX 75080
(214) 680-8460
Specialty: B,Stock Brokerage
Executive Search

Abel M Gonzalez
Gonzalez Abel M & Assoc
P O Box 681845
San Antonio, TX 78268
(210) 695-5555
Specialty: P
Contingency/Retainer Search

Office Manager
Group G
4099 McEwen Rd
Dallas, TX 75244
(214) 960-8444
Specialty: G
Executive Search

Mike Collins, Managing Assoc
Guidry East Barnes & Bono Inc
1414 W Randol Mill Rd Ste 200
Arlington, TX 76012
(800) 444-7145
(817) 274-3356 FAX
Specialty: H
Retainer Only Executive Search

Rodney J Gullo, Pres
Gullo R J & Associates
15710 John F Kennedy Blvd
Ste 110
Houston, TX 77032
(713) 590-9001
(713) 590-1503 FAX
Specialty: E,M,Refinery/
Petrochemicals
Contingency/Retainer Search

Office Manager
H S Group Inc
2925 L B J Freeway
Dallas, TX 75234
(214) 243-7037
Specialty: G
Executive Search

Office Manager
Halden & Associates
8711 E Pinnacle Peak Rd
P O Box 328
Scottsdale, AZ 85255
(602) 488-9634
Specialty: G
Executive Search

Office Manager
Hallmark Professional Search Inc
4213 Montgomery Blvd N E
Albuquerque, NM 87109
(505) 884-7101
Specialty: G
Executive Search

Office Manager
Halpin Personnel Services Inc
16630 Imperial Valley Dr
Houston, TX 77060
(713) 931-3100
Specialty: G
Executive Search

Office Manager
Hansar\Young International
11710 Pine Forest Dr
Dallas, TX 75230
(214) 361-9007
Specialty: G
Executive Search

Office Manager
Hardie James H
600 Sabine St
Austin, TX 78701
(512) 474-4474
Specialty: G
Executive Search

Vera E Harris CPC, Owner
Harris Personnel Resources
2201 N Collins Ste 260
Arlington, TX 76011
(817) 265-9190
(817) 543-3155 FAX
Specialty: C,E,M,P,S
Contingency/Retainer Recruiter

Office Manager
Health Care Recruiters Inc
4100 Spring Valley Rd
Dallas, TX 75244
(214) 386-7272
Specialty: G
Executive Search

Office Manager
Health Professionals of America Personnel Consultants
2616 South Loop West
Houston, TX 77054
(713) 669-0333
Specialty: G
Executive Search

Office Manager
Healthcare Recruiters International
5420 L B J Freeway
Dallas, TX 75240
(214) 770-2020
Specialty: G
Executive Search

James K Wimberly, Pres
Healthcare Recruiters Inc
4100 Spring Valley Road Ste 800
Dallas, TX 75244
(214) 386-7272
(214) 960-1309 FAX
Specialty: H
Contingency/Retainer Recruiter

Dan Smith, Owner
Healthcare Resources Group
3945 SE 15th St Ste 101
Oklahoma City, OK 73115-2247
(405) 677-7872
Specialty: H,S
Contingency Executive Search

Office Manager
Hebel R W & Associates
4821 Spricewood Springs Rd
Austin, TX 78759
(512) 338-9691
Specialty: G
Executive Search

Office Manager
Hedman Kent R & Associates
3312 Woodford Dr
Arlington, TX 76013
(817) 277-0888
Specialty: G
Executive Search

Office Manager
Heidrich And Struggles Inc
1999 Bryan St
Dallas, TX 75201
(214) 220-2130
Specialty: G
Executive Search

Office Manager
Henderson Taylor Consulting
14785 Preston Rd
Dallas, TX 75240
(214) 991-8782
Specialty: G
Executive Search

Office Manager
Hero Janice Vickery
6116 N Central Expressway
Dallas, TX 75206
(214) 360-0602
Specialty: G
Executive Search

Office Manager
Hill John L & Associates
17719 Butte Creek Rd
Houston, TX 77090
(713) 893-6834
Specialty: G
Executive Search

Office Manager
Hoffman Associates Inc
8655 E Via De Ventura
Scottsdale, AZ 85258
(602) 483-6120
Specialty: G
Executive Search

W L (Bill) Smith, Pres
International Search Division of Entec Inc
P O Box 470898
Tulsa, OK 74147
(918) 627-9070
(918) 524-8604 FAX
Specialty: C,E,M
Contingency Executive Search

William M Strawn, Pres
Houtz • Strawn Associates Inc
5000 Plaza On The Lake Ste 320
Austin, TX 78746
(512) 328-3313
(512) 328-7040 FAX
Specialty: H
Retainer Only Executive Search

Office Manager
Interview Legal Search
2020 North Loop West
Houston, TX 77018
(713) 956-0993
Specialty: G
Executive Search

Vera E Harris CPC, Owner
HPR Health Staff
2201 N Collins Ste 260
Arlington, TX 76011
(817) 261-3355
(817) 543-3155 FAX
Specialty: H
Contingency/Retainer Recruiter

Office Manager
J & B International Inc
2000 North Loop West
Houston, TX 77018
(713) 688-6448
Specialty: G
Executive Search

Office Manager
Ideal Services
20 Green Way Ste 660
Houston, TX 77046
(713) 621-6113
Specialty: E(Saudi)
Executive Search

Office Manager
J G Consultants
8350 N Central Expressway
Dallas, TX 75225
(214) 696-9196
Specialty: G
Executive Search

Jerry Gross, Partner
J Gross & Assoc
2722 Fircrest Ct
Stafford, TX 77477
(713) 261-5236 (Also Fax)
Specialty: C,E,M,T,General Management,Hi-Tech, Women & Minorities
Contingency/Retainer Search

Office Manager
James Dean & Associates
701 N Post Oak Rd
Houston, TX 77024
(713) 681-1456
Specialty: G
Executive Search

Office Manager
Jablo Partners
P O Box 795549
Dallas, TX 75379
(214) 701-8460
Specialty: G
Executive Search

Office Manager
James E Ticer Associates
268 El Duane Ct
Santa Fe, NM 87501
(505) 982-5252
Specialty: G
Executive Search

Office Manager
Jackman Financial Group Inc
17440 Dallas Pkwy
Dallas, TX 75287
(214) 733-0272
Specialty: G
Executive Search

Jim Blazek
James Group The
P O Box 54061
Hurst, TX 76054
(214) 268-8118
Specialty: G
Executive Search

Office Manager
Jackson & Coker
2711 L B J Freeway
Dallas, TX 75234
(214) 620-2900
Specialty: G
Executive Search

Office Manager
Jewett Gary
17021 E Nicklaus Dr
Fountain Hills, AZ 85268
(602) 837-0110
Specialty: G
Executive Search

John Davidson, Pres
John Davidson & Assoc Inc
3198 Royal Lane Ste 100
Dallas, TX 75229
(214) 352-7800
(714) 352-7808 FAX
Specialty: M(Food Processing)
Contingency/Retainer Search

John R Stephens, Pres
John R Stephens & Associates
7007 Gulf Frwy Ste 202
Houston, TX 77087
(713) 644-0067
(713) 644-4332 FAX
Specialty: E,,Construction, Pulp & Paper
Contingency/Retainer Search

John W Worsham, Pres
John W Worsham & Associates Inc
2001 Kirby Drive Ste 505
Houston, TX 77019-6033
(713) 522-6505
Specialty: B
Contingency Executive Search

John Wylie, Pres
John Wylie Associates Inc
1727 E 71st
Tulsa, OK 74136
(918) 496-2100
(918) 496-2557 FAX
Specialty: E,M,R
Contingency/Retainer Search

Office Manager
Joseph Chris & Associates
400 N Sam Houston Pkwy
Houston, TX 77060
(713) 931-8744
Specialty: G
Executive Search

Office Manager
KDM Associates Inc
13140 Colt Rd
Dallas, TX 75240
(214) 234-1491
Specialty: G
Executive Search

Office Manager
Kearney A T
4003 Bennedict Ln
Austin, TX 78746
(512) 327-4145
Specialty: G
Executive Search

Office Manager
Kearney A T Executive Search
6930 E 1st St
Scottsdale, AZ 85251
(602) 994-3032
Specialty: G
Executive Search

Office Manager
Kearney A T Inc
500 N Akard St
Dallas, TX 75201
(214) 969-0010
Specialty: G
Executive Search

Office Manager
Kearney A T Inc
5599 San Felipe St
Houston, TX 77056
(713) 626-4790
Specialty: G
Executive Search

Office Manager
Kenton Associates
1801 Royal Lane Ste 900
Dallas, TX 75227
(214) 248-0680
Specialty: G
Executive Search

Office Manager
Kenzer Corp
3030 L B J Freeway
Dallas, TX 75234
(214) 620-7776
Specialty: G
Executive Search

Office Manager
King Computer Search Inc
9221 L B J Freeway
Dallas, TX 75243
(214) 238-1021
Specialty: G
Executive Search

Office Manager
Kingston & Associates
3030 N Central Ave
Phoenix, AZ 85012
(602) 264-1484
Specialty: G
Executive Search

Office Manager
Klark & Associates
1616 West Loop South
Houston, TX 77027
(713) 622-2061
Specialty: G
Executive Search

Office Manager
Korn/Ferry International
500 N Akard St
Dallas, TX 75201
(214) 954-1834
Specialty: G
Executive Search

Sammye Jo Kressenberg, Pres
Kressenberg Associates
13140 Coit Road Ste 407
Dallas, TX 75240
(214) 234-1491
Specialty: E(Semiconductor), G,H(Rehabilitation Industry),I,S
Executive Search

Office Manager
Kristan Associates
5485 Belt Line Rd
Dallas, TX 75240
(214) 960-7010
Specialty: G
Executive Search

Office Manager
Kristan Associates Executive Search
12 Greenway Plaza Ste 1100
Houston, TX 77046
(713) 961-3040
(713) 961-3626 FAX
Specialty: G,S,M,Office Furnishings,Building Products
Retainer Only Executive Search

Office Manager
Lamalie Associates Inc
1601 Elm St
Dallas, TX 75201
(214) 754-0019
Specialty: G
Executive Search

Office Manager
Lamalie Associates Inc
1301 McKinney St
Houston, TX 77010
(713) 739-8602
Specialty: G
Executive Search

Office Manager
Largent Parks & Partners Inc
12770 Coit Rd
Dallas, TX 75251
(214) 980-0047
Specialty: G
Executive Search

Sid Lasky, Owner
Lasky & Co
6334 Gaston Ave Ste 214
Dallas, TX 75214
(214) 826-8450
(214) 826-1628 FAX
Specialty: E,M,R
Contingency/Retainer Search

Lea Randolph, Pres
Lea Randolph & Associates
10210 N Central Expressway
Dallas, TX 75231
(214) 987-4415
(214) 369-9548 FAX
Specialty: G,H
Contingency/Retainer Recruiter

Office Manager
Leadership Resources Inc
222 W Las Colinas Blvd
Irving, TX 75039
(214) 869-2260
Specialty: G
Executive Search

Office Manager
LeClair Sutton Assocs Inc
3508 Lindenwood Ave
Dallas, TX 75205
(214) 520-1774
Specialty: G
Executive Search

Office Manager
Lehman & Associates Inc
98 San Jacinto Blvd
Austin, TX 78701
(512) 478-1131
Specialty: G
Executive Search

Office Manager
Lehman George Associates Inc
211 Highland Cross Dr
Houston, TX 77073
(713) 443-0044
Specialty: G
Executive Search

Len Oppenheimer, Owner
Len Oppenheimer & Associates
8626 E MacKenzie Dr
Scottsdale, AZ 85251
(602) 990-1220
(602) 990-1220 FAX
Specialty: G
Executive Search

Office Manager
Leyendecker Douglas
6418 Pineshade Ln
Houston, TX 77008
(713) 862-3030
Specialty: G
Executive Search

T Paul Ligon
Ligon Paul Company
11241 Rosser Rd
Dallas, TX 75229
(214) 358-1727
Specialty: F,I,R,S,T, Communications,Management, Services
Executive Search

Office Manager
Lineback Associates
13111 Westheimer Rd
Houston, TX 77077
(713) 531-1910
Specialty: G
Executive Search

Office Manager
Litchfield & Willis Inc
5858 Westheimer Ste 403
Houston, TX 77057
(713) 975-8500
Specialty: G
Retainer Only Executive Search

Office Manager
Lockland Associates Inc
8950 N Central Expressway
Dallas, TX 75231
(214) 363-2441
(214) 890-7960
Specialty: G
Executive Search

Ron Loewenstein
Loewenstein & Assoc
5847 San Felipe Ste 990
Houston, TX 77057
(713) 952-1840
Specialty: E,S,Architectural, Automation,Chemicals, Environmental,HazardousWaste, Scientific/Technical
Executive Search

John P Albus, Owner
Lord & Albus Company
11902 Jones Rd Ste L-185
Houston, TX 77070
(713) 955-5673
Specialty: E,M,P,R,S,BioTech, Environmental
Contingency/Retainer Search

Office Manager
Lucas Associates Inc
2000 Bering Dr
Houston, TX 77057
(713) 735-6000
Specialty: G
Executive Search

Office Manager
Lyn-Jay International Executive Search
9200 Old Katy Road
Houston, TX 77055
(214) 644-5129
Specialty: G
Executive Search

Office Manager
M & M Associates
8000 IH 10 W
San Antonio, TX 78230
(512) 340-8772
Specialty: G
Executive Search

Heidi L Haring, Principal
Major Wilson & Africa
311 Market St 2nd Fl Ste 203
Dallas, TX 75202
(214) 744-1010
(214) 744-1020 FAX
Specialty: L
Contingency/Retainer Search

Tom Sheehan, Principal
Managed Care Recruiters
100 Decker Court Ste 280
Irving, TX 75062
(214) 650-1666
(214) 650-9004 FAX
Specialty: H,I
Contingency/Retainer Search

Rich Bolls, Branch Mgr
Management Recruiters
1360 Post Oak Blvd Ste 2110
Houston, TX 77056
(713) 850-9850
(713) 850-1429 FAX
Specialty: E,H,S
Contingency Executive Search

Louis Bellview, Mgr
Management Recruiters
317 S Friendswood Drive
Friendswood, TX 77546
(713) 996-008
(713) 996-5449 FAX
Specialty: E(Chemicals & Refining),G,I,H(Nurses)
Contingency Executive Search

Jim Rice, Principal
Management Recruiters
494 S Seguin Ste 201
New Braunfels, TX 78130-7938
(214) 629-6290
(210) 629-6264 FAX
Specialty: I
Contingency Executive Search

Robert S Bond
Management Recruiters
6500 West Freeway Ste 720
Ft Worth, TX 76116-2140
(817) 731-1500
Specialty: G
Executive Search

Johanna Bird, Mgr
Management Recruiters of Clearlake
17625 El Camino Real
Houston, TX 77058
(713) 286-7797
Specialty: E,H
Contingency/Retainer Recruiter

Lorraine L Keller, Mgr
Management Recruiters of Norhtwest Austin
8310 Capital of TX Hwy North
Ste 400
Austin, TX 78731
(512) 338-0880
(512) 338-0481 FAX
Specialty: R,BioTech/Pharmaceutical,Chemicals,Plastics
Executive Search

Martin L Hansen, Pres
Management Recruiters of Austin
3 Cielo Center Ste 650
1250 Capital of Texas Hwy S
Austin, TX 78746
(512) 327-8292
(512) 327-3901 FAX
Specialty: A,C,E,H,R,S
Contingency/Retainer Search

Tom Perkins, Gen Mgr
Management Recruiters of Santa Fe
320 Galisteo Ste 504
Santa Fe, NM 87501
(505) 982-2213
(505) 982-3506 FAX
Specialty: G
Contingency/Retainer Search

R S Lineback, Gen Mgr
Management Recruiters of Dallas
5310 Harvest Hill Road
Ste 110-LB105
Dallas, TX 75230-5805
(214) 788-1515
(214) 701-8242 FAX
Specialty: E,H,M,R
Contingency Executive Search

Erin Blanchette
Management Recruiters of Tucson
1730 E River Rd Ste 220
Tucson, AZ 85718
(602) 577-0515
Specialty: G
Executive Search

Office Manager
Management Recruiters-Dal N
5495 Belt Line Rd
Dallas, TX 75240
(214) 490-3399
Specialty: G
Executive Search

David L Orwig, Pres
Management Search Inc
2800 W Country Club Dr
Oklahoma City, OK 73116
(405) 842-3173
(405) 842-3173 FAX
Specialty: Agriculture
Contingency Recruiter

Office Manager
Markcting Resources Int'l
333 E North Belt Dr
Houston, TX 77060
(713) 591-7777
Specialty: G
Executive Search

Office Manager
Marburger Ray & Associates Inc
9800 Northwest Frwy
Houston, TX 77092
(713) 683-8798
Specialty: G
Executive Search

Office Manager
Marrs-McClane
14643 Dallas Pkwy Ste 360 LB36
Dallas, TX 75240
(214) 239-1199
Specialty: G
Executive Search

Tammy Rinaldi, Pres
Marilyn Austin CPC & Assoc
11999 Katy Frwy Ste 150
Houston, TX 77079
(713) 493-5706
(713) 493-2682 FAX
Specialty: B,C,F,G,H,I,L,M,O
Contingency Executive Search

Marvin L Silcott, Pres
Marvin L Silcott & Assoc Inc
7557 Rambler Rd Ste 1336
Dallas, TX 75231
(214) 369-7802
(214) 369-7875 FAX
Specialty: E,F,L,M,R,Bio
Tech/Genetic Engineering,
Energy,Evironmental
Retainer Only Executive Search

Marjorie Starr CPC
Marjorie Starr & Associates
2266 S Dobson Rd Ste 273
Mesa, AZ 85282
(602) 730-6050
(602) 730-6292 FAX
Specialty: H,S
Contingency/Retainer Search

Office Manager
Mauck Bill
3535 Briarpark Dr
Houston, TX 783-0497
(713) 783-0497
Specialty: G
Executive Search

William L Piatkiewicz, Pres
Medical Executive Search Assoc
3250 N Riverbend Cirle E
Tucson, AZ 85715
(602) 885-2552
(602) 885-2542 FAX
Specialty: E,H,M,R,S,Bio-Tech, Chemicals,Management, Pharmaceuticals
Contingency/Retainer Search

John O'Keefe, Owner
Medical Results Inc
3420 Executive Center Drive
Ste 114
Austin, TX 78731
(512) 343-1119
(512) 343-0142 FAX
Specialty: H,Also Medical
Contingency Executive Search

Kevin D Page, Principal
MegaSearch Inc
15425 North Frwy Ste 330
Houston, TX 77090
(713) 872-7800
(713) 872-7810 FAX
Specialty: E,G,T
Contingency/Retainer Search

Office Manager
Meredith J M & Assoc Inc
4001 N 32nd St
Phoenix, AZ 85018
(602) 954-7100
Specialty: G
Executive Search

Office Manager
Merritt Hawkins & Assoc
222 W Las Colinas Blvd
Irving, TX 75039
(214) 444-2200
Specialty: G
Executive Search

Office Manager
Michaels W Root & Co
5065 Westheimer Rd
Houston, TX 77056
(713) 965-9175
Specialty: G
Executive Search

Wayne C Strong
MicroSearch
7670 East Broadway Ste 106
Tucson, AZ 85710
(602) 298-7902
(602) 298-5426 FAX
Specialty: E(Semiconductor)
Contingency/Retainer Search

Office Manager
Miera Consultant International
4001 Indian School Rd N E
Albuquerque, NM 87110
(505) 268-7267
Specialty: G
Executive Search

Office Manager
Miller Karl Associates
538 Haggard
Plano, TX 75074
(214) 578-0785
Specialty: G
Executive Search

Office Manager
Mitchell Jim & Associates Inc
2626 South Loop West
Houston, TX 77054
(713) 660-6488
Specialty: G
Executive Search

Office Manager
Moerbe-Forman
5050 Quorum Dr
Dallas, TX 75240
(214) 404-8411
Specialty: G
Executive Search

Office Manager
Moore Thomas R Executive Sch
611 Ryan Plaza Dr
Arlington, TX 76011
(817) 548-8766
Specialty: G
Executive Search

Office Manager
MSI Healthcare
5215 N O'Connor Rd
Irving, TX 75062
(214) 869-3939
Specialty: G
Executive Search

Office Manager
Murphy Search Management
18484 Preston Rd Ste 102
Dallas, TX 75252
(214) 960-7200
Specialty: C,M
Executive Search

Office Manager
Must Joanne Research Specialist
9000 W Bellfort St
Houston, TX 77031
(713) 541-6804
Specialty: G
Executive Search

Office Manager
National Human Resource Group
35 Casa Verde
Austin, TX 78734
(512) 261-7770
Specialty: G
Executive Search

Office Manager
Nenstiel William H & Assoc
4430 N Civic Center Plaza
Scottsdale, AZ 85251
(602) 949-5164
Specialty: G
Executive Search

Arthur Newman
Newman Arthur Assoc Inc
4615 Southwest Fwy Ste 715
Houston, TX 77027-7106
(713) 439-0080
Specialty: G
Executive Search

Jack King, Pres
Newman-Johnson-King Inc
P O Box 58345
Houston, TX 77258
(713) 474-7422
(713) 474-9382 FAX
Specialty: E,G,M,R,S
Contingency/Retainer Search

Office Manager
Nixon & Associates
5602 Swiss Ave
Dallas, TX 75214
(214) 991-7727
Specialty: G
Executive Search

Office Manager
O'Rourke John & Associates
2630 Fountain View Dr
Houston, TX 77057
(713) 952-9488
Specialty: G
Executive Search

Steve Odell, Pres
Odell & Associates Inc
12700 Park Central Place
Ste 1800
Dallas, TX 75251
(214) 458-7900
Specialty: H,L
Contingency/Retainer Recruiter

John Kearley, Mgr
Opportunity Unlimited Inc
2720 W Mockingbird Ln
Dallas, TX 75235
(214) 357-9196
Specialty: C,E
Contingency/Retainer Recruiter

Don W Orr, Pres
Orr Executive Search
5125 N 16th St B-223
Phoenix, AZ 85016
(602) 274-2170
(602) 224-6043 FAX
Specialty: A(Direct Marketing/
Market Research/Brand
Management)
Contingency/Retainer Search

Office Manager
Overseas Opportunities
8915 Broadway St
Houston, TX 77061
(713) 649-6331
Specialty: G
Executive Search

Office Manager
Owens-Dallas Employment Services Corp
12830 Hillcrest Rd
Dallas, TX 75230
(214) 661-2431
Specialty: G
Executive Search

Office Manager
Page G S
5956 Sherry Ln
Dallas, TX 75225
(214) 392-1800
Specialty: G
Executive Search

Office Manager
Pan American Search Inc
600 Sunland Park Dr
El Paso, TX 79912
(915) 833-9991
Specialty: G
Executive Search

W L Pate Jr CPC, Pres
Pate Resources Group
595 Orleans Ste 707
Beaumont, TX 77701
(409) 833-4646
(409) 833-4646 FAX
Specialty: B,C,E,F,H,Physicians, L,P,S
Contingency Executive Search

Office Manager
Patson Ronald F
2500 Tanglewilde St
Houston, TX 77063
(713) 974-2068
Specialty: G
Executive Search

Office Manager
Pearson & Associates
11811 N Tatum Blvd
Phoenix, AZ 85028
(602) 953-9783
Specialty: G
Executive Search

Office Manager
Pencom Systems Inc
9050 N Capital of TX Hwy
Austin, TX 78759
(512) 343-1111
Specialty: G
Executive Search

Peter W Ambler, Owner
Peter W Ambler Company
14643 Dallas Pkwy Ste 537
Dallas, TX 75240
(214) 404-8712
(214) 404-8761 FAX
Specialty: C,E,F,G,H,M,P,R,S
Retainer Only Executive Search

Karen Louett,Pres
Practice Dynamics Inc
11222 Richmond Ste 125
Houston, TX 77082
(713) 531-0911
(713) 531-9014 FAX
Specialty: H(Physicians)
Contingency/Retainer Search

Richard H Darroh, Sr Partner
Piper-Morgan Associates Personnel Consultants
3355 W Alabama Ste 1120
Houston, TX 77098
(713) 840-9922
Specialty: E,F,P
Executive Search

Office Manager
Preng & Associates
2925 Briarpark Dr
Houston, TX 77042
(713) 266-2660
Specialty: G
Executive Search

Office Manager
Pool Henry & Partners
141 W Greenbriar Ln
Dallas, TX 75208
(214) 948-2006
Specialty: G
Executive Search

Office Manager
Pritchard & Associates Inc
908 Town & Country Blvd
Houston, TX 77024
(713) 467-8844
Specialty: G
Executive Search

Office Manager
Powell's Executive Personnel-Search Inc
14502 Brook Hollow
San Antonio, TX 78232
(512) 496-5464
Specialty: G
Executive Search

Kathy Lane, Pres
Pro-Employer
9461 LBJ Frwy Ste 116
Dallas, TX 75243
(214) 783-2777
(214) 783-4818 FAX
Specialty: H
Contingency Executive Search

Office Manager
ProCounsel
1222 Commerce St
Dallas, TX 75202
(214) 741-3014
Specialty: G
Executive Search

Office Manager
Professional Executive Recruiters
1200 Executive Dr East Ste 125
Richardson, TX 75081-2227
(214) 235-3984
Specialty: E,Construction
Executive Search

Office Manager
Professional Search
4250 E Camelback Rd Ste 180K
Phoenix, AZ 85018
(602) 952-2500
Specialty: G
Executive Search

John M Ledterman, Principal
Professional Team Search
4050 E Greenway Rd Ste 4
Phoenix, AZ 85032
(602) 482-1551
(602) 788-0710 FAX
Specialty: C,F,M,P,S
Contingency/Retainer Search

Anton Wylie, Pres
Professions In Medicine
12700 Hillcrest Rd Ste 190
Dallas, TX 75230
(214) 980-0018
Specialty: H(Physicians)
Executive Search

Office Manager
Prothero & Associates Inc
15150 Preston Rd
Dallas, TX 75248
(214) 788-0767
Specialty: G
Executive Search

Robert A Stone, Pres
R A Stone & Associates
14881 Quorum Drive Ste 325
Dallas, TX 75240
(214) 233-0483
(214) 991-4995 FAX
Specialty: A,Media,Entertainment
Retainer Only Executive Search

Randy Scott, Pres
R L Scott Associates
8851 Hwy 80 West Ste 201
Fort Worth, TX 76116
(817) 244-5449
Specialty: G(Mid to Upper Management),H(Psychiatric)
Contingency/Retainer Search

Bernard Silverman
R Saxon & Associates
7419 E Onyx Ct Ste 101
Scottsdale, AZ 85258
(602) 991-4460
(602) 991-2006 FAX
Specialty: C,Operations Research
Contingency/Retainer Search

Office Manager
Rand-Curtis Resources
7822 N Ridgeview Dr
Paradise Valley, AZ 85253
(602) 483-7565
Specialty: G
Executive Search

Office Manager
Ray Paul & Carre Orban Int'l
301 Commerce St
Fort Worth, TX 76102
(817) 334-0500
Specialty: G
Executive Search

Office Manager
Recruiters For Business & Industry
1533 N Lee Trevino Dr
El Paso, TX 79936
(915) 593-1555
Specialty: G
Executive Search

Office Manager
Resource Management Group
701 N Post Oak Rd
Houston, TX 77024
(713) 956-0001
Specialty: G
Executive Search

Office Manager
Resource Recruiters Inc
14001 Dallas N Pkwy
Dallas, TX 75240
(214) 934-6545
Specialty: G
Executive Search

Office Manager
Resources Unlimited
222 W Las Colinas Blvd
Irving, TX 75039
(214) 401-3318
Specialty: G
Executive Search

Office Manager
Richard Earl & Associates
3526 Grande Bulevar Blvd
Irving, TX 75262
(214) 570-3987
Specialty: G
Executive Search

L R Ritchie, Pres
Robert A Paul & Assoc
650 N Sam Houston Pkwy E
Ste 224
Houston, TX 77060
(713) 999-0054
(713) 999-1844 FAX
Specialty: E,Petrochemicals, Construction,Environmental & Safety,Energy,Technical,Senior & Plant Management
Contingency/Retainer Search

Fred Krafcik CPC, Owner
Robert George & Associates
1303-103 W Buckingham Ste 232
Garland, TX 75040
(214) 495-1271
(214) 495-0697 FAX
Specialty: C,E
Contingency Executive Search

Ken Gitlin, VP
Robert Half
1360 Post Oak Blvd Ste 1470
Houston, TX 77056
(713) 623-4700
Specialty: B,C,F
Contingency Executive Search

Office Manager
Robert Half International
4100 Rio Bravo St
El Paso, TX 79902
(915) 544-6699
Specialty: B,C,F
Executive Search

Office Manager
Robert Lowell International
12200 Park Central Dr
Dallas, TX 75251
(214) 233-2270
Specialty: G
Executive Search

Office Manager
Roddy Group Executive Search Consultants
5931 Don White Ln
Houston, TX 77088
(713) 445-7553
Specialty: G
Executive Search

Office Manager
Roddy Group Executive Search Consultants
10700 Northwest Frwy
Houston, TX 77092
(713) 782-7642
Specialty: G
Executive Search

Gayle Rodgers
Rodgers Ramsey Inc
3401 Louisiana Ste 240
Houston, TX 77002
(713) 529-7010
Specialty: H,I
Contingency/Retainer Recruiter

Office Manager
Rodriguez RA & Associates
10935 Ben Crenshaw Dr
El Paso, TX 79935
(915) 598-5028
Specialty: G
Executive Search

John A Roemer, Principal
Roemer Bartlett & Kate
P O Box 741265
Dallas, TX 75374-1265
(214) 699-1091
(214) 690-6370 FAX
Specialty: C,E(Software),P
Contingency/Retainer Search

Office Manager
Rogers Carroll & Associates
3323 Darbyshire Dr
Dallas, TX 75229
(214) 350-8536
Specialty: G
Executive Search

John E Mitchell Jr.
Romac & Associates
1700 Pacific Av
Dallas, TX 75201
(214) 720-0050
Specialty: B,F,Management,
Securities
Executive Search

Ben Dickerson, Pres
Roth Young Dallas
5344 Alpha Rd
Dallas, TX 75240
(214) 233-5000
(214) 233-8213 FAX
Specialty: H,M(Food),S(Food),
P(Food)
Contingency/Retainer Search

Larry Gladstone, Pres
Roth Young/Houston
2020 North Loop West Ste 260
Houston, TX 77018
(713) 957-8484
Specialty: H,S,T,Supermarket
Contingency/Retainer Search

Donna Johnson, Manager
Russell Group The
9699 N Hayden Rd Ste 108
Scottsdale, AZ 85258
(602) 998-3522
(602) 948-9654 FAX
Specialty: C,S,E(Software)
Executive Search

Office Manager
Russell Reynold Associates Inc
1000 Louisiana
Houston, TX 77002
(713) 658-1776
Specialty: G
Executive Search

Office Manager
Russell Reynolds Associates Inc
2001 Ross Ave
Dallas, TX 75201
(214) 220-2033
Specialty: G
Executive Search

Office Manager
RWS Partners in Search
5050 Quorum Dr
Dallas, TX 75240
(214) 386-7835
Specialty: G
Executive Search

Office Manager
S S & A Executive Search
4350 E Camelback Rd
Phoenix, AZ 85018
(602) 998-1744
Specialty: G
Executive Search

Office Manager
Sacco Kevin P
Executive Search
11811 N Tatum Blvd
Phoenix, AZ 85028
(602) 953-7670
Specialty: G
Executive Search

Office Manager
Salemi Stephen T Inc
3200 Southwest Frwy
Houston, TX 77027
(713) 963-8870
Specialty: G
Executive Search

John Steiner, Sales Mgr
Sales Consultants
1111 W Mockingbird Lane
Ste 1300
Dallas, TX 75247-5075
(214) 637-6011
(214) 637-4167 FAX
Specialty: S
Contingency/Retainer Recruiter

Al Britten, Gen Mgr
Sales Consultants
5111 N Scottsdale Rd Ste 156
Scottsdale, AZ 85250
(602) 946-1609
(602) 946-6718 FAX
Specialty: G,H,I,S,T
Contingency Executive Search

Jay Middlebrook, Pres
Sales Consultants of Austin
106 E 6th St Ste 430
Austin, TX 78701-3696
(512) 476-3555
(512) 476-1331 FAX
Specialty: E,G,H,R,S,
Environmental,Pharmaceuticals,
Security Systems,Medical
Executive Search

Office Manager
Sales Resources Inc
4350 E Camelback Rd
Phoenix, AZ 85018
(602) 952-0042
Specialty: G
Executive Search

Office Manager
Sandhurst Associates
4851 LBJ Frwy
Dallas, TX 75244
(214) 458-1212
Specialty: G
Executive Search

James E O'Daniel
Sanford Rose Assoc
10127 Morocco, Ste 116
San Antonio, TX 78216
(512) 341-9197
Specialty: G
Executive Search

Office Manager
Scannell & Hundley
14300 Cornerstone Village Dr
Houston, TX 77014
(713) 444-9592
Specialty: G
Executive Search

Office Manager
Schwartz M S & Co Inc
5956 Sherry Ln
Dallas, TX 75225
(214) 691-3939
Specialty: G
Executive Search

Harvey M Weiner, Pres
Search America Consultants For Executive Selection
12700 Hillcrest Rd Ste 172
Dallas, TX 75230
(214) 233-3302
(214) 233-1518 FAX
Specialty: T(Hospitality Industry-Private Club,Hotel,Recreation, Restaurant Mangement)
Retainer Only Executive Search

Gary Jewett, Owner
Search Associates
16810 E Avenue of the Fountains
Fountain Hills, AZ 85268
(602) 837-0571
Specialty: C,F,G,H,P,S
Contingency Executive Search

S Joseph Baker CPC, Pres
Search Consultants Int'l Inc
4545 Post Oak Place Ste 208
Houston, TX 77027
(713) 622-9188
(713) 622-9186 FAX
Specialty: E(Environmental, Chemicals,PetroChem,Energy)
Contingency/Retainer Search

Office Manager
Search Financial Inc
2911 Turtle Creek Blvd
Dallas, TX 75219
(214) 522-6433
Specialty: G
Executive Search

David G Jensen, Mg Dir
Search Masters Int'l
500 Foothills Dr Ste 2
Sedona, AZ 86336
(602) 282-3553
(602) 282-5881 FAX
Specialty: M,R,S(Bio-Technology)
Contingency/Retainer Search

Office Manager
Search Network The
14755 Preston Rd
Dallas, TX 75240
(214) 233-5303
Specialty: G
Executive Search

Office Manager
Shisler Axley & Associates
5430 LBJ Frwy Ste 1600
Dallas, TX 75240
(214) 387-8656
Specialty: Hi-Tech
Executive Search

Office Manager
Sink C W & Co Inc
5956 Sherry Ln
Dallas, TX 75225
(214) 369-6591
Specialty: G
Executive Search

Mike Varrichio, Mgr Dir
Source EDP
6606 L B J Frwy Ste 148
Dallas, TX 75240
(214) 387-1600
(214) 387-0204 FAX
Specialty: C,
Contingency/Retainer Search

Audrianne Zachara, Director
Source Engineering
4545 Fuller Dr Ste 100
Irving, TX 75038
(214) 717-5005
(214) 717-0075 FAX
Specialty: E
Contingency/Retainer Search

Robert DeVoe, Mg Partner
Source Finance
6606 L B J Frwy Ste 148
Dallas, TX 75240
(214) 387-2200
(214) 387-0204 FAX
Specialty: F
Executive Search

Office Manager
Southern Resources
12900 Preston Rd
Dallas, TX 75230
(214) 960-1637
Specialty: G
Executive Search

Office Manager
Southwest Rehab Consultants
2410 W Ruthrauff Rd
Tucson, AZ 85705
(602) 888-2262
Specialty: G
Executive Search

Office Manager
Sparks Thomas & Associates
2777 N Stemmons Frwy
Dallas, TX 75207
(214) 630-7814
Specialty: G
Executive Search

Sybil Goldberg, Owner
Spectra International
6991 E Camelback Rd Ste 13-305
Scottsdale, AZ 85251
(602) 481-0411
(602) 481-0525 FAX
Specialty: C,E,H,I,O,P,R,S,Retail
Contingency/Retainer Search

Office Manager
Spencer Stuart & Associates
1111 Bagby St
Houston, TX 77002
(713) 225-1621
Specialty: G
Executive Search

Office Manager
Spradley Legal Search
3131 McKinney Ave
Dallas, TX 75204
(214) 969-5900
Specialty: G
Executive Search

Sue DeLaurentis, Regional VP
Staff Extension Inc
4408 Spicewood Springs Road
Ste 200
Austin, TX 78759
(512) 338-1358
(512) 343-8373 FAX
Specialty: P
Interim & Permanent
Contingency/Retainer Search

Dick Steffensrud, Regional VP
Staff Extension Inc
5050 Quorum Drive Ste 637
Dallas, TX 75240
(214) 991-4737
(214) 991-5325 FAX
Specialty: P
Interim & Permanent
Contingency/Retainer Search

Bob Tann, Regional VP
Staff Extension Inc
3300 South Gessner Drive
Ste 251
Houston, TX 77063
(713) 784-8696
Specialty: P
Interim & Permanent
Contingency/Retainer Search

Office Manager
Stephens John R & Associates
Executive Search Consutants Inc
7007 Gulf Frwy
Houston, TX 77087
(713) 644-0067
(713) 644-4332 (Fax)
Specialty: G
Executive Search

Office Manager
Stehouwer & Associates Inc
2939 Mossrock
San Antonio, TX 78230
(512) 349-4995
Specialty: G
Executive Search

Office Manager
Steven A Williams & Associates
4309 Canyonside Tr
Austin, TX 78731
(512) 794-8600
Specialty: G
Executive Search

Office Manager
Steinfield & Associates
2626 Cole Avenue Ste 400
Dallas, TX 75204
(214) 220-0535
Specialty: G
Executive Search

Gary McLearen CPC, Principal
Summit Search
12407 Mopac North 100 Ste 326
Austin, TX 78758-5728
(512) 836-5005
(512) 836-5728 FAX
Specialty: M(Logistics & Distribution)
Executive Search

Dee Ray, Pres
Sumner Ray Technical Resources
4500 S Garnett Rd Ste 612
Tulsa, OK 74146
(918) 665-8686
(918) 665-8693 FAX
Specialty:E,M,Drafting,Technical
Permanent & Temporary
Contingency/Retainer Search

Office Manager
Tarrant County Employment & Training & Private Industry
2601 Scott Ave
Fort Worth, TX 76103
(817) 531-5680
Specialty: G
Executive Search

Office Manager
Surratt Travis
222 W Las Colinas Blvd
Irving, TX 75039
(214) 401-4112
Specialty: G
Executive Search

Office Manager
Taylor & Associates
6420 Hillcroft St
Houston, TX 77081
(713) 981-0710
Specialty: G
Executive Search

Tim Staton, Owner
T O Staton & Assoc Inc
6016 Valley Forge
Houston, TX 77057
(713) 935-9575
(713) 686-9599 FAX
Specialty: B,F
Contingency/Retainer Recruiter

Office Manager
Taylor Carl J & Co
2501 Oak Lawn Ave
Dallas, TX 75219
(214) 520-0442
Specialty: G
Executive Search

Office Manager
Talon Resources
4851 Keller Springs Rd
Dallas, TX 75248
(214) 380-8816
Specialty: G
Executive Search

Office Manager
Technical Search Inc
6776 Southwest Frwy
Houston, TX 77074
(713) 952-8855
Specialty: G
Executive Search

Office Manager
Technifind
5959 Gateway West Blvd
El Paso, TX 79925
(915) 775-1176
Specialty: G
Executive Search

Office Manager
The Clements Frank Company
6951 Midcrest Drive
Dallas, TX 75240
(214) 980-1400
Specialty: G
Executive Search

Office Manager
Telesolutions Of Arizona Inc
8655 E Via De Ventura Ste F127
Scottsdale, AZ 85258
(602) 483-1300
Specialty: G
Executive Search

E David Dawson, Pres
The Dawson Group
1213 Montpier Dr
Franklin, TN 37064
(615) 790-3302
(615) 790-0323 FAX
Specialty: I
Executive Search

David Stukalin, VP
Terry Stukalin Health Care Management Services Inc The
10777 Westheimer Rd Ste 950
Houston, TX 77042
(713) 781-0184
(713) 781-4550 FAX
Specialty: H(Hospital Management/Nursing Management)
Executive Search

Warren Samuel CPC, Pres
The Employment Assistance Group
17610 Midway Road 134 LB307
Dallas, TX 75287
(214) 407-0474
(214) 931-8374 FAX
Specialty: G
Retainer Only Executive Search

Alex Preston, Pres
The Energists
10260 Westheimer Ste 300
Houston, TX 77042
(713) 781-6881
(713) 781-2998 FAX
Specialty: Energy Industry
Executive Search

Cindy Bienski, Office Mgr
The Executive Consulting Group
701 N Post Oak Rd Ste 610
Houston, TX 77024
(713) 686-9500
(713) 686-9599 FAX
Specialty: B,F
Contingency/Retainer Search

Pia Curry, Owner
The Hiring Assistant
4442 Manning Lane
Dallas, TX 75220
(214) 350-8700
Specialty: B,E,G,M,P
Screen Job Ad Responses

Howard Bloom, Pres
The Howard C Bloom Co
5000 Quorum Drive Ste 160
Dallas, TX 75240
(214) 385-6455
(214) 385-1006 FAX
Specialty: L
Executive Search

F Carl Hensley CPC,CSP,Pres
The Personnel Office
24139 Boerne Stage Rd
San Antonio, TX 78255-9517
(512) 698-0300
Specialty: C,E,E,Corporate
Executives
Contingency/Retainer Recruiter

Larry C Nobles CPC, Pres
The Realty Group
5100 E Skully Dr Ste 660
Tulsa, OK 74135
(918) 622-0228
(918) 622-0290 FAX
Specialty: E,Environmental,
Industrial Hygiene,Safety
Contingency/Retainer Search

Martin J Jacobs, Mgr
The Rubicon Group
P O Box 2159
Scottsdale, AZ 85252-2159
(602) 423-9280
(602) 946-2461 FAX
Specialty: H(Physicians,
Administrative Nurses),I
Accuaries),L(Attorneys)
Contingency/Retainer Search

Linda L Center
The Search Center Inc
1155 Dairy Ashford, Ste 704
Houston, TX 77079-3011
(713) 589-8303
Specialty: Chemicals,Energy, Specialized Services(**Trading & Marketing Only**),Banking as it relates to Trading
Executive Search

Office Manager
Thomas Richardson
Rundin & Co
9525 Katy Frwy
Houston, TX 77024
(713) 932-0381
Specialty: G
Executive Search

Office Manager
Torrance Recruiting
P O Box 1984
Scottsdale, AZ 85252
(602) 946-9024
Specialty: G
Executive Search

J Brian Trambley CPC
Trambley The Recruiter
6731 Academy Rd N E Ste 9
Albuquerque, NM 87109
(505) 821-5440
(505) 821-4180 FAX
Specialty: E,M,R
Contingency Executive Search

Office Manager
Triad Associates
3627 E Indian School Rd
Phoenix, AZ 85018
(602) 224-5943
Specialty: G
Executive Search

Office Manager
Trotman Wheat & Associates
3316 Oak Grove
Dallas, TX 75204
(214) 954-1919
Specialty: G
Executive Search

Office Manager
Tucker Michael Associates
17304 Preston Rd
Dallas, TX 75252
(214) 733-6885
Specialty: G
Executive Search

Office Manager
Tuttle Neidhart Semyan Inc
12655 N Central Expwy
Dallas, TX 75243
(214) 991-3555
Specialty: G
Executive Search

Max R Shunk, Pres
Universal Search
12601 N Cave Creek Rd Ste 106
Phoenix, AZ 85022
(602) 971-9415
(602) 493-8696 FAX
Specialty: B(limited),C,E,F,G,H,
L,M,O,P,R,S
Contingency/Retainer Search

Bill Vick, Pres
Vick & Associates
3325 Landershire Ln Ste 1001
Plano, TX 75023-6218
(214) 612-8425
(214) 612-1924 FAX
Specialty: C (Microcomputers)
Contingency/Retainer Search

Office Manager
Unlimited Sources Inc
1 Riverway Dr Ste 1626
Houston, TX 77056
(713) 621-4629
Specialty: G
Executive Search

Office Manager
Vincent Darryl & Associates
12651 Briar Forest Dr
Houston, TX 77077
(713) 497-5240
Specialty: G
Executive Search

Office Manager
VanHorn Taylor & Assocs
2000 W Cessna Wy
Tucson, AZ 85737
(602) 544-0853
Specialty: G
Executive Search

Office Manager
VRL & Associates
P O Box 10295
Glendale, AZ 85318
(602) 938-3031
Specialty: G
Executive Search

Tony Vernon, Pres
Vernon Sage & Associates
4809 Brentwood Stair Rd Ste 514
Fort Worth, TX 76180
(817) 451-8785
(817) 451-8859 FAX
Specialty: G,H,M
Contingency/Retainer Search

Office Manager
Walsh Denis P & Associates
5402 Bent Bough Ln
Houston, TX 77088
(713) 931-9121
Specialty: G
Executive Search

Office Manager
Ward Howell Int'l Inc
1000 Louisiana St
Houston, TX 77002
(713) 655-7155
Specialty: G
Executive Search

Office Manager
Wardrup Associates Inc
2201 N Central Expwy Ste 116
Richardson, TX 75080
(214) 437-9333
Specialty: C,S,Hi-Tech
Executive Search

Office Manager
Watkins & Associates Executive Search Consultants Inc
7322 Southwest Frwy
Houston, TX 77074
(713) 777-5261
Specialty: G
Executive Search

Office Manager
Watson Legal Search
1616 West Loop South
Houston, TX 77027
(713) 622-3474
Specialty: G
Executive Search

Office Manager
Wesson Robert & Associates
14900 Landmark Blvd
Dallas, TX 75240
(214) 239-8613
Specialty: G
Executive Search

Office Manager
Wheeler Moore & Co
5930 LBJ Frwy
Dallas, TX 75240
(214) 386-8806
Specialty: G
Executive Search

Bruce Whitaker, Pres
Whitaker Fellows & Associates
820 Gessner Drive Ste 1500
Houston, TX 77024
(713) 465-1500
Specialty: E,H,L
Executive Search

Office Manager
White Pat & Associates
12337 Jones Rd
Houston, TX 77070
(713) 955-6886
Specialty: G
Executive Search

Office Manager
Wien & Associates
6920 Broadway Blvd
Tucson, AZ 85710
(602) 722-0406
Specialty: G
Executive Search

Office Manager
Winters Professional Recruiting Inc
45 NE Loop 410
San Antonio, TX 78216
(512) 377-3325
Specialty: G
Executive Search

Office Manager
Witt Associates
14755 Preston Rd
Dallas, TX 75240
(214) 386-5070
Specialty: G
Executive Search

Office Manager
Wood M & Associates
17440 Dallas Pkwy
Dallas, TX 75287
(214) 248-3344
Specialty: G
Executive Search

Jay Wright
Wright Group The
5902 Windmier Ct Ste 100
Dallas, TX 75252
(214) 733-7245
Specialty: G,S,Decision Support, Product Development
Executive Search

Office Manager
Young & Co
11710 Pine Forest Dr
Dallas, TX 75230
(214) 361-9005
Specialty: G
Executive Search

JOB SEEKERS SURVIVAL HINTS

Learn to stretch your money, especially if you are unemployed and looking for a job. Job hunting often takes longer than expected, so avoid creating added financial pressures by mismanaging your resources.

Some helpful hints to aid you in this area are the following:

- Identify and list all your outstanding bills, both the one-time and reoccurring items.

- Create a budget for the next six months to handle these expenses. Allow room in your budget for gasoline, tolls, and parking expenses.

- Get in the habit of collecting and using coupons at the grocery stores to stretch you dollar. Shop the sales and stock up on essentials when on sale.

- Be conservative in your spending, cut back but don't eliminate expenses for recreation. Learn to substitute activities such as a ride in the country, or a visit to a museum or zoo for a night out on the town. Go to the bargain matinee or discount movies instead of paying full price.

- Pay the minimum on your credit cards.

DALLAS & THE SOUTH WEST JOB SEEKERS SOURCEBOOK

Section 6

Database/Network/Referral Services

Overview

Database/Network/Referral services provide another viable avenue for candidates to follow in the course of their job search.

These services are often free or provided for a nominal fee. The advantage in using these services is to expand the exposure a job seeker will get in the available job market.

Use of database services is usually a **passive** activity until an interview is requested by a hiring company that has obtained access to your record and indicates an interest.

Use of these services should be done only to supplement other job search activities such as responding to specific newspaper ads, personal networking, using employment agencies or executive recruiters, or other employment services.

The value of any of these types of services to a job seeker depends upon several things:

- the quality and cost of the service,
- the kind of job being sought and your experience,
- the access or exposure that these services have to hiring companies.

Useful information on how to select and use a quality database, network, or referral service has been provided on the next few pages.

How to Select a Database, Network or Referral Service

Selecting a database/referral service to help you find a job or change jobs requires careful research on your part.

To avoid unnecessary expense, completing this research is a must! To increase the chances of obtaining a job through this approach means that you must qualify and then select only services that you wish to represent you in your job search. To assist you in this process we've outlined some important selection criteria that should be useful.

Selection Criteria:

The selection of the right database service to support your job search efforts should be based upon a combination of the following criteria:

Specialty Does the database service specialize in serving job seekers and hiring companies in your career field?

If so, the service will be useful in your job search. If they deal exclusively in your discipline, so much the better.

Experience How long has the database service been in business?

It is best to select a service that has been around at least one year. These services will already have established a network of contacts with hiring companies and will be better sources for job openings.

Referrals Was this service referred to you by someone else in your field?

If so, then a referral will give you a better idea of the quality and type of service being offered.

Location Is the service regional? And if so, where?

If so, then your exposure to the local job market may be much better by using a local regional database. However, if you are looking for a job away from where you live, then the answer to this question will allow you to focus your efforts on other services which provide either national databases or strong databases in other geographic areas.

Quality Does this service have a good reputation and do they present themselves in a professional manner?

The best way to determine this is to talk to other job seekers and to check with the Better Business Bureau. If you're unhappy with what you see or find, keep looking.

Cost Is the cost of this service within reason, considering the type of service being offered?

If yes, then the chances are better that participation in the service will give you broader exposure to a larger share of the employment market.

Questions to ask to qualify a Database/Network/Referral Service:

1. How long have they been in business?

   The longer a firm has been in the business, the more contacts they are likely to have, therefore the odds of their being able to help you are better.

2. How many client companies are they working with?

   The more client companies that use the database or referral service, the greater your opportunity of finding a job.

3. How easy is it for companies to use?

   Avoid those services that are difficult for companies to use, as chances are many of the companies being served aren't actively using the service.

4. How many people are being placed using their service?

   If they can't tell you or the number appears extremely low, then the odds are that this service isn't worth the money.

5. How long will your entry remain on file?

   If it is just for a short period of time, consider the renewal cost when comparing one service to another.

   Also a good service will allow you to request that your entry be removed once you have found a new position.

6. How easy is it for you to use?

   A good database or referral service should be relatively easy for you to use. More importantly, the service should provide the flexibility to accommodate your specific job experiences in a meaningful manner.

7. What does the service cost for you to use?

   Identify all of the costs associated with the use of the service. Measure the value of the service, by finding out how many companies are actively using the service. Divide this number into your cost to determine the your opportunity cost.

Using a Database, Network or Referral Service

To maximize your opportunity of using a database or referral service to reach an employer in search of someone with your skills, you need to follow a few important rules.

Employers perform specific searches to fill their job orders.

Therefore, do everything possible to help make their job easier. This includes being as specific as possible about all of your job skills and work history.

Employers searching a database see as many as a hundred entries per day.

This means that you must get noticed and stay noticed by them to be considered for a job opening. This is best done by being creative yet clear in your explanation of your work history.

Employers know their business, but they don't know you or how well you can perform your job.

This means that they need your help in getting to know you. Remember, you know your job history and performance record best, so tell them what you are good at.

Describe and identify the important features of previous accomplishments.

Furnish them with a means of measuring performance, such as a list of awards or reference letters.

Two thirds of all job hunters spend five hours or less a week on their job search.

Spend **full-time** on your job search, at least 30 hours a week.

Looking for a job is a job, a full-time job. If you want to succeed, you must be committed to the process and be willing to spend whatever it takes in time to be successful.

If the service doesn't handle the right type of hiring companies or doesn't show a large number of placements, then it may be not be best for you.

The most significant point to remember, is that database and referral services are **passive** approaches for seeking a job.

There is no guarantee that anyone will search the database and come up with your entry as a match.

<u>Therefore, it is extremely important that you continue to use other active approaches to further your job search.</u>

Sarah Morgan Taylor
Access/Networking in the Public Interest
96 Mt Auburn St
Cambridge, MA 02140
(617) 495-2178
Database of college graduates and job openings
Database Service

Office Manager
AIA Referral Network
American Institute of Architects
1735 New York Ave NW
Washington, DC 20006
Available to AIA members and student members. Job Seekers can call for position search and receive a print out of positions. Call or write for fee and resume format info.
Job Service

Office Manager
Air Transportation Association Resume Bank
1709 New York Ave, NW
Washington, DC 20006-5206
No phone Number available
Free resume forwarding service for airline industry employees
Referral Service

Roger Miller, Pres
American Association of Finance & Accounting
5757 Wilshire Blvd Ste 447
Los Angeles, CA 90056
(213) 852-1311
Resume Database Service for Accounting & Financial
Resume Database

Office Manager
American Institute of Biological Sciences (AIBS)
730 11th St NW
Washington, DC 20001-4584
(202) 628-1500
(800) 992-AIBS
Specialty: Offers Placement Services & Maintains Computerized Job Lists. Call or write for details
Professsional Association

Office Manager
American Public Health Association
1015 15th St NW
Washington, DC 20005
(202) 789-5600
Specialty: H Placement Services Available call or write for details
Professional Organization

James C Rodgers
American Society of Design Engineers
P O Box 931
Arlington Heights, IL 60006
(708) 259-7120
(708) 225-6517 FAX
Specialty: E Job Referrals available call or write for specifics
Professional Association

Office Manager
Association for Direction Instruction
P O Box 10252
Eugene, OR 97440
(503) 485-1293
Specialty: Association of public school and special education teachers and university instructors. Offers placement services. Call or write for specifics.
Professional Association

Office Manager
American Theatre Association
1010 Wisconsin Ave NW
6th Floor
Washington, DC 20007
(202) 342-7530
Specialty: Offers placement assistance call or write for specifics
Professional Association

Office Manager
Aviation Maintenance Foundation International
P O Box 2826
Redmond, WA 98073
(206) 828-3917
(206) 827-6895 FAX
Specialty: Aviation Maintenance Industry Placement Services available call or write for details
Trade Association

Office Manager
Artists in Print
665 3rd St
San Francisco, CA 94107
(415) 243-8244
Specialty: Job Referral for Graphic Artists
Referral Service

Colin Hanna
Bank Executives Network
300 S High St
West Chester, PA 19382
(215) 431-1900
Database service to banks of active job seekers
Database Service

Office Manager
BPI - Business People Inc
33 S 6th St Ste 2985
Minneapolis, MN 55402
(612) 370-0550
(612) 344-1648 FAX
Provides regional industry job fairs; Offers a resume mailing service for applicants unable to attend a job fair Resumes sent to all hiring copmanies represented at a job fair for $20
Job Fairs/Mailing Service

Office Manager
Brown's Best Job Lists
St Paul, MN 55102
(612) 331-6283
Specialty: Job Listing Service
Can connect you with 30-60 employers per month. Listing charge per month. Call for details
Job Listing Service

Harry Allcock, Mgr
Career Placement Registry
302 Swann Ave
Alexandria, VA 22301
(800) 368-3093
(703) 683-1085
Resume Database, $45 for six months activation
Database Service

Office Manager
College Media Advisors
MJ-300
Department of Journalism
Memphis State University
Memphis, TN 38152
(901) 678-2401
Specialty: Professional Assoc serving advisors,directors,college students etc interested in college & university student media.
Offers placement referrals Call or write for specifics.
Professional Association

Office Manager
CORS
One Pierce Place, Ste 300 East
Itasca, IL 60143
(708) 250-8677
(800) 323-1352
Database of job seekers for Employers Job Search Service
Candidate Finder Service

Office Manager
CU Career Connection
University of Colorado
Campus Box 133
Boulder, CO 80309-0133
Hot line of social services job openings. $20/two months for an access code. Touchtone phone is required to key code, field of interest & geographic area.
Job Service

Office Manager
Datamation Databank
265 S Main St
Akron, OH 44308
(216) 762-0279
Electronic Database, matches job with your qualifications, Free
Database Service

Office Manager
Executive Telecom System Inc
1000 Waterway Blvd
Indianapolis, IN 46202
(317) 633-2045
Resumes of active job seekers, obtained thru CareerPro offices
$35 for 24 weeks activation
Database Service for employers

Office Manager
Dial-A-Job
National Association of Interpretation
P O Box 1892
Ft Collins, CO 80522
Call (303) 491-7410 24 hours a day for a recording of full time, temporary & seasonal jobs in environment, education, interpretation, etc. Updated weekly.
Job Service

Office Manager
Federal Job Matching Service
Breakthrough Publications
P O Box 594
Millwood, NJ 10546
$30.00 fee to match your education and experience to federal job requirements and return a list. You need a special questionnaire and turnaround time is about 3 weeks. Call for specifics
Job Service

Office Manager
Employers' Jobnet
PO Box 325
Readstown, WI 54652
(608) 629-57499
Electronic Database of Job Openings
Database Service

Bob Mikesell, Mgr
First Interview
5500 Interstate N Parkway
River Edge One, Ste 425
Atlanta, GA 30328
(404) 952-1058
Database service to contingency employment agencies specializing in sales/marketing
Database Service

Mike Novak, Mgr
Graduating Engineers Employment Registry
Career Technologies Corp
138 Old River Rd
Andover, MA 01810
(508) 683-0098
Database service to companies interested in hiring engineers
Database Service

Office Manager
Health Personnel Options Traveling Service
2221 University Ave SE Ste 140
Minneapolis, MN 55414
Specialty: H,Nurse and health professionals (excludes physicians) are placed short term (4-26 weeks). No charge to candidates. You need special forms call for info.
Job Service

John Hawkins, Mgr
HRIN - College Recruitement Database
Executive Telecom System Inc
9585 Valparaiso Ct
Indianapolis, IN 46268
(317) 872-2045
Resumes of recent college graduates offered to hiring companies thru their Human Resources Information Network
Database Service

Brad Davis, Director
ICN
8855 Atlanta Ave, Ste 356
Huntington Beach, CA 92646
(714) 753-3312
Exchanges resumes on a referral basis within their network
Referral Service

Kenneth P Jeranek, Mgr
Insurance National Search
Kinsale-KPJ Consilum
68 W Main St
Oyster Bay, NY 11771
(516) 922-9450
Database of job seekers in the insurance industry
Database Service

Office Manager
Job Mart
National Water Well Association
6375 Riverside Dr
Dublin, OH 43017
(614) 761-3222
Specialty: Job Seekers complete resume forms/blind ad. Ads are circulated to employers who may pay a fee to see the full resume. Cost to jobseeker is $20/12 months. Positions include geologists, scientists & engineers.
Job Service

Office Manager
Job NAA
Newspaper Association Job Bank
11600 Sunrise Valley Dr
Reston, VA 22091
Office Manager
Specialty: Newspaper Postions
Call 24 hours a day for a national job bank.
Job Service

Office Manager
Jobline
BIOSOS
2100 Arch St
Philadelphia, PA 19103-1399
(215) 587-4800
(800) 523-4806
(215) 587-2016 FAX
Specialty: On Line Database of Employment Opportunities in life sciences disciplines including academic,government & industry
Database Service

Office Manager
Job Referral Service
National Contract Managers Association
1912 Woodford Rd
Vienna, VA 22182
Office Manager
Specialty: Contract Manager, free service. Submit association's form with ten copies of your resume. Resumes on file for 6 months. Call for details.
Job Service

Dwayne Miller, Mgr
JOBSource
Computerized Employment Systems
418 S Howes, Ste D
Ft Collins, CO 80521
(303) 493-1779
Database software for placement firms
Database Service

Office Manager
JobFest
800 Lee St
Des Plaines, IL
(708) 824-3378
Conducts Job Fairs
Job Fair Coordinator

Office Manager
kiNexus
640 N LaSalle St Ste 560
Chicago, IL 60610
(800) 828-0422
(312) 642-0616 FAX
Resume Database Service for College Graduates, Free
Database Service

Office Manager
Korn/Ferry International
600 Montgomery St, 31st Floor
San Francisco, CA 94111
(415) 956-1834
Database of job seekers
salaries $50K to $75,
available to clients
Database Service

Dr Ethel O Washington
National Association of Black Americans in Vocational Education (NAABAVE)
5057 Woodward Room 976
Detroit, MI 48202
(313) 494-1660
Specialty: Vocational Education
Placement Service available call or write for specifics
Professional Association

Office Manager
National Association of Black Accountants
900 Second St NE Ste 205
Washington, DC 20002
(202) 682-0222
(202) 682-33322 FAX
Specialty: F Offers placement service call or write for specifics
Professional Association

Office Manager
National Banking Network
2628 Barrett St
Virginia Beach, VA 23452
No telephone Number
Database service to contingency employment agencies specializing in banking
Database Service

Office Manager
National Association of Black Women Attorneys
3711 MaComb St NW
Washington, DC 20016
(202) 966-9393
Specialty: L Publishes Job Annoucements and is a job placement resource call or write for information
Professional Association

Office Manager
National Employment Network
PO Box 7169
Alexandria, VA 22307
No telephone Number
Database service to hiring companies
Database Service

Mary Ann Weber, Pres
National Insurance Recruiters Association
Shiloh Careers
PO Box 831
Brentwood, TN 37024-0831
(615) 373-3090
Database of job seekers in the insurance industry
Database Service

Office Manager
Nationwide Interchange Service
PO Box 21390
Canton, OH 44701-1390
(216) 455-1433
Private industry database of active job seekers, available to placement firms only. See your personal recruiter.
Database Service

Dr Steve Johnson
National Resume Bank
Job Coach
901 E Grove St
Bloomington, IL 61701
(309) 829-3931
Resume database, 3 month listing free to job seekers. Free access to employers. Developed by the Professional Association of Resume Writers
Database Service

Office Manager
Paralegal Placement Network
P O Box 710
Solebury, PA 19009
Office Manager
Specialty: L, Job Matching. $15 registration fee for two years. Call for form and specifics.
Job Service

Office Manager
National Teachers Clearinghouse
P O Box 1257
Boston, MA 02188-1257
Once registered you will receive reports of open positions matching your experience. Fees from $25-$100. Call for Specifics.
Job Service

Office Manager
Association of Government Accountants
2200 Mt Vernon Ave
Alexandria, VA 22301
Pay by the minute database of 500+ accountants, finance jobs. $1.95 first minute $.95 thereafter.
Job Service

Paul Servass, Mgr
Printers Resume Network
Curtis Publishing Co
1000 Waterway Blvd
Indianapolis, IN 46202
(317) 636-1000
Database of job seekers
from the printing industry
Database Service

Office Manager
Professional Resume File
National Research Council
Personnel Office
2101 Constitution Ave NW
Washington, DC 20418
Free Service. Research Field
Send a copy of your resume and
ask that it be placed in this
file.
Job Service

Tom Robinson, Mgr
Pronet
University Pronet
Bowman Alumni House
Stanford University
Stanford, CA 94305
(415) 723-7569
Database of available
college graduates
Database Service

Office Manager
Resume-Link
P O Box 218
Hillard, OH 43026
(800) 622-5441
Database of College Graduates
Database Service

Office Manager
Society of Certified Credit
Executives
P O Box 27357
St Louis, MO 63141
(314) 991-3030
Specialty: Organization of credit
executives who are certified
through the organization's
program. Offers placement
services call or write or details
Referral Service

Office Manager
Softsource
527 James St
Geneva, IL 60134
(708) 879-1009
(708) 879-0807 FAX
Critique resume, select
companies matching your
background,send letters for $2
per letter
Referral Service

Office Manager
Sole Electronic Job Referral Service
Society of Logistics Engineers
8100 Professional Pl Ste 211
New Carrollton, MD 20785
Free Service. Use your computer to connect to a national bulletin board of job listings.
Job Service

Office Manager
Talent Bank
Trans Century Corporation
1724 Kalorama Rd NW
Washington, DC 20009
Free Service. Refers resumes to international employers. Must obtain their form to submit your resume.
Job Service

D J Baniqued
Techmatch
162 N Franklin, Ste 602
Chicago, IL 60606
(312) 263-5507
(312) 263-4237 FAX
Database services
for: C,F,P,S
Database Service

Eric Sandberg, Sr VP
Texas S & L League
408 W 14th St
Austin, TX 78701
(512) 476-6131
Electronic Database of job seekers in Banking or Savings & Loan Industry
Database Service

Office Manager
U S Employment Opportunities-Banking/Finance
Washington Research Associates
2103 Lincoln St
Arlington, VA 22207
(703) 276-8260
Specialty: On Line data base of current openings in banking & finance. Call or write for details
Database Service

Office Manager
Women In Information Processing
Lock Box 39173
Washington, DC 20016
(202) 328-6161
Specialty: Organization of women in computer, office automation,robotics and telecommunications. Offers computerized resume bank,career counseling and resume help. Call or write for details.
Referral Service

Continue your networking by:

- getting your resume into the free network services
- signing up with a few of the low cost database services
- contacting your church and professional associations to ensure that you have all of their job leads
- checking with the placement office of the colleges that you attended

DALLAS & THE SOUTH WEST JOB SEEKERS SOURCEBOOK

Section 7

Career Consultant Services

Overview

Career consultants generally offer assistance to job seekers for a fee. The range of their services extends from simple resume preparation, psychological counseling, vocational testing, interview practice videotaping, to coaching on every aspect of a job search.

Career consultants provide the most benefit in helping a job seeker to focus their efforts constructively to obtain a new job or make a career change in the shortest period of time.

The majority of these career services provide tools to help a job seeker, but still require each individual to actively direct their own job search.

Professionals in this field should have the appropriate educational background and sufficient experience to provide the services required. Generally, they are likely to have a Masters degree or higher accompanied with substantial practical experience.

In your selection process, look for firms that will take the time and care to pre-screen an individual at no charge to determine their needs.

Career consultants offer a variety of services at costs that range from relatively inexpensive to expensive. You can expect to pay from $50 to $125 per hour on an hourly basis. Avoid paying for package deals that are not necessary.

Look for consultants that have your best interests as their priority, instead of the fees to be earned. Good consultants will not attempt to sell services not needed or requested by an individual.

To assist you in your endeavors to find a qualified career consultant or counselor, we have provided important information on the following pages for the selection and use of these types of services.

How to Select a Career Consultant

Finding the right career consultant for you can take time and careful research. This process should not be rushed, since in most cases it is the individual that pays for their services. As with anything, the benefits derived are proportional to amount of effort applied.

This selection process cannot and should not be ignored. To maximize your chances of obtaining a job by using a career counselor/consultant means that you must work hard to qualify and then select a the right one.

Your goal is to find one that will provide the most beneficial services to support you during your job search. To assist you in this process we've outlined some important selection criteria below that should be useful.

Selection Criteria:

The selection of the right career counselor/consultant to support your job search efforts should be based upon a combination of the following criteria:

Proximity Is the firm convenient for you to visit on a regular basis?

This is important when attempting to meet on a regular basis to work through the issues on your job search.

Specialty Does the consultant specialize in working with personnel in your career field and industry?

If so, they will be best able to understand your needs and will be the most experienced in providing you with useful information on how to find a new job. If they deal exclusively in your discipline, so much the better.

Experience How long has the career counselor/consultant been in the business? And how long have they been working with members of your profession?

It is best to select a consultant who has at least three years experience specializing in your industry. These people will already have established a network of contacts with a number of hiring companies and will be better sources of information about new job

Personality Does the consultant like you and do you like them? Do you "click" with the consultant?

If, yes, then you have a better shot at establishing and maintaining a good rapport with them on an ongoing basis.

Referrals Was this firm referred to you by someone else in your field?

In addition to positive responses for the preceding qualifiers, a referral will give you a better feeling about their professional ability.

Quality Does this firm have a good reputation and do the consultants present themselves in a professional manner?

The best way to determine this is to talk to other job seekers and to visit the consultant's office to get a feeling for how the service is performed. If you're unhappy with what you see or find, keep looking.

Credentials Does this consultant have the proper education and work experience to be of meaningful assistance to you?

If not, then keep looking. Remember, this is a service that you are paying for, so don't settle on less than the best.

Questions to ask to qualify a career consultant:

1. How long have they been in the business?

   The longer a firm has been in the business, the more contacts they are likely to have, therefore increasing the odds that the service will truly facilitate your job search.

2. How many job seekers are they working with?

   Avoid career consultants that have more than 20 active job seekers per counselor, because you'll be easily forgotten.

3. Do they belong to any national or local professional affiliations?

   Qualified career consultants will usually belong to at least one professional organization. In many cases, membership in these organizations requires that a member meet certain educational or experience requirements.

5. What is the cost of their service? What are the hidden costs?

   Look for those services which charge on an hourly basis, with additional charges for other services as needed. With these firms you have better control over your long term costs by only paying for what you need as opposed to one price for a "package".

Working with a Career Consultant

To maximize your success of having a career counselor/consultant to help you direct your professional career or find a new job, you need to remember a few important axioms.

Career counselor/consultants normally charge a package fee or an hourly rate for services.

Therefore, do everything possible to help make their job easier. This includes having a very good resume available for their use and being prepared and on time for your work sessions with them.

Good career consultants know their job, but they don't know you or how well you can perform your job.

This means that they need your help in getting to know you. Remember, you know your work history, skills, qualifications, and accomplishments best, so tell them what you are good at.

Describe and identify the important features of previous accomplishments. Furnish them with a means of measuring performance, such as a list of recognition awards or reference letters.

Career counselors/consultants are support personnel who will help you make decisions and focus your efforts to change careers or find a job.

The leg work to find a job is still your responsibility.

Career councelors/consultants really don't find people jobs, however their professional advice can be helpful in assisting you to find a job quicker.

If a consultant firm doesn't have the experience in your field or doesn't assist people in your particular circumstances, it may not be the firm for you to use.

If they have too many job seekers that they are attempting to serve, then they may be not be the best firm for you to use.

To find the best career consultant or counselor, do some comparison shopping and check references. Reputable firms will have many very good references and will gladly provide them to you.

Review any contract carefully before signing. It should be clear as to what services you will be provided, for the fee that you are paying.

Finally, the ultimate responsibility for handling a career change or finding a job is still your obligation. It requires that you work hard at this task. Using a career consultant is not a passive activity.

M Shaw, Owner
Accelerated Resumes
8200 Pat Booker Road Ste 381
San Antonio, TX 78233
(210) 979-1111
Specialty: Government/Military Conversions
Career Consultant

Dwain Bowline, Pres
Affiliated Therapists of OK
2121 E 51st St Ste 109
Tulsa, OK 74105
(918) 742-9900
Specialty: Career & Vocational Counseling, Outplacement
Career Consultant

Ercument Cetner, Data Coordinator
Alamo Resume & Personnel
1616 San Pedro Avenue Ste 2
San Antonio, TX 78212
(210) 735-JOBS
(210) 735-2216 FAX
Specialty: G
Career & Vocational Counseling

Office Manager
Aluma Group Aptitude Testing
425 W Wilshire Blvd
Oklahoma City, OK 73132
(405) 848-8797
Specialty: G
Career & Vocational Counseling

Office Manager
Appel Victor H Phd
4131 Spicewood Springs Rd
Austin, TX 78759
(512) 345-5070
Specialty: G
Career & Vocational Counseling

Office Manager
Aptitude Inventory Measurement Service (AIMS)
12160 Abrams Ste 314
Dallas, TX 75243
(214) 234-8378
Specialty: Aptitude Testing and Career Information
Career & Vocational Counseling

Office Manager
Austin Community College
5930 Middle Fiskville Rd
Austin, TX 78752
(512) 483-7007
Specialty: G
Career & Vocational Counseling

Office Manager
Austin Counseling Center
504 W 17th St
Austin, TX 78701
(512) 495-9044
Specialty: G
Career & Vocational Counseling

Office Manager
Bellamy Douglas EDD
Psychologist P C
12900 Preston Rd
Dallas, TX 75230
(214) 404-8888
Specialty: G
Career Counsultant

Office Manager
Bernhard Haldane Associates
7335 S Lewis Ave
Tulsa, OK 74136
(918) 491-9151
Specialty: G
Career & Vocational Counseling

Office Manager
Besson Taunee
6330 LBJ Frwy
Dallas, TX 75240
(214) 239-1399
Specialty: G
Career & Vocational Counseling

Office Manager
Blankman Shoshona MA
Pathfinding Counseling
6100 Seagull Ln NE
Albuquerque, NM 87109
(505) 880-1618
Specialty: G
Career & Vocational Counseling

Office Manager
Blankman Shoshona MA
Pathfinding Counseling Service
6100 Seagull St NE
Albuquerque, NM 87109
(505) 880-1618
Specialty: G
Career & Vocational Counseling

Office Manager
Breihan Bob
1203 Lavaca St
Austin, TX 78701
(512) 469-9447
Specialty: G
Career & Vocational Counseling

Office Manager
Brownfield Kathryn Ed D-LPC
2651 E 21st St
Tulsa, OK 74104
(918) 744-4242
Specialty: G
Career & Vocational Counseling

Office Manager
C B M School of Computer Business
406 W Durango
San Antonio, TX 78204
(512) 224-9286
Specialty: G
Career & Vocational Counseling

Office Manager
C L Carter Jr & Associates Inc
Hibernia Bank Building
Richardson, TX 75080
(214) 234-3296
Specialty: G
Career & Vocational Counseling

Dwain Bowline, President
Career & Educational Consultants
219 W 5th Avenue
Briston, OK 74010
(918) 367-2673
Specialty: Career,Life & Financial Aid Planning
Career Consultant

Joyce Shoop MS, Counselor
Career Action Assoc PC
12655 N Central Expressway
Ste 1012
Dallas, TX 75243

(214) 392-7337
Specialty: G

- **Education & Life/Work Planning**
- **Individual Career Assessment**
- **Individual & Corporate Seminars**
- **Corporate Outplacement**

Career Consultant

Rebecca Hayes, Counselor
Career Action Assoc PC
1325 8th Avenue
Ft Worth, TX 76104

(817) 763-9528
Specialty: G

- **Education & Life/Work Planning**
- **Individual Career Assessment**
- **Individual & Corporate Seminars**
- **Corporate Outplacement**

Career Consultant

Office Manager
Career Assessment Services
6301 Gaston Ave
Dallas, TX 75214
(214) 823-2256
Specialty: G
Career Consultant

Office Manager
Career Center
4163 A Montgomery Blvd NE
Albuquerque, NM 87109
(505) 880-1618
Specialty: G
Career & Vocational Counseling

Office Manager
Career Center
4163 A Montgomery Blvd NE
Albuquerque, NM 87109
(505) 883-4513
Specialty: G
Career & Vocational Counseling

Robert F Sarmiento PhD, Psychologist
Career Clinic
9525 Katy Frwy Ste 210
Houston, TX 77024-1414

(713) 465-2456
(713) 468-2868
Specialty: Career Testing & Counseling

- **Career Testing**
- **Professional Counseling**
- **Job Search Strategies**
- **Outplacement**
- **Personnel Testing**

Career/Outplacement Counseling

Dr Michael Magee, Psychologist
Career Consultation Center
1250 E Cliff Drive
El Paso, TX 79902

(915) 532-2976
Specialty: G

- **Vocational,personality,**
- **intelligence and academic**
- **achievement testing.**
- **Learning disabilities and**
- **attention deficit**
- **evaluation**

Career & Vocational Counseling

Office Manager
Career Design Associates Inc
2818 S Country Club Rd
Garland, TX 75041
(214) 278-4701
Specialty: G
Career Consultant

Office Manager
Career Development Center
1964 W Gray
Houston, TX 77018
(713) 521-0489
Specialty: G
Career & Vocational Counseling

Office Manager
Career Development Institute
6800 Park Ten Blvd
San Antonio, TX 78213
(512) 737-2100
Specialty: G
Career & Vocational Counseling

Office Manager
Career Development Services
4823 S Sheridan Rd
Tulsa, OK 74145
(918) 665-1162
Specialty: G
Career & Vocational Counseling

Richard Citrin, PhD
Jon Crook, PhD
Career Development Specialists/ Iateria Institute
1152 Country Club Lane
Fort Worth, TX 76112
(817) 654-9600
(817) 654-2246 FAX
Specialty: Job Club, Career Testing & Evaluation
Career Consultant

Taunee Besson, President
Career Dimensions
6330 L B J Freeway Ste 136
Dallas, TX 75240
(214) 239-1399
Specialty: G
Career Consultant

Office Manager
Career Directions
4025 Woodland Park Blvd
Arlington, TX 76013
(817) 461-0200
Specialty: Job Search Strategies
Career & Vocational Counseling

Office Manager
Career Directions Center
4550 NW Loop 410
San Antonio, TX 78229
(512) 735-7443
Specialty: G
Career & Vocational Counseling

Office Manager
Career Focus Associates
1700 Coit Road
Plano, TX 75057
(214) 596-1233
Specialty: Career Assessment, Job Search Skills,Resumes
Career & Vocational Counseling

Office Manager
Career Guidance & Resource Ctr
701 San Mateo Blvd N E
Albuquerque, NM 87108
(505) 255-1109
Specialty: G
Career & Vocational Counseling

Office Manager
Career Guidance & Resource Center
701 San Mateo Blvd NE
Albuquerque, NM 87108
(505) 255-1109
Specialty: G
Career & Vocational Counseling

Melodye H Lembo M Ed, Director
Career Guidance Center
1240 Southbridge Court Ste 104
Hurst, TX 76034

(817) 282-2620
Specialty: Testing, Exploration,Guidance

- **Voc. Testing-Adolescents & Adults**
- **Career Planning & Counseling**
- **College or Voc. Guidance**
- **Displaced,Burnout,Career Change**
- **Corporate Personnel Screening**

Career Consultants

Office Manager
Career Horizons
3420 E Shea Blvd
Phoenix, AZ 85028
(602) 494-9823
Specialty: G
Career & Vocational Counseling

Office Manager
Career Horizons
4034 E McDowell Rd
Phoenix, AZ 85008
(602) 231-0298
Specialty: G
Career & Vocational Counseling

Office Manager
Career Management Resources
5215 N O'Connor Road
Irving, TX 75062
(214) 556-0786
Specialty: Career Transitions
Career & Vocational Counseling

Office Manager
Career Marketing Inc
2603 Augusta Dr
Houston, TX 77057
(713) 784-5474
Specialty: G
Career & Vocational Counseling

David M Dorrell, Career Coordinator
Career Resources
5804 N Grand
Oklahoma City, OK 73118
(405) 842-5155
(405) 842-6357 FAX
Specialty: G
Career Consultant/Resume Service

Office Manager
Career Visions Inc
1100 Louisiana
Houston, TX 77002
(713) 759-0227
Specialty: G
Employment Agency/Recruiter

Office Manager
Career Strategies
1414 W Randol Road Ste 100
Arlington, TX 76012
(214) 274-0093
Specialty: Career Design
Career & Vocational Counseling

Office Manager
Careerbanc
24 E Greenway Plaza
Houston, TX 77046
(713) 623-2570
Specialty: G
Career & Vocational Counseling

Office Manager
Career Technical Centre
P O Box 166632
Irving, TX 75016
(214) 283-5418
Specialty: G
Career & Vocational Counseling

Office Manager
Careerpath Consultants
8632 Fredericksburg Rd Ste 215
San Antonio, TX 78240
(512) 599-1114
Specialty: G
Career & Vocational Counseling

Rick Davis, President
Career Transition Centers
2910 E Camelback Road Ste 230
Phoenix, AZ 85016
(602) 955-7002
(602) 955-0765 FAX
Specialty: A,B,C,E,F,H,M,P,R,S,T
Career Consultant Service

Carol Duncan
Carol Duncan Enterprises Inc
12900 Preston Road
Dallas, TX 75230
(214) 385-1130
Specialty: Job Search & Transition,Counseling,Resume Assistance
Career & Vocational Counseling

Carl E McElroy, Owner
CEMAC
2321 Wyatt Ct
Fort Worth, TX 76119
(817) 536-9773
(817) 536-9773 FAX
Specialty: Testing/Assessment And Training
Career Counsultant

Office Manager
Center For Continuing Careers
2909 Hillcroft St
Houston, TX 77057
(713) 952-9021
Specialty: G
Career & Vocational Counseling

Office Manager
Chadwell Carrell M PHD
3500 Oak Lawn Ave
Dallas, TX 75219
(214) 526-3505
Specialty: G
Career Consultant

Office Manager
College Money
P O Box 12927
San Antonio, TX 78212
(512) 735-2252
Specialty: G
Career & Vocational Counseling

Office Manager
Corporate Dynamics
511 E John Carpenter Frwy
Dallas, TX 75247
(214) 869-2470
Specialty: G
Career Consultant

Office Manager
Counseling Services Of Houston
1964 W Gray
Houston, TX 77019
(713) 521-9391
Specialty: G
Career & Vocational Counseling

Office Manager
Davis Sandra L MS
4307 Newton Ct
Dallas, TX 75219
(214) 522-2104
Specialty: G
Career Consultant

Office Manager
Deems Associates
7835 E Redfield Rd Ste 106
Scottsdale, AZ 85260
(602) 483-8242
Specialty: G
Career & Vocational Counseling

Office Manager
Donohue Peggy
1221 Abrams Road
Dallas, TX 75214
(214) 699-0774
Specialty: G
Career & Vocational Counseling

Office Manager
Erwin William M PhD
7744 Broadway
San Antonio, TX 78209
(512) 821-5905
Specialty: G
Career & Vocational Counseling

Charles D Bearden
Executive Horizons Inc
1661 E Camelback Rd Ste 250
Phoenix, AZ 85016
(602) 230-1551
Specialty: G
Career & Vocational Counseling

Office Manager
Faschingbauer Thomas R PhD
5015 Montrose Blvd
Houston, TX 77006
(713) 523-6765
Specialty: G
Career & Vocational Counseling

Office Manager
Forty Plus of Houston
2909 Hillcroft St
Houston, TX 77057
(713) 952-7587
Specialty: G
Career & Vocational Counseling

Office Manager
Full Circle Counseling
600 N Main St
McAllen, TX 78501
(210) 618-2673
Specialty: G
Career & Vocational Counseling

Office Manager
Future Trax
1601 S Shepherd Ste 24
Houston, TX 77019
(713) 526-5970
Specialty: G
Career & Vocational Counseling

Office Manager
GCI Personnel Management
2600 E Griffin Pkwy
Mission, TX 78752
(210) 631-3308
Specialty: G
Career & Vocational Counseling

Office Manager
Goodwill Industries
5000 San Mateo Blvd N E
Albuquerque, NM 87109
(505) 881-6402
Specialty: G
Career & Vocational Counseling

Office Manager
Goodwill Industries
5000 San Mateo Blvd N E
Albuquerque, NM 87109
(505) 881-6402
Specialty: G
Career & Vocational Counseling

Office Manager
Grangaard Daniel R
1812 Centre Creek Dr
Austin, TX 78754
(512) 339-7511
Specialty: G
Career & Vocational Counseling

Office Manager
Hartshore Jonathan-Worklife Counseling
3401 Carlisle N E
Albuquerque, NM 87110
(505) 889-3333
Specialty: G
Career & Vocational Counseling

Office Manager
Hartshorne Jonathan-Worklife Counseling
3401 Carlisle Blvd NE
Albuquerque, NM 87110
(505) 889-3333
Specialty: G
Career & Vocational Counseling

Lois Henry PhD, Principal
Henry & Associates
6900 East Cambelback Road
Ste 700
Scottsdale, AZ 85251

(602) 941-1137
(602) 990-0002 FAX
Specialty: Self Marketing/Interviewing

- **Career-Life Counseling**
- **Individual Testing**
- **Career Change & Search Assistance**
- **Personal Counseling**
- **Corporate Consultation**

Career Consulting

Office Manager
Hofmeister Joyce & Schlabach
5847 San Felipe
Houston, TX 77057
(713) 789-5500
Specialty: G
Career & Vocational Counseling

Office Manager
Houston International Univ
3333 Fannin St
Houston, TX 77004
(713) 528-0275
Specialty: G
Career & Vocational Counseling

Office Manager
Hunt Patton & Brazeal
5215 E 71st St
Tulsa, OK 74114
(918) 747-8386
Specialty: G
Career & Vocational Counseling

Office Manager
International Business College
4121 Montana Ave
El Paso, TX 79903
(915) 566-8643
Specialty: G
Career & Vocational Counseling

Office Manager
Johnson O'Connor Research Foundation Inc
3200 Wilcrest Dr
Houston, TX 77042
(713) 783-3411
Specialty: G
Career & Vocational Counseling

Dr Kahn
Kahn Alfred J PhD
4615 Post Oak Place Ste 200
Houston, TX 77027
(713) 621-5044
(713) 840-8312 FAX
Specialty: G
Career & Vocational Counseling

Office Manager
Kelley Betty PhD
3620 Wyoming Blvd NE Ste 208A
Albuquerque, NM 87111
(505) 296-0323
Specialty: G
Career & Vocational Counseling

Office Manager
Kelly Betty PHD
3620 Wyoming Blvd NE
Ste 208 A
Albuquerque, NM 87111
(505) 296-0323
Specialty: G
Career & Vocational Counseling

Office Manager
Life Work International
17049 El Camino Real
Houston, TX 77058
(713) 486-5433
Specialty: G
Career & Vocational Counseling

Office Manager
Lulac Educational Svc Center
2220 Broadway St
Houston, TX 77012
(713) 641-2463
Specialty: G
Career & Vocational Counseling

Office Manager
Mancuso Cullen J Phd
2651 E 21st St
Tulsa, OK 74114
(918) 747-8386
Specialty: G
Career & Vocational Counseling

Office Manager
Morgenstern Evan
4227 N 32nd St
Phoenix, AZ 85018
(602) 956-9447
Specialty: G
Career & Vocational Counseling

Office Manager
Network Rehabitation
300 Thunderbird Dr
El Paso, TX 79912
(915) 585-2044
Specialty: G
Career & Vocational Counseling

Office Manager
New Directions Counseling Center
8140 N Mo-Pac Expwy
Building 2 Ste 230
Austin, TX 78759
(512) 343-9496
Specialty: G
Career & Vocational Counseling

Office Manager
New Mexico Job Corp Outreach Screening & Placement Agency
156 Wyatt Dr
Las Cruces, NM 88005
(505) 525-8191
Specialty: G
Career & Vocational Counseling

Office Manager
NewStart Career Counseling
3080 N Civic Center Plaza
Scottsdale, AZ 85251
(602) 947-3311
Specialty: G
Career & Vocational Counseling

Office Manager
OCM Inc
5700 Harper Dr NE
Albuquerque, NM 87109
(505) 822-1223
Specialty: G
Career & Vocational Counseling

Office Manager
Offerle Joan M PhD
7320 N MoPac Expwy
Austin, TX 78731
(512) 346-2044
Specialty: G
Career & Vocational Counseling

Office Manager
Options Resource & Career Ctr
1200 Blalock Rd
Houston, TX 77055
(713) 465-1118
Specialty: G
Career & Vocational Counseling

Wm R McCright, Owner
Production Associates
POB 470301
Tulsa, OK 74147-0301
(918) 622-7038
(918) 622-6385 FAX
Specialty: Talent Casting Services for Television,Motion Pictures & Print-Advertising
Career Consultant Service

Office Manager
Professional Career Associates
9430 Research Blvd at Mo-Pac
Austin, TX 78759
(512) 338-9144
Specialty: G
Career & Vocational Counseling

Office Manager
Professional Counseling Svcs
1221 Abrams Rd
Dallas, TX 75214
(214) 699-0774
Specialty: Life Changes & Transition
Career Consultant

Office Manager
Purpose Quest
3916 Juan Tabo NE Ste 19
Albuquerque, NM 87111
(505) 299-9094
Specialty: G
Career & Vocational Counseling

Office Manager
Purpose Quest
3916 Juan Tabo Blvd NE Ste 19
Albuquerque, NM 87111
(505) 299-9094
Specialty: G
Career & Vocational Counseling

Office Manager
RCG
8333 Douglas Rd
Dallas, TX 75225
(214) 363-9928
Specialty: G
Career Consultant

Office Manager
Reading & Guidance Center Inc
3703 Yoakum Blvd
Houston, TX 77006
(713) 528-0244
Specialty: G
Career & Vocational Counseling

Office Manager
Rehabilitation Services Associates Inc
3505 Turtle Creek Blvd
Dallas, TX 75219
(214) 520-9800
Specialty: G
Career & Vocational Counseling

Office Manager
Sabol Donald E
11230 West Ave
San Antonio, TX 78213
(512) 341-8824
Specialty: G
Career & Vocational Counseling

Office Manager
Schor Mark M PHD
13339 N Central Expressway
Dallas, TX 75243
(214) 4709101
Specialty: G
Career & Vocational Counseling

Office Manager
Searle Martha F
2403 San Mateo Blvd N E
Albuquerque, NM 87110
(505) 880-0204
Specialty: G
Career & Vocational Counseling

Office Manager
Second Wind Program
605 Baylor St
Austin, TX 78703
(512) 474-8550
Specialty: G
Career & Vocational Counseling

Office Manager
Shumsky & Shumsky Inc
7887 San Felipe St
Houston, TX 77063
(713) 784-6610
Specialty: G
Career & Vocational Counseling

Office Manager
Sternes Glenn F PhD
3000 Weslayan Ste 340
Houston, TX 77027
(713) 622-7806
Specialty: G
Career & Vocational Counseling

Tonya M Hughes, Sr Mkt Rep
Superior Programming Services Inc
2950 North Loop West Suite 130
Houston, TX 77092
(713) 956-0200
(713) 956-0258 FAX
Specialty: C,Consulting
Career Consultant Service

Rodney L Lowman PhD, Dir
The Development Laboratories
611 Stuart Street Ste 205
Houston, TX 77006
(713) 527-9235
(713) 527-8130 FAX
Specialty: Psychological evaluation/treatment/career -work issues
Career & Vocational Counseling

Office Manager
TrainingWorks Inc
4911 N Portland Ave
Oklahoma City, OK 73112
(405) 942-7400
Specialty: G
Career Consultants

Pat Brown, Pres
Travel Placement Specialists
3311 Richmond Avenue Ste 230
Houston, TX 77098
(713) 942-0662
(713) 942-0665 FAX
Specialty: T,Travel Industry
Career Consultant Service

Office Manager
Truit John F
12800 Briar Forest Dr
Houston, TX 77088
(713) 497-7844
Specialty: G
Career & Vocational Counseling

Office Manager
Valley Vocational Services
2512 E Thomas Rd
Phoenix, AZ 85016
(602) 957-1234
Specialty: G
Career & Vocational Counseling

Office Manager
VanDenHeuvel Joseph G PhD
126 Monroe N E
Albuquerque, NM 87108
(505) 262-1472
Specialty: G
Career & Vocational Counseling

Office Manager
VanDenHeuvel Joseph G PHD
126 Monroe St NE
Albuquerque, NM 87108
(505) 262-1472
Specialty: G
Career & Vocational Counseling

Office Manager
VGS Inc
505 Baines
Brookshire, TX 77423
(713) 375-5110
Specialty: G
Career & Vocational Counseling

Office Manager
VGS Inc
1475 W Gray
Houston, TX 77019
(713) 520-6675
Specialty: G
Career & Vocational Counseling

Office Manager
VGS Inc
2600 Southwest Frwy
Houston, TX 77098
(713) 659-1800
Specialty: G
Career & Vocational Counseling

Office Manager
Villwock Jaclyn E EdD
820 Gessner Dr
Houston, TX 77055
(713) 464-1529
Specialty: G
Career & Vocational Counseling

Office Manager
Visage Professional Services
10226 Glenkirk Dr
Houston, TX 77089
(713) 481-0990
Specialty: G
Career & Vocational Counseling

Office Manager
Vocational Evaluation Center
306 Thunderbird Dr
El Paso, TX 79912
(915) 584-1124
Specialty: G
Career & Vocational Counseling

William M Helton Jr
PhD,Psychologist
William H Helton Jr PhD
721 N Fielder Road Ste C
Arlington, TX 76012
(817) 460-5831
Specialty: G
Career & Vocational Counseling

Office Manager
Williams & McDaniel Inc
10777 Westheimer Rd
Houston, TX 77042
(713) 780-2188
Specialty: G
Career & Vocational Counseling

Office Manager
Willins Pat MA PhD
2325 San Pedro Dr N E
Albuquerque, NM 87110
(505) 883-8484
Specialty: G
Career & Vocational Counseling

Office Manager
Willins Pat MA PHD
2325 San Pedro Dr NE
Albuquerque, NM 87110
(505) 883-8484
Specialty: G
Career & Vocational Counseling

Office Manager
Wilson Edward J M Ed IPC
2715 Bissonnet St
Houston, TX 77005
(713) 524-6377
Specialty: G
Career & Vocational Counseling

Office Manager
Women's Resource Center YWCA
823 S Gary Pl
Tulsa, OK 74104
(918) 582-7555
Specialty: G
Career & Vocational Counseling

Office Manager
Work Connection Inc The
1222 N Main Ave
San Antonio, TX 78212
(512) 226-1468
Specialty: G
Career & Vocational Counseling

Office Manager
Worklife Counseling
3401 Carlisle N E
Albuquerque, NM 87110
(505) 889-3333
Specialty: G
Career & Vocational Counseling

Office Manager
World of Work Inc
4102 Bellaire Blvd
Houston, TX 77025
(713) 664-4774
Specialty: G
Career & Vocational Counseling

Office Manager
World of Work Inc
2923 N 67 Place
Scottsdale, AZ 85251
(602) 946-1884
Specialty: G
Career & Vocational Counseling

DALLAS & THE SOUTH WEST JOB SEEKERS SOURCEBOOK

Section 8

Outplacement Services

Outplacement services generally offer assistance to job seekers for a fee that is usually paid for by one's previous employer (Corporate Sponsored).

The range of their services extends from simple resume preparation, vocational testing, use of an office (complete with telephone and secretarial support), to coaching on every aspect of the job search.

Outplacement services offer a variety of services at costs that range from relatively inexpensive to expensive. In the majority of the cases, the cost of such services is covered by the previous employer, especially if the employer has just gone through a restructuring.

The value of any of these services to a job seeker depends upon several things: the quality of the service, the kind of work being sought, the access or exposure that these services have to hiring companies and your own level of experience.

It should be noted that outplacement services provide the most benefit by helping job seekers focus their efforts constructively to obtain new jobs in the shortest period of time.

Outplacement services provide the tools to help job seekers expedite their job search, but still require individuals to actively direct their own job search.

The next few pages contain important information on how to:

- Select an outplacement service for help
- Work with an outplacement service for maximum results

How to Select an Outplacement Service

Finding the right outplacement firm for you can take time and careful research. This process should not be rushed, since different firms offer distinct levels of outplacement support at a variety of different costs.

Taking time to pick the right service will ensure that you are satisfied that you are getting the best service for the money spent, regardless as to who is paying the fee.

This careful selection process cannot and should not be ignored. To maximize your chances of obtaining a job with the aid of an outplacement firm means that you must work hard to qualify and then select a service that provides the most beneficial service package to support your job search efforts.

To assist you in this process we've outlined some important selection criteria below.

Selection Criteria:

The selection of the best outplacement firm to support your job search efforts should be based upon a combination of the following criteria:

Specialty Does the consultant specialize in working with personnel in your career field and industry?

If so, they will most likely be better prepared to understand your needs and will be the most helpful in providing you with useful information on how and where to find a new job. If they deal exclusively in your discipline, so much the better.

Experience How long has this outplacement firm been in the business? And how long have they been working with members of your profession?

It is best to select an outplacement firm that has at least three years experience specializing in your industry. Seasoned firms will have an established network of contacts with a number of hiring companies and should be a better source for assisting you to locate job openings.

Personality Does the outplacement consultant like you and do you like them? Do you "click"?

If yes, then you have a better shot at establishing and maintaining a good rapport with them on an ongoing basis. This is especially important for those times when you have a need to discuss potential job offers or personal family matters related to your career change or job search.

Proximity Is the firm convenient for you to visit on a regular basis?

This is important since many of the services provided by an outplacement firm are only provided on premise.

Quality Does this firm have a good reputation and do they present themselves in a professional manner?

The best way to determine this is to talk to other job seekers and to visit the outplacement firm's office to size them up. If you're unhappy with what you see or find, keep looking. If your employer is paying the fee then have a discussion with your Human Resources department about your observations and conclusions.

Cost How much does this service cost?

Evaluate the services received against your cost.

Referrals Was this firm referred to you by someone else?

Given that you have positive responses for the preceding qualifiers, a referral will give you a better feeling about their professional ability.

Background Does this consultant have the proper education and work experience to be of meaningful assistance to you?

If not, then keep looking. Remember, this is a service that someone, maybe you, is paying for, so don't settle on less than the best.

Questions to ask to qualify an outplacement service:

1. How long have they been in the business?

   The longer a firm has been in the business, the more contacts they are likely to have, therefore the odds of their being able to help you are better.

2. Number of job seekers in your field that they work with monthly?

   Firms handling a minimum of five people in your field per month are best suited to help you manage your career change.

3. How many job seekers are they working with?

   Avoid those firms that have more than 30 active job seekers per counselor, because you'll be easily forgotten.

4. How many client companies are they working with?

   Firms which average two or three companies per counselor are about the right size to support you in your job search. Those firms attempting to handle a larger number of hiring companies per counselor may be spreading their resources too thin.

5. What services do they provide and for how long?

   Outplacement firms differ widely in the type, quality, and amount of services which they provide to their clients.

   Many of them just offer their services to corporate sponsors.

   It is very important to find the firm that provides the best range of services for the least cost.

Working with an Outplacement Firm

To maximize your success of having an outplacement firm help you redirect your professional career or find a new job, you need to remember a few important axioms.

Outplacement firms normally get paid a package fee or a hourly rate for their services.

Therefore, do everything possible to make it easier for them to help you. This includes having a very good resume available for their use, being prepared and on time for your work sessions with them.

Good outplacement firms know their job, but they don't know you or how well you can perform on the job.

To do their job right, they will need your help in getting to know you. Be cooperative in completing assignments, furnishing information, and applying techniques learned.

In addition to supplying the typical day to day support, these services often offer training in various job search methodologies -- <u>apply what you learn</u>.

Recap:

If an outplacement firm doesn't have the experience in your field, it may not be the firm for you to use.

If the firm have too many job seekers that they are attempting to serve, then they may be not be the best firm for you to use.

Using a good qualified outplacement firm can be very beneficial to help initiate, organize, and execute a job search.

To find the best firm for your needs, do some comparison shopping and check references. Any reputable firm will gladly provide them for you.

An outplacement firm is a service designed to facilitate your job search efforts, but putting the effort into finding a job is still the job seeker's responsibility.

Office Manager
Aaron Resources Inc
P O Box 73029
Houston, TX 77273
(713) 583-7881
Specialty: G
Outplacement Consultants

Office Manager
Accountabilities Personnel Consultants
1980 Post Oak Blvd
Houston, TX 77056
(713) 961-5603
Specialty: G
Outplacement Consultants

Office Manager
Ackerman Johnson Inc
9311 San Pedro Ave
San Antonio, TX 78216
(512) 525-7955
Specialty: G
Outplacement Consultants

Mary Palusiak
Action Life Plans
602 West Seventh Street
Austin, TX 78701
(512) 469-0088
Specialty: Career And Vocational Counseling
Outplacement Consultant

Office Manager
AddTec
6101 Balcones Dr
Austin, TX 78731
(512) 452-9300
Specialty: G
Outplacement Consultants

Office Manager
Adminstaff
5450 Bee Caves Rd
Austin, TX 78746
(512) 328-9083
Specialty: G
Outplacement Consultants

Office Manager
Affirmative Action Programs Svcs
P O Box 33212
San Antonio, TX 78265
(512) 590-3639
Specialty: G
Outplacement Consultants

Office Manager
Alternative Resources Corp
1800 West Loop South
Houston, TX 77027
(713) 871-9900
Specialty: G
Outplacement Consultants

Office Manager
Anchor Personnel
P O Box 218710
Houston, TX 77218
(713) 496-4740
Specialty: G
Outplacement Consultants

Office Manager
Ashford Staffing Corp
1001 S Dairy Ashford St
Houston, TX 77077
(713) 558-9484
Specialty: G
Outplacement Consultants

Office Manager
Baker Resource Group Inc
4545 Post Oak Place Dr
Houston, TX 77027
(713) 622-9184
Specialty: G
Outplacement Consultants

Office Manager
Barrett International
5346 Windswept Ln
Houston, TX 77056
(713) 497-7670
Specialty: G
Outplacement Consultants

Office Manager
Belto & Associates
12651 Briar Forest Dr
Houston, TX 77077
(713) 497-7670
Specialty: G
Outplacement Consultants

J R Hickey, Reg VP
Bernard Haldane Associates
3030 NW Expressway St
Oklahoma City, OK 73112

(405) 948-7668
(405) 948-7869 FAX
Specialty: G

- **Private And Corporate Outplacement**
- **Job Search Guidance And Assistance**
- **48 Offices Nationwide & In Canada**
- **Founded 1947**

Outplacement Consultants

Office Manager
Blackhawk Services
10301 Northwest Frwy
Houston, TX 77092
(713) 681-5286
Specialty: G
Outplacement Consultants

Office Manager
Bronstein Reuben & Associates
9801 Westheimer Rd
Houston, TX 77042
(713) 785-3722
Specialty: G
Outplacement Consultants

Robert F Sarmiento PhD, Psychologist
Career Clinic
9525 Katy Frwy Ste 210
Houston, TX 77024-1414
(713) 465-2456
(713) 468-2868
Specialty: Career Testing
Career/Outplacement Counseling

Office Manager
Bullock Personnel Inc
1020 NE Loop 410
San Antonio, TX
(512) 828-7301
Specialty: G
Outplacement Consultants

Office Manager
Career Concepts of Oklahoma
5601 NW 72nd St
Oklahoma City, OK 73132
(405) 721-7542
Specialty: G
Outplacement Consultants

Office Manager
Business Mediation Services
4362 Fiesta Ln
Houston, TX 77004
(713) 748-2085
Specialty: G
Outplacement Consultants

Office Manager
Career Guidance Center
1240 Southridge Ct
Arlington, TX 76010
(817) 282-2620
Specialty: G
Outplacement Consultants

William Helton
Career Assessment
721 N Fielder Rd
Arlington, TX 76012
(817) 460-5831
Specialty: G
Outplacement Consultants

Office Manager
Career Management Services
4900 Richmond Squ Ste 201
Oklahoma City, OK 73118
(405) 840-5312
Specialty: G
Outplacement Consultants

Office Manager
Career Network Personnel
1235 North Loop West
Houston, TX 77055
(713) 868-3955
Specialty: G
Outplacement Consultants

Office Manager
Career Technical Centre
P O Box 166632
Irving, TX 75016
(214) 283-5418
Specialty: G
Outplacement Consultants

Office Manager
Catalyst Career Consultants
2520 Longview St
Austin, TX 78705
(512) 474-7773
Specialty: G
Outplacement Consultants

Office Manager
Challenger Gray & Christmas Inc
5001 LBJ Frwy
Dallas, TX 75244
(214) 786-1816
Specialty: G
Outplacement Consultants

Office Manager
Challenger Gray & Christmas Inc
201 Main St
Fort Worth, TX 76104
(817) 332-2880
Specialty: G
Outplacement Consultants

Office Manager
Challenger Gray & Christmas Inc
4801 Woodway Dr
Houston, TX 77056
(713) 820-3500
Specialty: G
Outplacement Consultants

Office Manager
Chase Personnel Services Inc
8401 Westheimer Rd
Houston, TX 77063
(713) 785-4448
Specialty: G
Outplacement Consultants

Office Manager
Connally & Associates
P O Box 361
LaPorte, TX 77572
(713) 478-5014
Specialty: G
Outplacement Consultants

Office Manager
Craft Personnel Consultants
5225 Katy Frwy
Houston, TX 77007
(713) 862-6100
Specialty: G
Outplacement Consultants

Office Manager
Diversified Employment Svcs
13750 San Pedro Ave
San Antonio, TX 78232
(512) 490-3377
Specialty: G
Outplacement Consultants

Office Manager
Drake Beam Morin Inc
1221 McKinney
Houston, TX 77010
(713) 739-7000
Specialty: G
Outplacement Consultants

Office Manager
Eckardt Jeanne Personnel Svcs
10575 Katy Frwy
Houston, TX 77024
(713) 935-9500
Specialty: G
Outplacement Consultants

Office Manager
Elaine Best & Assoicates Inc
4151 Southwest Frwy
Houston, TX 77027
(713) 623-6466
Specialty: G
Outplacement Consultants

Office Manager
Energy Search Recruiters
7324 Southwest Frwy
Houston, TX 77074
(713) 777-1128
Specialty: G
Outplacement Consultants

Office Manager
Engineering & Environmental Personnel Inc
7018 Neff St
Houston, TX 77074
(713) 772-7957
Specialty: G
Outplacement Consultants

Office Manager
Farrington & Associates
8580 Katy Frwy
Houston, TX 77024
(713) 932-6077
Specialty: G
Outplacement Consultants

Office Manager
Farris James Associates
4900 Richmond Squ Ste 201
Oklahoma City, OK 73118
(405) 848-0535
Specialty: G
Outplacement Consultants

Norbert Vallee, Exec Dir
Forty Plus of Dallas Inc
13601 Preston Road Ste 301
Dallas, TX 75240
(412) 991-9917
Specialty: Employment Assessment,Peer Support, Resume, Networking & Interview Skills
Outplacement Non Profit Support Group

Office Manager
Future's Unlimited
6070 Gateway Blvd East
El Paso, TX 79905
(915) 772-9242
Specialty: G
Outplacement Consultants

Office Manager
Global Career Network
6706 Stonewater St
Houston, TX 77084
(713) 859-8655
Specialty: G
Outplacement Consultants

Office Manager
Houston Creative Connections Inc
701 N Post Oak Rd
Houston, TX 77024
(713) 957-2393
Specialty: G
Outplacement Consultants

Laura J Ayoub, Pres
Human Element
416 N Stanton Ste 303
El Paso, TX 79901
(915) 544-5698
(915) 534-7738 FAX
Specialty: Personnel Management
Outplacement Consultants

Office Manager
IBS Financial Services Inc
1800 West Loop South
Houston, TX 77027
(713) 623-4427
Specialty: G
Outplacement Consultants

Office Manager
In-Bond Central Inc
4150 Rio Bravo St
El Paso, TX 79902
(915) 533-9191
Specialty: G
Outplacement Consultants

Office Manager
Industrial Labor Services
1714 Collingsworth St
Houston, TX 77009
(713) 224-0202
Specialty: G
Outplacement Consultants

Office Manager
Jones Cary M
5433 Westheimer Rd
Houston, TX 77056
(713) 629-4984
Specialty: G
Outplacement Consultants

Joy Reedbelt PhD, Pres
Joy Reedbelt Assoc Inc
5804 N Grand
Oklahoma City, OK 73118
(405) 842-6336
(405) 842-6357 FAX
Specialty: G
Outplacement Consultants

Office Manager
Katz & Associats
4105 Westbank Dr
Austin, TX 78746
(512) 328-0183
Specialty: G
Outplacement Consultants

Office Manager
Kieffer Kaye
504 W 17th St
Austin, TX 78701
(512) 495-9044
Specialty: G
Outplacement Consultants

Office Manager
Lee Wells Personnel Consultants Inc
3220 Louisiana St
Houston, TX 77006
(713) 627-1000
Specialty: G
Outplacement Consultants

Office Manager
Lewis Coy Incorporated
800 Bering Dr
Houston, TX 77057
(713) 974-1123
Specialty: G
Outplacement Consultants

Office Manager
LPC Personnel
7887 Katy Frwy
Houston, TX 77024
(713) 680-9898
Specialty: G
Outplacement Consultants

Office Manager
Marian Group Inc The
510 Bering Dr
Houston, TX 77057
(713) 975-1410
Specialty: G
Outplacement Consultants

Office Manager
Martin David H & Associates
P O Box 5581
Austin, TX 78763
(512) 477-4771
Specialty: G
Outplacement Consultants

Office Manager
Medex Management Services
4801 Woodway Dr
Houston, TX 77056
(713) 623-4445
Specialty: G
Outplacement Consultants

Office Manager
Milam Design Services Inc
7748 W Hwy 290
Austin, TX 78736
(512) 288-7747
Specialty: G
Outplacement Consultants

Office Manager
Military Recruiting Institute
9888 Bissonnet St
Houston, TX 77036
(713) 995-6987
Specialty: G
Outplacement Consultants

Office Manager
Mims Legal Search Consultants
2000 Bering Dr
Houston, TX 77057
(713) 787-1027
Specialty: G
Outplacement Consultants

Office Manager
National Search Inc
15219 Beacham Dr
Houston, TX 77070
(713) 251-3100
Specialty: G
Outplacement Consultants

Office Manager
Nelson Haper & Associates
2400 E Arizona Biltmore Cir
Ste 2250
Phoenix, AZ 85016
(602) 381-0011
Specialty: G
Outplacement Consultants

Office Manager
Nelson Harper & Associates
4760 N Oracle Rd
Tucson, AZ 85705
(602) 293-1292
Specialty: G
Outplacement Consultants

Office Manager
Nelson Len & Associates Inc
5440 Babock Rd
San Antonio, TX 78240
(512) 690-9191
Specialty: G
Outplacement Consultants

Office Manager
NSC Companies Inc
2630 Fountain View Dr
Houston, TX 77057
(713) 952-2500
Specialty: G
Outplacement Consultants

Office Manager
Oaks Personnel Services Inc
5847 San Felipe
Houston, TX 77057
(713) 782-1010
Specialty: G
Outplacement Consultants

Office Manager
Outpath Sensitive Outplacement Counseling
611 Ryan Plaza Drive
Arlington, TX 76011
(817) 277-9919
Specialty: Biofeedback Training, Career Assessment
Outplacement Consultants

Office Manager
Patterson Connie
1616 West Loop South
Houston, TX 77027
(713) 621-7770
Specialty: G
Outplacement Consultants

Office Manager
Personnel Resources
1700 West Loop South
Houston, TX 77027
(713) 623-2206
Specialty: G
Outplacement Consultants

Office Manager
Prejean John F
2200 S Post Oak Rd
Houston, TX 77056
(713) 840-0703
Specialty: G
Outplacement Consultants

Office Manager
Pritchard & Associates Inc
908 Town & Country Blvd
Houston, TX 77024
(713) 467-8844
Specialty: G
Outplacement Consultants

Office Manager
Pro Resource Group
10575 Katy Frwy
Houston, TX 77024
(713) 827-0999
Specialty: G
Outplacement Consultants

Office Manager
Pro Vocational Testing Ctr
5704 N Rockwell Dr
Oklahoma City, OK 73132
(405) 848-6007
Specialty: G
Outplacement Consultants

Office Manager
Professional Contract Finanacial Services Inc
11757 Katy Frwy
Houston, TX 77079
(713) 558-1150
Specialty: G
Outplacement Consultants

John M Ledterman, Principal
Professional Team Search
4050 E Greenway Rd Ste 4
Phoenix, AZ 85032
(602) 482-1551
(602) 788-0710 FAX
Specialty: C,F,M,P,S
Individual/Corporate Outplacement

Office Manager
Quest Personnel Resources Inc
50 Briar Hollow Ln
Houston, TX 77027
(713) 961-0605
Specialty: G
Outplacement Consultants

Office Manager
Recruit Ad Group
1100 NW Loop 410
San Antonio, TX 78213
(512) 525-8146
Specialty: G
Outplacement Consultants

Office Manager
Recruiters Inc
15425 North Frwy
Houston, TX 77090
(713) 872-9200
Specialty: G
Outplacement Consultants

Office Manager
Renaldo Patti
11607 Elmcroft
Houston, TX 77099
(713) 498-6661
Specialty: G
Outplacement Consultants

Office Manager
Right Associates
6987 N Oracle Rd
Tucson, AZ 85726
(602) 575-5264
Specialty: G
Outplacement Consultants

Office Manager
Rosie Walts Personnel Svc Inc
10850 Richmond Ave
Houston, TX 77042
(713) 784-0882
Specialty: G
Outplacement Consultants

Office Manager
Russek Dee Personnel
12337 Jones Rd
Houston, TX 77070
(713) 890-4500
Specialty: G
Outplacement Consultants

Office Manager
Salem Technical Services
8140 N Mo-Pac Expwy
Building 3 Ste 130
Austin, TX 78759
(512) 346-0600
Specialty: G
Outplacement Consultants

Sally White
Sally White & Associates Inc
2201 N Collins St
Arlington, TX 76011
(817) 274-5027
Specialty: G
Outplacement Consultants

Office Manager
Sandri-Roberts & Associates
10575 Katy Frwy
Houston, TX 77024
(713) 935-9300
Specialty: G
Outplacement Consultants

Office Manager
Scientific Placement
Inc Employment
800 Tully Rd
Houston, TX 77079
(713) 496-6100
Specialty: G
Outplacement Consultants

Office Manager
Stanford Paula
4027 N Classen Blvd
Oklahoma City, OK 73118
(405) 524-0575
Specialty: G
Outplacement Consultants

Office Manager
Team Security
9513 Carnegie Ave
El Paso, TX 79925
(915) 592-7555
Specialty: G
Outplacement Consultants

Office Manager
Teamsource
2305 Donley Dr
Donley, TX 78758
(512) 834-0585
Specialty: G
Outplacement Consultants

Office Manager
Texas Technical Search
7324 Southwest Frwy
Houston, TX 77074
(713) 777-2204
Specialty: G
Outplacement Consultants

Office Manager
Trace Consultants Inc
9888 Bissonnet St
Houston, TX 77036
(713) 995-6303
Specialty: G
Outplacement Consultants

Office Manager
Truitt John F
12800 Briar Forest Dr
Houston, TX 77077
(713) 497-7844
Specialty: G
Outplacement Consultants

Office Manager
UltraStaff
3730 Kirby Dr
Houston, TX 77098
(713) 522-7100
Specialty: G
Outplacement Consultants

Office Manager
Vista Consulting Group
7007 Gulf Frwy
Houston, TX 77087
(713) 645-5488
Specialty: G
Outplacement Consultants

Office Manager
Vista Vocational Resources
4803 Fredericksburg
San Antonio, TX 78229
(512) 340-8157
Specialty: G
Outplacement Consultants

Office Manager
Walker N Darlene Inc
10777 Northwest Frwy
Houston, TX 77092
(713) 688-0703
Specialty: G
Outplacement Consultants

Nancy Welborne
Welborne Nancy MED
1414 W Randol Mill Rd
Arlington, TX 76012
(817) 274-0093
Specialty: G
Outplacement Consultants

David W Farmer, Consultant
Whitney Smith Co
500 Throckmorton Ste 3002
Fort Worth, TX 76102
(817) 877-4120
(817) 877-3846 FAX
Specialty: B,C,F,M,P,Real Estate
Outplacement, Corporate or
Individual Outplacement

Office Manager
Wolff R L & Associates
2400 Augusta Dr
Houston, TX 77057
(713) 266-9921
Specialty: G
Outplacement Consultants

DALLAS & THE SOUTH WEST JOB SEEKERS SOURCEBOOK

Section 9

Resume Preparation Services

Resume preparation firms help an individual prepare a professional looking resume for making the best impression on hiring companies. As such, these firms vary in the services that they offer.

Some provide just simple typing and copying support. Others offer resume preparation using a laser printer that offers a variety of type fonts to create a better appearance.

Still others have developed a carefully thought out approach to the preparation of a structured resume. These types of services use professional writers to enhance the presentation of an individual's job history. These firms also charge more, but they put much more effort into the creation and printing of a document that will gain attention to help you obtain a job sooner.

Spending a little time to comparison shop and review samples of their work will pay off in the long haul. Your resume is your first, and sometimes the only, opportunity to make an impression. The right firm will get the job done for you, but your input is critical to the successful creation of this product.

The next few pages contain important information which will assist you in understanding how to:

- Select a resume preparation firm to help you
- Work with a resume preparation firm

How to Select a Resume Preparation Service

Finding the correct resume preparation service is a fairly easy task, given that you spend a little time on advance research. This process should not be bypassed, since having a professional looking resume is the most important first step of any job search.

To maximize your chances of selecting the best resume preparation service to meet your needs, you must first determine what are your needs and then qualify a service according to THESE needs. To assist you in this process we've outlined some useful selection criteria.

Selection Criteria:

The selection of the right resume preparation service to use to prepare a professional looking resume should be based upon a combination of the following criteria:

Experience How long has the resume preparation service been in the business?

It is best to select a service that has at least three years experience specializing in preparing resumes. These people will already have established a good reputation and will most likely know how to assist you in creating that best first impression on paper.

Proximity Is the service convenient for you to visit several times?

This is important when attempting to meet to proof your resume and when it is necessary to obtain additional copies of your resume.

Personality Do you "click" with the resume preparer?

If, yes, then you have a better shot at establishing and maintaining a good rapport with them and in obtaining the best prepared resume.

Referrals Was this firm referred to you by someone else?

Given that you have positive responses for the preceding qualifiers, a referral will give you a better feeling about their professional ability.

Quality Does this agency have a good reputation and do they present themselves in a professional manner?

The best way to determine this is to talk to other job seekers and to visit the resume preparer's office to size them up. If you're unhappy with what you see or find, keep looking.

Services What services are provided by the resume preparer?

Some firms just do typing and formatting, others provide full service support which includes a detailed evaluation of your work history. The latter of these firms tend to provide a better service for those people inexperienced in putting together a good resume.

Networks Is this consultant a member of a professional affiliation?

If yes, then the chances are that they must meet some level of professional standards for their industry. This in turn usually means that they are experienced and qualified enough to be able to do a good job on your resume.

Cost What is the total cost of the service?

It is important to understand what your cost is in relationship to the services being provided. Full service firms that spend time to analyze your job history and work with you one-on-one should cost more that just a typing service.

Questions you should ask to qualify a resume preparation firm:

1. How long have they been in the business?

   The longer a firm has been in the business, the more experience that they are likely to have, therefore the odds of their being able to help you are better.

2. How many job seekers from your field have they worked with?

   Firms handling a large number of people in your field will best understand some of the buzz words in the industry and be less prone to make mistakes when preparing your resume.

3. How much does this service cost? And how long will it take?

   Look for the hidden costs such as costs for extra copies of resumes. Find out if there is a charge for rush orders or delivery.

4. Are they able to offer you a variety of type fonts and sizes to customize your resume?

   The better services will have this capability.

5. What is the background of the staff you will be working with?

   Finding a service which has experience in career consulting and professional writing would be the best choice to serve your needs if you need more than just typing.

Working with a Resume Preparation Firm

To succeed in having a resume preparation firm do a good job for you when preparing your resume, you need to remember a few important points.

Resume preparation firms normally get paid a package fee for their services.

Therefore, do everything possible to help make their job easier. This includes having a good write up of your job history available for their use, being prepared and on time for your work sessions with them.

Good resume preparation firms know their job, but they don't know anything about you or your work background.

To provide you with the best possible service they need your help in documenting your work history. Remember, you know your work experience better than anyone, so tell them what you are good at.

Identify and describe in detail the important features of previous accomplishments. Furnish specific information for measuring performance, such as a list of recognition awards or reference letters.

The final product is your responsibility.

Therefore, proof and reproof each version of the resume until you are completely satisfied. Check font types, margin spacing, and the alignment of similar entries.

K.I.S.S. (Keep it simple stupid)

Avoid having your resume appear too cluttered, be specific, and if needed allow your resume to go to two pages (but never three).

If a resume preparation firm hasn't been in business very long, it may not be the firm for you to use.

Finally, review any contract carefully before signing. It should be clear as to what services you will be provided for the fee that you are paying.

Office Manager
A A A Express Printing
4503 Menaul Blvd N E
Albuquerque, NM 87110
(505) 888-3500
Specialty: G
Resume Service

Brooke Andrews, Writer/Editor
A New Beginning: Business Communications & Resumes
777 W Southern Avenue Ste 103
Mesa, AZ 85210
(602) 844-2300
(602) 844-2302 (Fax Call First)
Specialty: Interview, Write,Laser print
Resume Service

Office Manager
A Professional Resume Place
1106 N Hwy 360
Irving, TX 76011
(214) 647-8568
Specialty: G
Resume Service

Office Manager
A To Z Resume & Writing Service
9414 E San Salvadore Dr
Scottsdale, AZ 85258
(602) 451-8846
Specialty: G
Resume Service

Office Manager
A Typing Joy
5747 W Missouri Ave
Glendale, AZ 85301
(602) 931-3307
Specialty: G
Resume Service

Office Manager
Absolutely Write
3100 Jan Pl N E Ste F-205
Albuquerque, NM 87111
(505) 271-2500
Specialty: G
Resume Service

Office Manager
Accent On You!
4635 S Lakeshore Dr Ste #136
Tempe, AZ 85282
(602) 345-4576
Specialty: G
Resume Service

Office Manager
Accent On Your Resume Writing
1826 W Broadway Rd #43
Mesa, AZ 85041
(602) 898-7637
Specialty: G
Resume Service

Office Manager
Accent Resumes
1414 W Randol Mill Rd Ste 100
Arlington, TX 76012
(817) 274-0093
Specialty: G
Resume Service

Office Manager
Action Resume Business Svc
3120 W Britton Rd
Oklahoma City, OK 73120
(405) 755-0440
Specialty: G
Resume Service

Ercument Cetiner, Data Coordinator
Alamo Resume & Personnel
1616 San Pedro Avenue Ste 2
San Antonio, TX 78212
(210) 735-JOBS
(210) 735-2216 FAX
Specialty: G
Resume Service

Office Manager
Alphagraphic Printshops of The Future
2160 N Alma School Rd
Chandler, AZ 85224
(602) 821-0985
Specialty: G
Resume Service

Office Manager
Alphagraphics Printshops of the Future
1750 Alma Rd
Richardson, TX 75081
(214) 234-3033
Specialty: G
Resume Service

Office Manager
Alphagraphics Printshops of The Future
5104 W Northern Av
Glendale, AZ 85301
(602) 842-0088
Specialty: G
Resume Service

Office Manager
Amelia's Resume & Business Svc
7527 Silver Cloud
Houston, TX 77086
(713) 440-9265
Specialty: G
Resume Service

Office Manager
American Career Group
3333 E Camelback Rd Ste 250
Phoenix, AZ 85018
(602) 381-1667
Specialty: G
Resume Service

Office Manager
American Resume Service
2610 W Beauty Home Rd
Phoenix, AZ 85017
(602) 242-2141
Specialty: G
Resume Service

Office Manager
Ande & Associates
84 NE Loop 410
San Antonio, TX 78216
(512) 366-2556
Specialty: G
Resume Service

Office Manager
Arizona Desktop Publishing
P O Box 6426
Yuma, AZ 85366
(602) 782-6267
Specialty: G
Resume Service

Office Manager
Arizona Resume Experts
10640 N 28th Dr Ste C-205
Phoenix, AZ 85029
(602) 866-7454
Specialty: G
Resume Service

Babbie Migl, Mgr
ASAP Secretarial Services
9200 Broadway Ste 125-C
San Antonio, TX 78217-5916
(210) 822-4118
(210) 829-0226 FAX
Specialty: Laser Resumes,Letters
Resume Service

Office Manager
Austin's Finest Resume & Writing Service
2900 S IH 35
Austin, TX 78704
(512) 445-4777
Specialty: G
Resume Service

Office Manager
B G Enterprises
530 Dallas St NE
Albuquerque, NM 87108
(505) 265-6624
Specialty: G
Resume Service

Ben Benton, Owner
Ben Benton & Company
124 N San Francisco St Ste 100
Flagstaff, AZ 86001
(602) 779-5300
Specialty: Resumes & Cover Letters
Resume Service

Office Manager
Best Rates Resumes USA
5800 N 19th Ave Ste 215
Phoenix, AZ 85015
(602) 242-0222
Specialty: G
Resume Service

Office Manager
Best Resume Service
3010 S Harvard Ave
Tulsa, OK 74114
(918) 745-0598
Specialty: G
Resume Service

Office Manager
Bly & Associates Inc
4528 S Sheridan Rd
Tulsa, OK 74145
(918) 664-6411
Specialty: G
Resume Service

Office Manager
Bottom Line The
2786 Hwy 47
Los Lunas NM 87031
(505) 864-2165
Specialty: G
Resume Service

Office Manager
Career Directions Center
4550 NW Loop 410
San Antonio, TX 78229
(512) 735-7443
Specialty: G
Resume Service

Office Manager
Career Focus Associates
1700 Coit Rd
Plano, TX 75075
(214) 596-1233
Specialty: G
Resume Service

Office Manager
Career Management Services
4900 Richmond Squ Ste 201
Oklahoma City, OK 73118
(405) 840-5312
Specialty: G
Resume Service

Pamela Lampert, Owner
Career Pro Resume Centers
2310 W Bell Rd Ste 8
Phoenix, AZ 85023
(602) 863-1166
(602) 863-6985 FAX
Specialty: Career Counseling, Interview Training
Resume Service

Daivd M Dorrell, Career Cord
Career Resources Inc
5804 N Grand
Oklahoma City, OK 73118
(405) 842-5155
(405) 842-6357 FAX
Specialty: G
Resume Service

Sandra McDonald, Proprietor
CareerPro Resume Services
177 E Ft Lowell Rd
Tucson, AZ 85705
(602) 293-9284
(602) 293-2825 FAX
Specialty: Technical,Grant & Resume Writing
Resume Service

Terri N Powers, Owner
Complete Commercial Writing Service
355 Nara Visa NW Ste C
Albuquerque, NM 87107
(505) 344-6371
(505) 344-2502 FAX
Specialty: Professional Writer (Columnist) Unique Resumes
Resume Preparation

Office Manager
Confidentially Yours
7701 N Lamar Blvd
Austin, TX 78752
(512) 451-5089
Specialty: G
Resume Service

Jack Esposito, Mgr
Copy Center
9040 N 19th Ave
Phoenix, AZ 85021
(602) 870-3006
(602) 943-9172 FAX
Specialty: Resume Preparation, Laser Print/IBM MAC Copies
Resume Service

Office Manager
Creative Image Resume Inc
2233 W Lindsey
Norman, OK 73069
(405) 364-8434
Specialty: G
Resume Service

Office Manager
Diana's Secretarial Service
5862 Cromo Dr
El Paso, TX 79912
(915) 584-5686
Specialty: G
Resume Service

Office Manager
Express Resume
1709 Moon St N E
Albuquerque, NM 87112
(505) 293-5008
Specialty: G
Resume Service

Office Manager
J & S Secretarial Services
P O Box 6307
Taos, NM 87571
(505) 758-8488
Specialty: G
Resume Service

Jeanne W Johnson, Owner
Jeanne's Office Service
6300 Ridglea Pl
Fort Worth, TX 76116
(817) 735-1727
Specialty: G
Resume Preparation

Bro Chuck Bell, Pres
Job $ource
1030 N Francis Ave
Oklahoma City, OK 73106
(405) 235-8900
Specialty: Resume Preparation & Job Search Assistance
Skills Marketing Firm

Office Manager
Job Support Center
2745 E Skelly Dr
Tulsa, OK 74105
(918) 742-8700
Specialty: G
Resume Service

Office Manager
K & K Professional Greetings Inc
P O Box 15068
Rio Rancho, NM 87174
(505) 891-4044
Specialty: G
Resume Service

Office Manager
Kinko's Copies
13637 N Tatum
Paradise Valley, AZ 85253
(602) 494-4399
Specialty: G
Resume Service

Office Manager
Legal Type Documents
85th Ave & Grand
Peoria, AZ 85345
(602) 878-6755
Specialty: G
Resume Service

Dean Clark, Pres
Legend CompuType Services
9894 Bissonnet Ste 860
Houston, TX 77036-8229
(713) 776-1000
(713) 776-1058 FAX
Specialty: G
Resume Preparation Service

Linda Charles, Owner
Linda's Typing Service
1521 N Beaver St Ste D
Flagstaff, AZ 86001
(602) 779-1004
(602) 773-4831 FAX
Specialty: Laser,Fax,Copy Service
Resume Service

Office Manager
Martha Ann Zivley Typing Service
2707 Hemphill Park
Austin, TX 78705
(512) 472-3210
Specialty: Resume Prepartion
Resume Service

Office Manager
MBA Resume Services
1000 Bay Area Blvd Ste 201
Houston, TX 77058
(713) 280-5100
Specialty: G
Resume Service

D H Fries, Manager
MBA Services
10700 Richmond Avenue Ste 100
Houston, TX 77042
(713) 783-9494
(713) 953-9870 FAX
Specialty: Creative Writing & Editing

- **Published Proffesional Writers**
- **Full Satisfaction Gurantee**
- **Documented Client Results**
- **All Levels & All Industries**

Resume Preparation Service

Office Manager
Miracle Resumes
6732 S Utica Ave
Tulsa, OK 74136
(918) 494-4941
Specialty: G
Resume Service

Office Manager
National Resume Service Inc
5100 N Brookline
Oklahoma City, OK 73112
(405) 943-0465
Specialty: G
Resume Service

Kyle Key, Mgr
Polaris Print & Copy
3006 Medical Arts St
Austin, TX 78705
(512) 476-6505
(512) 476-6506 FAX
Specialty: High Resolution
Laser Printer
Resume Service

Vera E Harris CPC, Owner
Pro-Med Resume Service
2201 N Collins Ste 260
Arlington, TX 76011
(817) 265-7965
(817) 543-3155 FAX
Specialty: G
Resume Preparation Service

Office Manager
Professional Resume & Writing Service
1550 E University Dr
Mesa, AZ 85203
(602) 890-2502
Specialty: G
Resume Service

Office Manager
Professional Resume & Writing Services
1301 Northwest Hwy
Garland, TX 75041
(214) 840-2369
Specialty: G
Resume Service

Office Manager
Professional Resume Center
4513 N 12th St
Phoenix, AZ 85014
(602) 265-0678
Specialty: G
Resume Service

Office Manager
Professional Resume Service
9430 Research Blvd
Austin, TX 78759
(512) 346-9114
Specialty: G
Resume Service

Office Manager
Professional Resume Service
6130 Montana Ave
El Paso, TX 79925
(915) 772-8247
Specialty: G
Resume Service

Francel Goff, Owner
Professional Resume Service
620-A East Main Street
Farmington, NM 87401
(505) 327-9992
Specialty: Writing,Formating,
Laser Printing
Resume Service

Office Manager
Professional Resumes
1901 Central Dr
Bedford, TX 76021
(214) 267-0633
Specialty: G
Resume Service

C M LaMotte, Pres
Professional Services-PES Inc
2533 Virginia N E Ste E&F
Albuquerque, NM 87110-4660
(505) 298-6006
(505) 291-5410 FAX
Specialty: Interview Training
Resume Preparation

John M Ledterman, Principal
Professional Team Search
4050 E Greenway Rd Ste 4
Phoenix, AZ 85032
(602) 482-1551
(602) 788-0710 FAX
Specialty: C,F,M,P,S
Resume Preparation Service

Office Manager
Resume Place The
2121 E 51st St
Tulsa, OK 74105
(918) 749-9400
Specialty: G
Resume Service

Office Manager
Resume Plus
8123 L B J Frwy
Dallas, TX 75251
(214) 871-9663
Specialty: G
Resume Service

Office Manager
Resume Pros
4347 S Hampton Rd
Dallas, TX 75232
(214) 339-2000
Specialty: G
Resume Service

Office Manager
Resume Service of San Antonio
4423 NW Loop 410
San Antonio, TX 78229
(512) 340-6981
Specialty: G
Resume Service

Office Manager
Resume Specialists of Arlington
1408 E Mitchell St
Arlington, TX 76010
(817) 483-6100
Specialty: G
Resume Service

Office Manager
Resume Writer's Ink
5601 NW 72nd St
Oklahoma City, OK 73132
(405) 721-7542
Specialty: G
Resume Service

Office Manager
Resume X-Press
8000 IH 10 West
San Antonio, TX 78230
(512) 344-1996
Specialty: G
Resume Service

Office Manager
Resumes Etc
13841 N 19th Ave
Phoenix, AZ 85029
(602) 863-6535
Specialty: G
Resume Service

Office Manager
Resumes Plus
4162 S Cooper St
Arlington, TX 76015
(817) 465-1165
Specialty: G
Resume Service

Office Manager
Resumes Plus
3201 Airport Frwy
Bedford, TX 76111
(817) 283-2849
Specialty: G
Resume Service

Robert McGahee, Mgr
Resumes That Win
6116 N Central Expwy Ste 508
Dallas, TX 75206
(214) 692-1122
(214) 692-5185 FAX
Specialty: Full Service Resume Preparation/Degreed Staff
Resume Service

Darrell C Rasmussen, Sr Writer
Resumes That Win
845 E Arapaho Rd Ste 107
Richardson, TX 75081
(214) 234-2274
(214) 238-0275 FAX
Specialty: G
Resume Service

Julie Roache
SCSA
3420 E Shea Blvd
Phoenix, AZ 85028
(602) 996-0613
(602) 996-0614 FAX
Specialty: Laser Printing
Resume Service

Office Manager
Secretary The
102 W Apache St
Farmington, NM 87401
(505) 327-9646
Specialty: G
Resume Service

Office Manager
South Texas Type
2202 S 77 Sunshine Strip
Harlingen, TX 78550
(210) 421-2905
Specialty: G
Resume Service

Sunny Butler, Owner
Sunny's Secretarial Service
5862 Cromo Drive Ste 150
El Paso, TX 79912-5510
(915) 584-3799
(915) 584-2566 FAX
Specialty: G
Resume Service

Neil Turk, Owner
Superior Systems & Secretarial Services
7007 Gulf Frwy Ste 133
Houston, TX 77087
(713) 645-9609
(713) 645-6076
Specialty: Preparation,Laser Printing,Personal Consultation
Resume Service

Kendra Bounds, Admin Mgr
Teamsource
2320 Donley Drive Ste A
Austin, TX 78758
(512) 834-0585
(512) 834-9693 FAX
Specialty: M
Resume Preparation Service

David W Farmer, Consultant
Whitney Smith Co
500 Throckmorton Ste 3002
Fort Worth, TX 76102
(817) 877-4120
(817) 877-3846 FAX
Specialty: B,C,F,M,P,Real Estate
Resume Preparation Service

Office Manager
Word Crafter The
109 Brooks St Box 6307
Taos, NM 87571
(505) 758-4164
Specialty: G
Resume Service

Office Manager
Word Power
608 Wonway St
Las Cruces, NM 88005
(505) 522-8665
Specialty: G
Resume Service

NET-RESEARCH PLACEMENT FIRM CONTACT FORM

Firm Name: ______________________________

Address: ______________________________

City: ______________________________

State: __________ Zip: __________

Phone: (______) ______________________

FAX: (______) ______________________

Recruiter: ______________________________

Specialty: ______________________________

CONTACT LOG

	DATE	COMMENTS
1		
2		
3		
4		
5		

INTERVIEWS ARRANGED

DATE	TIME	COMPANY	CONTACT

Feel Free to copy this form

NET-RESEARCH HIRING COMPANY CONTACT FORM

Firm Name: ______________________________

Address: ______________________________

City: ______________________________

State: __________ Zip: __________

Phone: (______) ______________________

FAX: (______) ______________________

Position: ______________________________

Salary: ______________________________

BENEFITS SUMMARY

BENEFIT	Y/N	COMMENTS
Medical		
Dental		
Vacation		
Insurance		
Parking		
Business Car		
Other		

INTERVIEWS ARRANGED

DATE	TIME	CONTACT	COMMENTS

Feel Free to copy this form

READER FEEDBACK FORM

We would like to make the next edition of the "*Dallas & The South West Job Seekers SourceBook*" even better than this one. You, our readers and the users of this source book can help use with your comments and suggestions. Here is your opportunity to tell us what we're doing right and what we're doing wrong. So, please take a minute of your time and complete this form to:

- Tell us how we can make our next edition of the "*Dallas & The South West Job Seekers SourceBook*" more helpful;
- Tell us about any changes we should make to any entries; and
- Let us know of any useful job sources that we have overlooked.

If you run out of space, just attach another sheet. Please send your comments to: Net-Research, 160 S. Bolingbrook Rd, Suite 114, Bolingbrook, Illinois 60440. We must hear from you by **December 31, 1993** to include your suggestions in our next edition.

Thanks for your help to make our source books better.

Donald D. Walker

Comments and Suggestions:

____

____

____

(More room available on the reverse side)

Comments & Suggestions (Continued)

Purely Optional: Please include you name, address, and evening phone number in case we need to reach you for more information.

NET-RESEARCH SOURCEBOOK ORDER FORM

To obtain additional copies of this or other Net-Research Job Seekers SourceBooks, complete and return this order form. Your order will be shipped within 10 days or when published).

ORDER FORM BK-2: (* = Available Summer 1993)

		Job Seekers SourceBook	Price	x Copies =	Total
___		Chicago & Illinois	$ 13.95	_____	$ ______
___		Boston & New England	$ 13.95	_____	$ ______
___		LA & Southern Calif.	$ 14.95	_____	$ ______
___		Pacific Northwest	$ 14.95	_____	$ ______
___		Dallas & The SouthWest	$ 14.95	_____	$ ______
___	*	Southern States	$ 13.95	_____	$ ______
___		Ohio Valley	$ 14.95	_____	$ ______
___	*	Mid-Atlantic	$ 14.95	_____	$ ______
___		Southern Atlantic Coast	$ 14.95	_____	$ ______
___	*	Plaines States	$ 13.95	_____	$ ______
___	*	Mountain States	$ 13.95	_____	$ ______
___	*	New York/New Jersey	$ 14.95	_____	$ ______
___		Northern Great Lakes	$ 14.95	_____	$ ______
___		**Entire set of Source Books**	**$162.50**	_____	$ ______

Shipping and Handling (1st Copy) $ 3.00
Additional Copies = Number of copies X $1.00 = ______

Total Bill: **$** ______

Payment Method Preferred: ___ Check Enclosed ___ VISA/MC

Card Number: ______________________________

Expiration Date: ___________________________

Signature Required: _________________________

Send Order To: (Please Print Clearly)

Name: ______________________________________

Address: ____________________________________

City: ______________________ St. _____ Zip: ________

Return this form to:
Net-Research, 16731 East Iliff #B 183, Aurora, Colorado 80013

NET-RESEARCH CONTACT SERVICE ORDER FORM

To assist our readers to quickly contact employment a   and executive recruiters that serve particular specialties, Net-Research provides the followin service: Resume and cover letter typin 1st Class mail of these materials to selective firms by specialty and   area. 20 copies of the resume, a copy of the cover letter, and a list of all a   or recruiters contacted is returned to purchaser via 2-day mail. To take advanta   of this offer, complete and return this order form. Your order will be shipped within 10 days.

ORDER FORM CS-2: (* = Available Summer 1993)

__Job Seekers SourceBook Regions__

___ Chicago & Illinois
___ Boston & New England
___ LA & Southern Calif.
___ Pacific Northwest
___ Dallas & The SouthWest
___ * Southern States
___ Ohio Valley
___ * Mid-Atlantic
___ Southern Atlantic Coast
___ * Plaines States
___ * Mountain States
___ * New York/New Jersey
___ Northern Great Lakes

__Type Firm to Contact__

____ Employment Agency
____ Executive Search Firm
____ Both

__Specific Specialties__

____
____

__Color of Bond Paper__

_____ Light Blue
_____ Ivory
_____ Light Gray

Base price (twenty firms contacted) $ 49.90
(Includes all shipping and handling, plus 20 copies of the resume returned to purchaser)
Additional firms contacted ($1.50 each) X ____ = ______

Total Bill: **$** ______

__Payment Method Preferred:__ ___ Check Enclosed ___ VISA/MC

Card Number: ______________________________

Expiration Date: ______________________________

Signature Required: ______________________________

Send Order To: (Please Print Clearly) (Enclose readable resume and cover letter text) Cover letter limited to one page, resume to two)

Name: ______________________________

Address: ______________________________

City: ______________________ St. ______ Zip: ________

Return form to: Net-Research, 16371 East Iliff #B 183, Aurora, Colorado 80013

NET-RESEARCH DATABASE ORDER FORM

The entries contained within each Source Book can also be obtained on a diskette, which comes with **free** software that allows the user access by: specialty, type firm, zip codes, or telephone area codes. To obtain database copies of this or other Net-Research Source Books, complete and return this order form. Your order will be shipped within 10 days.

ORDER FORM DB-2: (* = Available Summer 1993)

		Job Seekers SourceBook	Price x	Copies =	Total
___		Chicago & Illinois	$ 24.95	_____	$ ______
___		Boston & New England	$ 24.95	_____	$ ______
___		LA & Southern Calif.	$ 24.95	_____	$ ______
___		Pacific Northwest	$ 24.95	_____	$ ______
___		Dallas & The SouthWest	$ 24.95	_____	$ ______
___	*	Southern States	$ 24.95	_____	$ ______
___		Ohio Valley	$ 24.95	_____	$ ______
___	*	Mid-Atlantic	$ 24.95	_____	$ ______
___		Southern Atlantic Coast	$ 24.95	_____	$ ______
___	*	Plaines States	$ 24.95	_____	$ ______
___	*	Mountain States	$ 24.95	_____	$ ______
___	*	New York/New Jersey	$ 24.95	_____	$ ______
___		Northern Great Lakes	$ 24.95	_____	$ ______
___		**Entire set of databases**	**$275.00**	_____	$ ______

Shipping and Handling (1st Copy) $ 3.00
Additional Copies = Number of copies X $1.00 = ______

Total Bill: **$** ______

Payment Method Preferred: ___ Check Enclosed ___ VISA/MC

Card Number: ______________________________

Expiration Date: ______________________________

Signature Required: ______________________________

Send Order To: (Please Print Clearly)

Name: ______________________________

Address: ______________________________

City: ______________________ St. ______ Zip: __________

Return form to: Net-Research, 16371 East Iliff #B 183, Aurora, Colorado 80013

NET-RESEARCH WORD PROCESSING ORDER FORM

The entries contained within each Source Book can also be obtained on a diskette as a WordPerfect "Mail Merge" file. This allows the user to quickly generate cover letters using WordPerfect. To obtain copies of this or other Net-Research Source Books in WordPerfect "Mail Merge" format, complete and return this order form. Your order will be shipped within 10 days.

ORDER FORM MM-2: (* = Available Winter 1993)

		Job Seekers SourceBook	Price	x Copies =	Total
___		Chicago & Illinois	$ 24.95	_____	$ _____
___		Boston & New England	$ 24.95	_____	$ _____
___		LA & Southern Calif.	$ 24.95	_____	$ _____
___		Pacific Northwest	$ 24.95	_____	$ _____
___		Dallas & The SouthWest	$ 24.95	_____	$ _____
___	*	Southern States	$ 24.95	_____	$ _____
___		Ohio Valley	$ 24.95	_____	$ _____
___	*	Mid-Atlantic	$ 24.95	_____	$ _____
___		Southern Atlantic Coast	$ 24.95	_____	$ _____
___	*	Plaines States	$ 24.95	_____	$ _____
___	*	Mountain States	$ 24.95	_____	$ _____
___	*	New York/New Jersey	$ 24.95	_____	$ _____
___		Northern Great Lakes	$ 24.95	_____	$ _____
___		**Entire set of databases**	**$275.00**	_____	$ _____

Shipping and Handling (1st Copy) $ 3.00
Additional Copies = Number of copies X $1.00 = _____

Total Bill: **$** _____

Payment Method Preferred: ___ Check Enclosed ___ VISA/MC

Card Number: ______________________________

Expiration Date: ______________________________

Signature Required: ______________________________

Send Order To: (Please Print Clearly)

Name: ______________________________

Address: ______________________________

City: ______________________ St. _____ Zip: _______

Return form to: Net-Research, 16371 East Iliff #B 183, Aurora, Colorado 80013